The Poetical Works of Alexander Pope - Volume I

Alexander Pope

Esprios.com

THE POETICAL WORKS OF ALEXANDER POPE

VOL. I.

With Memoir, Critical Dissertation, and Explanatory Notes

by THE REV. GEORGE GILFILLAN

M. DCCC. LVI.

LIFE OF ALEXANDER POPE

Alexander Pope was born in Lombard Street, London, on the 21st of May 1688—the year of the Revolution. His father was a linen-merchant, in thriving circumstances, and said to have noble blood in his veins. His mother was Edith or Editha Turner, daughter of William Turner, Esq., of York. Mr Carruthers, in his excellent Life of the Poet, mentions that there was an Alexander Pope, a clergyman, in the remote parish of Reay, in Caithness, who rode all the way to Twickenham to pay his great namesake a visit, and was presented by him with a copy of the subscription edition of the " Odyssey, " in five volumes quarto, which is still preserved by his descendants. Pope's father had made about L10,000 by trade; but being a Roman Catholic, and fond of a country life, he retired from business shortly after the Revolution, at the early age of forty-six. He resided first at Kensington, and then in Binfield, in the neighbourhood of Windsor Forest. He is said to have put his money in a strong box, and to have lived on the principal. His great delight was in his garden; and both he and his wife seem to have cherished the warmest interest in their son, who was very delicate in health, and their only child. Pope's study is still preserved in Binfield; and on the lawn, a cypress-tree which he is said to have planted, is pointed out.

Pope was a premature and precocious child. His figure was deformed—his back humped—his stature short (four feet)—his legs and arms disproportionably long. He was sometimes compared to a spider, and sometimes to a windmill. The only mark of genius lay in his bright and piercing eye. He was sickly in constitution, and required and received great tenderness and care. Once, when three years old, he narrowly escaped from an angry cow, but was wounded in the throat. He was remarkable as a child for his amiable temper; and from the sweetness of his voice, received the name of the Little Nightingale. His aunt gave him his first lessons in reading, and he soon became an enthusiastic lover of books; and by copying printed characters, taught himself to write. When eight years old, he was placed under the care of the family priest, one Bannister, who taught him the Latin and Greek grammars together. He was next removed to a Catholic seminary at Twyford, near Winchester; and while there, read Ogilby's " Homer" and Sandys's " Ovid" with great delight. He had not been long at this school till he wrote a severe lampoon, of two hundred lines' length, on his master—so truly was the " boy the father of the man" —for which demi-Dunciad he was severely flogged. His father, offended at this, removed him to a London school, kept by a Mr Deane. This man taught the poet nothing; but his residence in London gave him the opportunity of attending the theatres. With these he was so captivated, that he wrote a kind of play, which was acted by his schoolfellows, consisting of speeches from Ogilby's " Iliad, " tacked together with verses of his own. He became acquainted with Dryden's works, and went to Wills's coffee-house to see him. He says, " Virgilium tantum vidi. " Such transient meetings of literary orbs are among the most interesting passages in biography. Thus met Galileo with Milton, Milton with Dryden, Dryden with Pope, and Burns with Scott. Carruthers strikingly remarks, " Considering the perils and uncertainties of a literary life—its precarious rewards, feverish anxieties, mortifications, and disappointments, joined to the tyranny of the Tonsons and Lintots, and the malice and envy of dunces, all of which Dryden had long and bitterly experienced—the aged poet could hardly have looked at the delicate and deformed boy, whose preternatural acuteness and sensibility were seen in his dark eyes, without a feeling approaching to grief, had he known that he was to fight a battle like that under which he was himself then sinking, even though the Temple of Fame should at length open to receive him. " At twelve, he wrote the " Ode to Solitude; " and shortly after, his satirical piece on Elkanah Settle, and some of his translations and imitations. His next period, he says, was in Windsor Forest, where for several years he did nothing but read the classics and indite poetry. He wrote a tragedy, a comedy, and four books of an Epic called " Alexander, " all of which afterwards he committed to the flames. He translated also a portion of Statius, and Cicero " De Senectute, " and " thought himself the greatest genius that ever was. " His father encouraged him in his studies, and when his verses did not please him, sent him back to " new turn" them, saying, " These are not good rhymes. " His principal favourites were Virgil's " Eclogues, " in Latin; and in English, Spencer, Waller, and Dryden—admiring Spencer, we presume, for his luxuriant fancy, Waller for his smooth versification, and Dryden for his vigorous sense and vivid sarcasm. In the Forest, he became acquainted with Sir William Trumbull, the retired secretary of state, a man of general accomplishments, who read, rode, conversed with the youthful poet; introduced him to old Wycherley, the dramatist; and was of material service to his views. With Wycherley, who was old, doted, and excessively vain, Pope did not continue long intimate. A coldness, springing from some criticisms which the youth ventured to make on the veteran's poetry, crept in between them. Walsh of Abberley, in Worcestershire, a man of good sense and taste, became, after a perusal of the " Pastorals" in MS., a warm friend and kind adviser of Pope's, who has immortalised him in more than one of his poems. Walsh told Pope that there had never hitherto appeared in Britain a poet who was at once great and correct, and exhorted him to aim at accuracy and elegance.

When fifteen, he visited London, in order to acquire a more thorough knowledge of French and Italian. At sixteen, he wrote the " Pastorals, " and a portion of " Windsor Forest, " although they were not published for some time afterwards. By his incessant exertions, he now began to feel his constitution injured. He imagined himself dying, and sent farewell letters to all his friends, including the Abbe Southcot. This gentleman communicated Pope's case to Dr Ratcliffe, who gave him some medical directions; by following which, the poet recovered. He was advised to relax in his studies, and to ride daily; and he prudently followed the advice. Many years afterwards, he repaid the benevolent Abbe by procuring for him, through Sir Robert Walpole, the nomination to an abbey in Avignon. This is only one of many proofs that, notwithstanding his waspish temper, and his no small share of malice as well as vanity, there was a warm heart in our poet.

In 1707, Pope became acquainted with Michael Blount of Maple, Durham, near Reading; whose two sisters, Martha and Teresa, he has commemorated in various verses. On his connexion with these ladies, some mystery rests. Bowles has strongly and plausibly urged that it was not of the purest or most creditable order. Others have contended that it did not go further than the manners of the age sanctioned; and they say, " a much greater license in conversation and in epistolary correspondence was permitted between the sexes than in our decorous age! " We are not careful to try and settle such a delicate question—only we are inclined to suspect, that when common decency quits the *words* of male and female parties in their mutual communications, it is a very ample charity that can suppose it to adhere to their *actions*. And nowhere do we find grosser language than in some of Pope's prose epistles to the Blounts.

His " Pastorals, " after having been handed about in MS., and shewn to such reputed judges as Lord Halifax, Lord Somers, Garth, Congreve, &c., were at last, in 1709, printed in the sixth volume of Tonson's " Miscellanies. " Like all well-finished commonplaces, they were received with instant and universal applause. It is humiliating to contrast the reception of these empty echoes of inspiration, these agreeable *centos*, with that of such genuine, although faulty poems, as Keat's " Endymion, " Shelley's " Queen Mab, " and Wordsworth's " Lyrical Ballads. " Two years later, (in 1711), a far better and more characteristic production from his pen was ushered anonymously into the world. This was the " Essay on Criticism, " a work which he had first written in prose, and which discovers a ripeness of judgment, a clearness of thought, a condensation of style, and a command over the information he possesses, worthy of any age in life, and almost of any mind in time. It serves, indeed, to shew what Pope's true forte was. That lay not so much in poetry, as in the knowledge of its principles and laws, —not so much in creation, as in criticism. He was no Homer or Shakspeare; but he might have been nearly as acute a judge of poetry as Aristotle, and nearly as eloquent an expounder of the rules of art and the glories of genius as Longinus.

In the same year, Pope printed " The Rape of the Lock, " in a volume of Miscellanies. Lord Petre had, much in the way described by the poet, stolen a lock of Miss Belle Fermor's hair, —a feat which led to an estrangement between the families. Pope set himself to reconcile them by this beautiful poem, —a poem which has embalmed at once the quarrel and the reconciliation to all future time. In its first version, the machinery was awanting, the " lock" was a desert, the " rape" a natural event, —the small infantry of sylphs and gnomes were slumbering uncreated in the poet's mind; but in the next edition he contrived to introduce them in a manner so easy and so exquisite, as to remind you of the variations which occur in dreams, where one wonder seems softly to slide into the bosom of another, and where beautiful and fantastic fancies grow suddenly out of realities, like the bud from the bough, or the fairy-seeming wing of the summer-cloud from the stern azure of the heavens.

A little after this, Pope became acquainted with a far greater, better, and truer man than himself, Joseph Addison. Warburton, and others, have sadly misrepresented the connexion between these two famous wits, as well as their relative intellectual positions. Addison was a more amiable and childlike person than Pope. He had much more, too, of the Christian. He was not so elaborately polished and furbished as the author of " The Rape of the Lock; " but he had, naturally, a finer and richer genius. Pope found early occasion for imagining Addison his disguised enemy. He gave him a hint of his intention to introduce the machinery into " The Rape of the Lock. "

Of this, Addison disapproved, and said it was a delicious little thing already—*merum sal*. This, Pope, and some of his friends, have attributed to jealousy; but it is obvious that Addison could not foresee the success with which the machinery was to be managed, and did foresee the difficulties connected with tinkering such an exquisite production. We may allude here to the circumstances which, at a later date, produced an estrangement between these celebrated men. When Tickell, Addison's friend, published the first book of the " Iliad, " in opposition to Pope's version, Addison gave it the preference. This moved Pope's indignation, and led him to assert that it was Addison's own composition. In this conjecture he was supported by Edward Young, who had known Tickell long and intimately, and had never heard of him having written at college, as was averred, this translation. It is now, however, we believe, certain, from the MS. which still exists, that Tickell was the real author. A coldness, from this date, began between Pope and Addison. An attempt to reconcile them only made matters worse; and at last the breach was rendered irremediable by Pope's writing the famous character of his rival, afterwards inserted in the Prologue to the Satires, —a portrait drawn with the perfection of polished malice and bitter sarcasm, but which seems more a caricature than a likeness. Whatever Addison's faults, his conduct to Pope did not deserve such a return. The whole passage is only one of those painful incidents which disgrace the history of letters, and prove how much spleen, ingratitude, and baseness often co-exist with the highest parts. The words of Pope are as true now as ever they were" the life of a wit is a warfare upon earth; " and a warfare in which poisoned missiles and every variety of falsehood are still common. We may also here mention, that while the friendship of Pope and Addison lasted, the former contributed the well-known prologue to the latter's " Cato. "

One of Pope's most intimate friends in his early days was Henry Cromwell—a distant relative of the great Oliver—a gentleman of fortune, gallantry, and literary taste, who became his agreeable and fascinating, but somewhat dangerous, companion. He is supposed to have initiated Pope into some of the fashionable follies of the town. At this time, Pope's popularity roused one of his most formidable foes against him. This was that Cobbett of criticism, old John Dennis, —a man of strong natural powers, much learning, and a rich, coarse vein of humour; but irascible, vindictive, vain, and capricious. Pope had provoked him by an attack in his " Essay on Criticism, " and the savage old man revenged himself by a running fire of fierce diatribes against that " Essay" and " The Rape of the Lock. " Pope waited till Dennis had committed himself by a powerful but furious assault on Addison's " Cato" (most of which Johnson has preserved in his Life of Pope); and then, partly to court Addison, and partly to indulge his spleen at the critic, wrote a prose satire, entitled, " The Narrative of Dr Robert Norris on the Frenzy of J. D." In this, however, he overshot the mark; and Addison signified to him that he was displeased with the spirit of his narrative, —an intimation which Pope keenly resented. *This* scornful dog would not eat the dirty pudding that was graciously flung to him; and Pope found that, without having conciliated Addison, he had made Dennis's furnace of hate against himself seven times hotter than before.

In 1712 appeared " The Messiah, " " The Dying Christian to his Soul, " " The Temple of Fame, " and the " Elegy on the Memory of an Unfortunate Lady. " Her story is still involved in mystery. Her name is said to have been Wainsbury. She was attached to a lover above her degree, —some say to the Duke of Berry, whom she had met in her early youth in France. In despair of obtaining her desire, she hanged herself. It is curious, if true, that she was as deformed in person as Pope himself. Her family seems to have been noble. In 1713, he published " Windsor Forest, " an " Ode on St Cecilia's Day, " and several papers in the *Guardian*—one of them being an exquisitely ironical paper, comparing Phillip's pastorals with his own, and affecting to give them the preference—the extracts being so selected as to damage his rival's claims. This year, also, he wrote, although he did not publish, his fine epistle to Jervas, the painter. Pope was passionately fond of the art of painting, and practised it a good deal under Jervas's instructions, although he did not reach great proficiency. The prodigy has yet to be born who combines the characters of a great painter and a great poet.

About this time, Pope commenced preparations for the great work of translating Homer; and subscription-papers, accordingly, were issued. Dean Swift was now in England, and took a deep interest in the success of this undertaking, recommending it in coffee-houses, and introducing the subject and Pope's name to the leading Tories. Pope met the Dean for the first time in Berkshire, where, in one of his fits of savage disgust at the conflicting parties of the period, he had retired to the house of a clergyman, and an intimacy commenced which was only terminated by death. We have often regretted that Pope had not selected some author more suitable to his genius than Homer. Horace or Lucretius, or even Ovid, would have been more congenial. His imitations of Horace shew us what he might have made of a complete translation. What a brilliant thing a version of Lucretius, in the style of the " Essay on Man, " would have been! And his " Rape of the Lock" proves that he had considerable sympathy with the elaborate fancy, although not with the meretricious graces of Ovid. But with Homer, the severely grand, the simple, the warlike, the lover and painter of all Nature's old original forms—the ocean, the mountains, and the stars—what thorough sympathy could a man have who never saw a real mountain or a battle, and whose enthusiasm for scenery was confined to purling brooks, trim gardens, artificial grottos, and the shades of Windsor Forest? Accordingly, his Homer, although a beautiful and sparkling poem, is not a satisfactory translation of the " Iliad, " and still less of the " Odyssey. " He has trailed along the naked lances of the Homeric lines so many flowers and leaves that you can hardly recognise them, and feel that their point is deadened and their power gone. This at least is our opinion; although many to this day continue to admire these translations, and have even said that if they are not Homer, they are something better.

The " Iliad" took him six years, and was a work which cost him much anxiety as well as labour, the more as his scholarship was far from profound. He was assisted in the undertaking by Parnell (who wrote the Life of Homer), by Broome, Jortin, and others. The first volume appeared in June 1715, and the other volumes followed at irregular intervals. He began it in 1712, his twenty-fifth year, and finished it in 1718, his thirtieth year. Previous to its appearance, his remuneration for his poems had been small, and his circumstances were embarrassed; but the result of the subscription, which amounted to L5320, 4s., rendered him independent for life.

While at Binfield, he had often visited London; and there, in the society of Howe, Garth, Parnell, and the rest, used to indulge in occasional excesses, which did his feeble constitution no good; and once, according to Colley Cibber, he narrowly escaped a serious scrape in a house of a certain description, —Colley, by his own account, " helping out the tomtit for the sake of Homer! " This statement, indeed, Pope has denied; but his veracity was by no means his strongest point. After writing a " Farewell to London, " he retired, in 1715, to Twickenham, along with his parents; and remained there, cultivating his garden, digging his grottos, and diversifying his walks, till the end of his days.

Some years before, he had become acquainted with Lady Mary Wortley Montague, the most brilliant woman of her age—witty, fascinating, beautiful, and accomplished—full of enterprise and spirit, too, although decidedly French in her tastes, manners, and character. Pope fell violently in love with her, and had her undoubtedly in his eye when writing " Eloisa and Abelard, " which he did at Oxford in 1716, shortly after her going abroad, and which appeared the next year. His passion was not requited, —nay, was treated with contempt and ridicule; and he became in after years a bitter enemy and foul-mouthed detractor of the lady, although after her return, in 1718, she resided near him at Twickenham, and they seemed outwardly on good terms.

In 1717, and the succeeding year, Pope lost successively his father, Parnell, Garth, and Rowe, and bitterly felt their loss. He finished, as we have seen, the " Iliad" in 1718; but the fifth and sixth volumes, which were the last, did not appear till 1720. Its success, which at the time was triumphant, roused against him the whole host of envy and detraction. Dennis, and all Grub Street with him, were moved to assail him. Pamphlets after pamphlets were published, all of which, after reading with writhing anguish, Pope had the resolution to bind up into volumes—a great collection of calumny, which he preserved, probably, for purposes of future revenge. His own friends, on the other hand, hailed his work with applause, —Gay writing a most graceful and elegant poem, in *ottava rima*, entitled, " Mr Pope's Welcome Home from Greece, " in which his different friends are pictured as receiving him home on the shores of Britain, after an absence of six years. Bentley, that stern old Grecian, avoided the extremes of a howling Grub Street on the one hand, and a flattering aristocracy on the other, and expressed what is, we think, the just opinion when he said, " It is a pretty poem, but it is not Homer. "

In 1721, he issued a selection from the poems of Parnell, and prefixed a very beautiful dedication to the Earl of Oxford, commencing with—

> " Such were the notes thy once-loved poet sung,
> Till death untimely stopp'd his tuneful tongue.
> Oh, just beheld and lost, admired and mourn'd,
> With softest manners, gentlest arts adorn'd!"

In 1722, he engaged to translate the " Odyssey. " He employed Broome and Fenton as his assistants in the work; and the portions translated by them were thought as good as his. He remunerated them very handsomely. Of this work, the first three quarto volumes appeared in 1725; and the fourth and fifth, which completed the work, the following year. Pope sold the copyright to Lintot for L600.

He was busy at this time, too, with an edition of Shakspeare, —not quite worthy of either poet. It appeared in six volumes, quarto, in 1725. His preface was good, but he was deficient in antiquarian lore; and his mortification was extreme when Theobald, destined to figure in " The Dunciad, " a mere plodding hack, not only in his " Shakspeare Restored, " exposed many blunders in Pope's edition; but issued, some years afterwards, an edition of his own, which was much better received by the public.

In 1726, there was a great gathering of the Tory wits at Twickenham. Swift had come from Ireland, and resided for some time with Pope. Bolingbroke came over occasionally from Dawley; and Gay was often there to laugh with, and be laughed at by, the rest. Swift had " Gulliver's Travels" —the most ingenious and elaborate libel against man and God ever written—in his pocket, nearly ready for publication; and we may conceive the grim, sardonic smile with which he read it to his friends, and their tumultuous mirth. Gay was projecting his " Beggars' Opera, " and Pope preparing some of his witty " Miscellanies. " At the end of two months, the Dean was hurried home by the tidings of Stella's illness. He left the " Travels" behind him, for the copyright of which Pope procured L300, —a sum counted then very large, and which Swift generously handed over to Pope.

In September this year, when returning in Lord Bolingbroke's coach from Dawley, the poet was overturned in a little rivulet near Twickenhan, and nearly drowned. The unfortunate little man! One is reminded of Gulliver's accident in the Brobdignagian cream-pot. In trying to break the glasses of the coach, which were down, he severely cut his right hand, and lost the use of two of his fingers, — an addition to his other deformities not very desirable; and we suspect that Pope thought Voltaire (who had met him at Bolingbroke's) but a miserable comforter, when, in a letter of pretended condolence, he asked—" Is it possible that those fingers which have written 'The Rape of the Lock, ' and dressed Homer so becomingly in an English coat, should have been so barbarously treated? Let the hand of Dennis or of your poetasters be cut off; yours is sacred. " It was perhaps in keeping that those mutilated fingers were soon to be employed in attacking Dennis, and that the embittered poet was about, with the half of his hand, but with the whole of his heart, to write " The Dunciad. "

In the end of April 1727, we find Swift again in Twickenham, where his irritation at the continued ascendancy of Sir Robert Walpole served to infuse more venom into the " Miscellanies" concocted between him and Pope, —two volumes of which appeared in June this year. Gay, also, and the ingenious and admirable Dr Arbuthnot, contributed their quota to these volumes. Swift speedily fell ill with that giddiness and deafness which were the *avant-couriers* of his final malady; and in August he left Twickenham, and in October, London and England, for ever.

In these " Miscellanies" there appeared the famous " Memoirs of Martinus Scriblerus, " written chiefly by Pope, in which he lashed the various proficients in the bathos, under the names of flying fishes, swallows, parrots, frogs, eels, &c., and appended the initials of well-known authors to each head. This roused Grub Street, whose malice had nearly fallen asleep, into fresh fury, and he was bitterly assailed in every possible form. Like Hyder Ali, he now—to travesty Burke—" in the recesses of a mind capacious of such things, determined to leave all Duncedom an everlasting monument of vengeance, and became at length so confident of his force, so collected in his might, that he made no secret whatever of his dreadful resolution, but, compounding all the materials of fun, sarcasm, irony, and invective, into one black cloud, he hung for a while on the declivities of Richmond Hill; and whilst the authors were idly and stupidly gazing on this menacing meteor which blackened all their horizon, it suddenly burst and poured down the whole of its contents on the garrets of Grub Street. Then issued a scene of (ludicrous) woe, the like of which no eye had seen, no heart conceived, and which no tongue can adequately tell. All the horrors of literary war before known or heard of—(MacFlecknoe, the Rehearsal, &c.)—were mercy to the new tempest of havoc which burst from the brain of this remorseless poet. A storm of universal laughter filled every bookseller's shop, and penetrated into the remotest attics. The miserable dunces, in part, were stricken mad with rage—in part, dumb with consternation. Some fled for refuge to ale, and others to ink; while not a few fell, or feared to fall, into the 'jaws of famine. '" This singular poem was written in 1727. It was first printed surreptitiously (*i. e.*, with the connivance of the author) in Dublin, and then reprinted in London. The first perfect edition, however, did not appear in London till 1729. On the day of its publication, according to Pope, a crowd of authors besieged the publisher's shop; and by entreaties, threats, nay, cries of treason, tried to hinder its appearance. What a scene it must have been—of teeth gnashing above ragged coats, and eyes glaring through old periwigs—of faces livid with famine and ferocity; while, to complete the confusion, hawkers, booksellers, and even lords, were mixed with the crowd, clamouring for its issue! And as, says Pope, " there is no stopping a torrent with a finger, out it came. " The consequence he had foreseen. A universal howl of rage and pain burst from the aggrieved dunces, on whose naked sides the hot pitch had fallen. They pushed their rejoinders beyond the limits of civilised literary warfare; and although Pope had been coarse in his language, they were coarser far, and their blackguardism was not redeemed by wit or genius. Pope felt, or seemed to feel, entire indifference as to these assaults. On some of them, indeed, he could afford to look down with contempt, on account of their obvious *animus* and gross language. Others, again, were neutralised by the fact, that their authors had provoked reprisals by their previous insults or ingratitude to Pope. Many, however, were too obscure for his notice; and some, such as Aaron Hill and Bentley, did not deserve to be classed with the Theobalds and Ralphs. To Hill, he, after some finessing, was compelled to make an apology. Altogether, although this production increased Pope's fame, and the conception of his power, it did not tend to shew him in the most amiable light, or perhaps to promote his own comfort or peace of mind. After having emptied out his bile in " The Dunciad, " he ought to have become mellower in temper, and resigned satire for ever. He continued, on the contrary, as ill-natured as before; and although he afterwards flew at higher game, the iron had entered into his soul, and he remained a satirist, and therefore an unhappy man, for life.

In 1731 appeared an " Epistle on Taste, " which was very favourably received; only his enemies accused him of having satirised the Duke of Chandos in it, —a man who had befriended Pope, and had lent him money. Pope denied the charge, although it is very possible, both from his own temperament, and from the frequent occurrence of similar cases of baseness in literary life, that it may have been true. Nothing is more common than for those who have been most liberally helped, to become first the secret, and then the open, enemies of their benefactors. In 1732 appeared his epistle on " The Use of Riches, " addressed to Lord Bathurst. These two epistles were afterwards incorporated in his " Moral Essays. "

As far back as 1725, Pope had been revolving the subject of the " Essay on Man; " and, indeed, some of its couplets remind you of " pebbles which had long been rolled over and polished in the ocean of his mind. " It has been asserted, but not proved, that Lord Bolingbroke gave him the outline of this essay in prose. It is unquestionable, indeed, that Bolingbroke exercised influence over Pope's mind, and may have suggested some of the thoughts in the Essay; but it is not probable that a man like Pope would have set himself on such a subject simply to translate from another's mind. He published the first epistle of the Essay, in 1732, anonymously, as an experiment, and had the satisfaction to see it successful. It was received with rapture, and passed through several editions ere the author was known; although we must say that the value of this reception is considerably lessened, when we remember that the critics could not have been very acute who did not detect Pope's " fine Roman hand" in every sentence of this brilliant but most unsatisfactory and shallow performance.

In the same year died dear, simple-minded Gay, who found in Pope a sincere mourner, and an elegant elegiast; and on the 7th of June 1733, expired good old Mrs Pope, at the age of ninety-four. Pope, who had always been a dutiful son, erected an obelisk in his own grounds to her memory, with a simple but striking inscription in Latin. During this year, he published the third part of the " Essay on Man, " an epistle to Lord Cobham, On the Knowledge and Characters of Man, and an Imitation of the First Satire of the Second Book of Horace. In this last, he attacks, in the most brutal style, his former love Lady Mary W. Montague, who replied in a piece of coarse cleverness, entitled, " Verses to the Imitator of the First Satire of the Second Book of Horace, " —verses in which she was assisted by Lord Harvey, another of Pope's victims. He wrote, but was prudent enough to suppress, an ironical reply.

In 1734 appeared his very clever and highly-finished epistle to Dr Arbuthnot (now entitled the " Prologue to the Satires"), who was then languishing toward death. Arbuthnot, from his deathbed, solemnly advised Pope to regulate his satire, and seems to have been afraid of his personal safety from his numerous foes. Pope replied in a manly but self-defensive style. He is said about this time to have in his walks carried arms, and had a large dog as his protector; but none of the dunces had courage enough to assail him. Dennis, who was no dunce, might have ventured on it—but he had become miserably infirm, poor, and blind; and Pope had heaped coals of fire on his head, by contributing a Prologue to a play which was acted for his behoof.

Our author's life becomes now little else than a record of multiplying labours and increasing infirmities. In 1734 appeared the fourth part of the " Essay on Man, " and the Second Satire of the Second Book of Horace. In 1735 were issued his " Characters of Women: An Epistle to a Lady" (Martha Blount). In this appears his famous character of Atossa—the Duchess of Marlborough. It is said—we fear too truly—that these lines being shewn to her Grace, as a character of the Duchess of Buckingham, she recognised in them her own likeness, and bribed Pope with a thousand pounds to suppress it. He did so religiously—as long as she was alive—and then published it! In the same year he printed a second volume of his " Miscellaneous Works, " in folio and quarto, uniform with the " Iliad" and " Odyssey, " including a versification of the Satires of Donne; also, anonymously, a production disgraceful to his memory, entitled, " Sober Advice from Horace to the Young Gentlemen about Town, " in which he commits many gross indecorums of language, and annexes the name of the great Bentley to several indecent notes. It is said that Bentley, when he read the pamphlet, cried, " 'Tis an impudent dog, but I talked against his Homer, and the *portentous cub never forgives.* "

The " Essay on Man" and the " Moral Epistles" were designed to be parts of a great system of ethics, which Pope had long revolved in his mind, and wished to incarnate in poetry. At this time occurred the strange, mysterious circumstances connected with the publication of his letters. It seems that, in 1729, Pope had recalled from his correspondents the letters he had written them, of many of which he had kept no copies. He was induced to this by the fact, that after Henry Cromwell's death, his mistress, Mrs Thomas, who was in indigent circumstances, had sold the letters which had passed between Pope and her keeper, to Curll the bookseller, who had published them without scruple. When Pope obtained his correspondence, he, according to his own statement, burned a great many and laid past the others, after having had a copy of them taken, and deposited in Lord Oxford's library. And his charge against Curll was, that he obtained surreptitiously some of these letters, and published them without Pope's consent. But, ere we come to the circumstances of the publication, several other things require to be noticed. In 1733, Curll, anxious to publish a Life of Pope, advertised for information; and, in consequence, one P. T., who professed to be an old friend of Pope's and his father's, wrote

Curll a letter, giving an account of Pope's ancestry, which tallied exactly with what Pope himself, in a note to one of his poems, furnished the following year. P.T., in a second letter, offered to the publisher a large collection of Pope's letters, and inclosed a copy of an advertisement he had drawn out to be published by Curll. Strange as it seems, Curll took no notice of the proposal till 1735, when, having accidentally turned up a copy of P. T.'s advertisement, he sent it to Pope, with a letter requesting an interview, and mentioning that he had some papers of P. T.'s in reference to his family history, which he would shew him. Pope replied by three advertisements in the papers, denying all knowledge of P. T. or his collection of letters or MSS. P.T. then wrote Curll that he had printed the letters at his own expense, seeking a sum of money for them, and appointing an interview at a tavern to shew him the sheets. This was countermanded the next day, P.T. professing to be afraid of Pope and his " bravoes, " although how Pope was to know of this meeting was, according to Curll, " the cream of the jest. "

Soon after, a round, fat man, with a clergyman's gown and a barrister's band, called on Curll, at ten o'clock at night. He said his name was Smith, that he was a cousin of P. T.'s, and shewed the book in sheets, along with about a dozen of the original letters. After a good deal of negotiation with this personage, Curll obtained fifty copies of P. T.'s printed copies, and issued a flaming advertisement announcing the publication of Pope's letters for thirty years, and stating that the original MSS. were lying at his shop, and might be seen by any who chose, —although not a single MS. seems to have been delivered. Smith, the day that the advertisement appeared, handed over, for a sum of money, about three hundred volumes to Curll. But as in the advertisement it was stated that various letters of lords were included, and as there is a law amongst regulations of the Upper House that no peer's letters can be published without his consent, at the instance of the Earl of Jersey, and in consequence, too, of an advertisement of Pope's, the books were seized, and Curll, and the printer of the paper where the advertisement appeared, were ordered to appear at the bar for breach of privilege. P.T. wrote Curll to tell him to conceal all that passed between him and the publisher, and promising him more valuable letters still. Curll, however, told the whole story; and as, when the books were examined, not a single lord's letter was found among them, Curll was acquitted, his books restored to him, the lords saying that they had been made the tools of Pope; and he proceeded to advertise the correspondence, in terms most insulting to Pope, who now felt himself compelled (!) to print, by subscription, his genuine letters, which, when printed, turned out, strange to tell, to be identical with those published by the rapacious bookseller! On viewing the whole transaction, we incline with Johnson, Warton, Bowles, Macaulay, and Carruthers, to look upon it as one of Pope's ape-like stratagems—to believe that P. T. was himself, Smith his agent, and that his objects were partly to outwit Curll, to mystify the public, to gratify that strange love of manoeuvring which dwelt as strongly in him as in any matchmaking mamma, and to attract interest and attention to the genuine correspondence when it should appear. Pope, it was said, could not " drink tea without a stratagem, " and far less publish his correspondence without a series of contemptible tricks—tricks, however, in which he was true to his nature—*that* being a curious compound of the woman and the wit, the monkey and the genius[1].

In 1737, four of his Imitations of Horace were published, and in the next year appeared two Dialogues, each entitled " 1738, " which now form the Epilogue to the Satires. One of them was issued on the same day with Johnson's " London. " In that year, too, he published his " Universal Prayer, " —a singular specimen of latitudinarian thought, expressed in a loose simplicity of language, quite unusual with its author. The next year he had intended to signalise by a third Dialogue, which he commenced in a vigorous style, but which he did not finish, owing to the dread of a prosecution before the Lords; and with the exception of letters (one of them interesting, as his last to Swift), his pen was altogether idle. In 1740, he did nothing but edit an edition of select Italian Poets. This year, Crousaz, a Swiss professor of note, having attacked (we think most justly) the " Essay on Man" as a mere Pagan prolusion—a thin philosophical smile cast on the Gordian knot of the mystery of the universe, instead of a *sword* cutting, or trying to cut, it in sunder—Warburton, a man of much talent and learning, but of more astuteness and anxiety to exalt himself, came forward to the rescue, and, with a mixture of casuistical cunning and real ingenuity, tried, as some one has it, " to make Pope a Christian, " although, even in Warburton's hands, like the dying Donald Bane in " Waverley, " he " makes but a queer Christian after all; " and his system, essentially Pantheistic, contrives to ignore the grand Scripture principles of a Fall, of a Divine Redeemer, of a Future World, and the glorious light or darkness which these and other Christian doctrines cast upon the Mystery of Man. If, however, Warburton, with all his scholastic subtlety, failed to make Pope a Christian, he made him a warm friend; Allen, Pope's acquaintance, a rich father-in-law; and himself, by and by, the

Bishop of Gloucester. Sophistry has seldom, although sometimes, been thus richly rewarded.

The last scene of Pope's tiny and tortured existence was now at hand. But ere it closed, it must close like Dryden's, characteristically, with an author's quarrel. Colley Cibber had long been a favourite of Pope's ire, and had as often retorted scorn, till at last, by laughing upon the stage at Pope's play (partly Gay's), entitled, " Three Hours After Marriage, " he roused the bard almost to frenzy; and Pope set to work to remodel " The Dunciad; " and, dethroning Theobald, set up Cibber as the lawful King of the Dull, —a most unfortunate substitution, since, while Theobald was the ideal of stolid, solemn stupidity, Cibber was gay, light, pert, and clever; full of pluck, too, and who overflowed in reply, with pamphlets which gave Pope both a headache and a heartache whenever he perused them.

Pope had never been strong, and for many years the variety and multitude of his frailties had been increasing. He had habitually all his life been tormented with headaches, for which he found the steam of strong coffee the chief remedy. He had hurt his stomach, too, by indulging in excess of stimulating viands, such as potted lampreys, and in copious and frequent *drams*. He was assailed at last by dropsy and asthma; and on the 30th of May 1744, he breathed his last, fifty-six years of age. He had long, he said, " been tired of the world, " and died with philosophic composure and serenity. He took the sacrament according to the form of the Roman Catholic Church; but merely, he said, because it " looked right. " A little before his death, he called for his desk, and began an essay on the immortality of the soul, and on those material things which tend to weaken or to strengthen it for immortality, — enumerating generous wines as among the latter influences, and spirituous liquors among the former! His last words were, " There is nothing that is meritorious but virtue and friendship; and, indeed, friendship itself is only a part of virtue. " Thus, " motionless and moanless, " without a word about Christ—the slightest syllable of repentance— and with a scrap of heathen morality in his mouth, died the brilliant Alexander Pope. Who is ready to say, " May my last end be like his" ? His favourite Martha Blount behaved, according to some accounts, with disgusting unconcern on the occasion. So true it is, " there is no friendship among the wicked, " even although the heartless Bolingbroke, too, was by, and seems to have succeeded in squeezing out some crocodile tears, as he bent over the dying poet, and said, " O God! what is man? " His remains were, according to his wish, deposited in Twickenham church, near his parents, where the single letter P on the stone alone distinguishes the spot.

Pope's character, apart from his poetry, which we intend criticising in our next volume, was not specially interesting or elevated. He was a spoiled child, a small self-tormentor, —full to bursting with petty spites, mean animosities, and unfounded jealousies. While he sought, with the fury of a pampered slave, to trample on those authors that were beneath him in rank or in popularity, he could on all occasions fawn with the sycophancy of a eunuch upon the noble, the rich, and the powerful. Hazlitt speaks of Moore as a " pug-dog barking from the lap of a lady of quality at inferior passengers. " The description is far more applicable to Pope. We have much allowance to make for the influence exerted on his mind by his singularly crooked frame and sickly habit of body, by his position as belonging to a proscribed faith, and by his want of training in a public school; but after all these deductions, we cannot but deplore the spectacle of one of the finest, clearest, and sharpest minds that England ever produced, so frequently reminding you of a bright sting set in the body, and steeped in the venom, of a wasp. And yet, withal, he possessed many virtues, which endeared him to a multitude of friends. He was a kind son. He was a faithful and devoted friend. He loved, if not *man*, yet many men with deep tenderness. A keen politician he was not; but, so far as he went along with his party, he was true to the common cause. In morals, he was greatly superior, in point of external decorum, to most of the wits of the time; but in falsehood, finesse, treachery, and envy, he stood at the bottom of the list, without that plea of poverty, or wretchedness, or despair, which so many of them might have urged. Uneasy, indeed, he always, and unhappy he often, was; but very much of his uneasiness and unhappiness sprung from his own fault. He attacked others, and could not bear to be attacked in return. He was a bully and a coward. He threw himself into a thorn-hedge, and was amazed that he came out covered with scratches and blood. While he shone in satirising many kinds of vice, he laid himself open to retort by his own want of delicacy. He, as well as Swift, was fond of alluding in his verse to polluted and forbidden things. *There*, and there alone, his taste deserted him; and there is something disgusting and unnatural in the combination of the elegant and the obscene— the coarse in sentiment and the polished in style. And whatever may be said for many of the amiable traits of the Man, there is very little to be said for the general tendency—so far as healthy morality and Christian principle are concerned—of the writings of the Poet.

CONTENTS

PREFACE
PASTORALS—
    Spring, the First Pastoral, or Damon
    Summer, the Second Pastoral, or Alexis
    Autumn, the Third Pastoral, or Hylas and AEgon
    Winter, the Fourth Pastoral, or Daphne
MESSIAH
AN ESSAY ON CRITICISM—
    Part First
    Part Second
    Part Third
THE RAPE OF THE LOCK—
    Canto I.
    Canto II.
    Canto III.
    Canto IV.
    Canto V.
WINDSOR-FOREST
ODE ON ST CECILIA'S DAY
TWO CHORUSES TO THE TRAGEDY OF BRUTUS—
    Chorus of Athenians
    Chorus of Youths and Virgins
TO THE AUTHOR OF A POEM ENTITLED SUCCESSIO
ODE ON SOLITUDE
THE DYING CHRISTIAN TO HIS SOUL
ELEGY TO THE MEMORY OF AN UNFORTUNATE LADY
PROLOGUE TO MR ADDISON'S TRAGEDY OF CATO
IMITATIONS OF ENGLISH POETS—
    Chaucer
    Spenser—
    The Alley,
    Waller—
    Of a Lady Singing to her Lute
    On a Fan of the Author's Design
    Cowley—

    The Garden
    Weeping
    Earl of Rochester—
      On Silence
    Earl of Dorset—
      Artemisia
      Phryne
    Dr Swift—
      The Happy Life of a Country Parson
THE TEMPLE OF FAME
ELOISA TO ABELARD
EPISTLE TO ROBERT EARL OF OXFORD AND EARL MORTIMER
EPISTLE TO JAMES CRAGGS, ESQ.
EPISTLE TO MR JERVAS
EPISTLE TO MISS BLOUNT
EPISTLE TO MRS TERESA BLOUNT
TO MRS M.B. ON HER BIRTHDAY
TO MR THOMAS SOUTHERN, ON HIS BIRTHDAY, 1742
TO MR JOHN MOORE
TO MR C., ST JAMES'S PLACE
EPITAPHS—
    On Charles Earl of Dorset
    On Sir William Trumbull
    On the Hon. Simon Harcourt
    On James Craggs, Esq.
    Intended for Mr Rowe
    On Mrs Corbet
    On the Monument of the Honourable Robert Digby, and his Sister
      Mary
    On Sir Godfrey Kneller
    On General Henry Withers
    On Mr Elijah Fenton
    On Mr Gay
    Intended for Sir Isaac Newton
    On Dr Francis Atterbury
    On Edmund Duke of Buckingham
    For One who would not be Buried in Westminster Abbey
    Another, on the same

On two Lovers struck dead by Lightning
AN ESSAY ON MAN—
    Epistle I.
    Epistle II.
    Epistle III.
    Epistle IV.
EPISTLE TO DR AKBUTHNOT; OR, PROLOGUE TO THE SATIRES
SATIRES AND EPISTLES OF HORACE IMITATED—
    Satire I. To Mr Fortescue
    Satire II. To Mr Bethel
THE FIRST EPISTLE OF THE FIRST BOOK OF HORACE—
    To Lord Bolingbroke
THE SIXTH EPISTLE OF THE FIRST BOOK OF HORACE—
    To Mr Murray
THE FIRST EPISTLE OF THE SECOND BOOK OF HORACE—
    To Augustus
THE SECOND EPISTLE OF THE SECOND BOOK OF HORACE—
    Book I. Epistle VII.
    Book II. Satire VI.
    Book IV. Ode I.
    Part of the Ninth Ode of the Fourth Book
THE SATIRES OF DR JOHN VERSIFIED—
    Satire II.
    Satire IV.
EPILOGUE TO THE SATIRES: IN TWO DIALOGUES—
    Dialogue I.
    Dialogue II.

POPE'S POETICAL WORKS.

PREFACE. [2]

I am inclined to think that both the writers of books, and the readers of them, are generally not a little unreasonable in their expectations. The first seem to fancy that the world must approve whatever they produce, and the latter to imagine that authors are obliged to please them at any rate. Methinks, as on the one hand, no single man is born with a right of controlling the opinions of all the rest; so, on the other, the world has no title to demand that the whole care and time of any particular person should be sacrificed to its entertainment. Therefore I cannot but believe that writers and readers are under equal obligations for as much fame, or pleasure, as each affords the other.

Every one acknowledges, it would be a wild notion to expect perfection in any work of man: and yet one would think the contrary was taken for granted, by the judgment commonly passed upon poems. A critic supposes he has done his part, if he proves a writer to have failed in an expression, or erred in any particular point: and can it then be wondered at, if the poets in general seem resolved not to own themselves in any error? For as long as one side will make no allowances, the other will be brought to no acknowledgments.

I am afraid this extreme zeal on both sides is ill-placed; poetry and criticism being by no means the universal concern of the world, but only the affair of idle men who write in their closets, and of idle men who read there.

Yet sure, upon the whole, a bad author deserves better usage than a bad critic; for a writer's endeavour, for the most part, is to please his readers, and he fails merely through the misfortune of an ill judgment; but such a critic's is to put them out of humour, —a design he could never go upon without both that and an ill temper.

I think a good deal may be said to extenuate the fault of bad poets. What we call a genius, is hard to be distinguished by a man himself from a strong inclination: and if his genius be ever so great, he cannot at first discover it any other way than by giving way to that prevalent propensity which renders him the more liable to be mistaken. The only method he has is to make the experiment by writing, and appealing to the judgment of others: now if he happens to write ill (which is certainly no sin in itself) he is immediately made an object of ridicule. I wish we had the humanity to reflect, that even the worst authors might, in their endeavour to please us, deserve something at our hands. We have no cause to quarrel with them but for their obstinacy in persisting to write; and this too may admit of alleviating circumstances. Their particular friends may be either ignorant or insincere; and the rest of the world in general is too well bred to shock them with a truth which generally their booksellers are the first that inform them of. This happens not till they have spent too much of their time to apply to any profession which might better fit their talents, and till such talents as they have are so far discredited as to be but of small service to them. For (what is the hardest case imaginable) the reputation of a man generally depends upon the first steps he makes in the world; and people will establish their opinion of us from what we do at that season when we have least judgment to direct us.

On the other hand, a good poet no sooner communicates his works with the same desire of information, but it is imagined he is a vain young creature given up to the ambition of fame; when perhaps the poor man is all the while trembling with the fear of being ridiculous. If he is made to hope he may please the world, he falls under very unlucky circumstances: for, from the moment he prints, he must expect to hear no more truth than if he were a prince, or a beauty. If he has not very good sense (and indeed there are twenty men of wit for one man of sense), his living thus in a course of flattery may put him in no small danger of becoming a coxcomb: if he has, he will consequently have so much diffidence as not to reap any great satisfaction from his praise; since, if it be given to his face, it can scarce be distinguished from flattery, and if in his absence, it is hard to be certain of it. Were he sure to be commended by the best and most knowing, he is as sure of being envied by the worst and most ignorant, which are the majority; for it is with a fine genius as with a fine fashion, all those are displeased at it who are not able to follow it: and it is to be feared that esteem will seldom do any man so much good as ill-will does him harm. Then there is a third class of people, who make the largest part of mankind, those of ordinary or indifferent capacities; and these (to a man) will hate, or suspect him: a hundred honest gentlemen will dread him as a wit, and a hundred innocent women as a satirist. In a word, whatever be his fate in poetry, it is ten to one but he must give up all the reasonable aims of life for it. There are indeed some advantages accruing from a genius to poetry, and they are all I can think of: the agreeable power of self-amusement when a man is idle or alone; the privilege of being admitted into the best company; and the freedom of saying as many careless things as other people, without being so severely remarked upon.

I believe, if any one, early in his life, should contemplate the dangerous fate of authors, he would scarce be of their number on any consideration. The life of a wit is a warfare upon earth; and the present spirit of the learned world is such, that to attempt to serve it (any way) one must have the constancy of a martyr, and a resolution to suffer for its sake. I could wish people would believe, what I am pretty certain they will not, that I have been much less concerned about fame than I durst declare till this occasion, when methinks I should find more credit than I could heretofore: since my writings have had their fate already, and it is too late to think of prepossessing the reader in their favour. I would plead it as some merit in me, that the world has never been prepared for these trifles by prefaces, biased by recommendations, dazzled with the names of great patrons, wheedled with fine reasons and pretences, or troubled with excuses. I confess it was want of consideration that made me an author; I writ because it amused me; I corrected because it was as pleasant to me to correct as to write; and I published because I was told I might please such as it was a credit to please. To what degree I have done this, I am really ignorant; I had too much fondness for my productions to judge of them at first, and too much judgment to be pleased with them at last. But I have reason to think they can have no reputation which will continue long, or which deserves to do so: for they have always fallen short, not only of what I read of others, but even of my own ideas of poetry.

If any one should imagine I am not in earnest, I desire him to reflect that the ancients (to say the least of them) had as much genius as we: and that to take more pains, and employ more time, cannot fail to produce more complete pieces. They constantly applied themselves not only to that art, but to that single branch of an art, to which their talent was most powerfully bent; and it was the business of their lives to correct and finish their works for posterity. If we can pretend to have used the same industry, let us expect the same immortality: though if we took the same care, we should still lie under a further misfortune: they writ in languages that became universal and everlasting, while ours are extremely limited both in extent and in duration. A mighty foundation for our pride! when the utmost we can hope is but to be read in one island, and to be thrown aside at the end of one age.

All that is left us is to recommend our productions by the imitation of the ancients; and it will be found true, that, in every age, the highest character for sense and learning has been obtained by those who have been most indebted to them. For, to say truth, whatever is very good sense must have been common sense in all times; and what we call learning is but the knowledge of the sense of our predecessors. Therefore they who say our thoughts are not our own, because they resemble the ancients, may as well say our faces are not our own, because they are like our fathers: and indeed it is very unreasonable that people should expect us to be scholars, and yet be angry to find us so.

I fairly confess that I have served myself all I could by reading; that I made use of the judgment of authors dead and living; that I omitted no means in my power to be informed of my errors, both by my friends and enemies: but the true reason these pieces are not more correct, is owing to the consideration how short a time they and I have to live: one may be ashamed to consume half one's days in bringing sense and rhyme together; and what critic can be so unreasonable as not to leave a man time enough for any more serious employment, or more agreeable amusement?

The only plea I shall use for the favour of the public is, that I have as great a respect for it as most authors have for themselves; and that I have sacrificed much of my own self-love for its sake, in preventing not only many mean things from seeing the light, but many which I thought tolerable. I would not be like those authors who forgive themselves some particular lines for the sake of a whole poem, and *vice versa* a whole poem for the sake of some particular lines. I believe no one qualification is so likely to make a good writer as the power of rejecting his own thoughts; and it must be this (if anything) that can give me a chance to be one. For what I have published, I can only hope to be pardoned; but for what I have burned, I deserve to be praised. On this account the world is under some obligation to me, and owes me the justice in return to look upon no verses as mine that are not inserted in this collection. And perhaps nothing could make it worth my while to own what are really so, but to avoid the imputation of so many dull and immoral things as, partly by malice, and partly by ignorance, have been ascribed to me. I must further acquit myself of the presumption of having lent my name to recommend any miscellanies or works of other men; a thing I never thought becoming a person who has hardly credit enough to answer for his own.

In this office of collecting my pieces, I am altogether uncertain whether to look upon myself as a man building a monument, or burying the dead. If time shall make it the former, may these poems (as long as they last) remain as a testimony that their author never made his talents subservient to the mean and unworthy ends of party or self-interest; the gratification of public prejudices or private passions; the flattery of the undeserving or the insult of the unfortunate. If I have written well, let it be considered that 'tis what no man can do without good sense, —a quality that not only renders one capable of being a good writer, but a good man. And if I have made any acquisition in the opinion of any one under the notion of the former, let it be continued to me under no other title than that of the latter.

But if this publication be only a more solemn funeral of my remains, I desire it may be known that I die in charity and in my senses, without any murmurs against the justice of this age, or any mad appeals to posterity. I declare I shall think the world in the right, and quietly submit to every truth which time shall discover to the prejudice of these writings; not so much as wishing so irrational a thing, as that every body should be deceived merely for my credit. However, I desire it may then be considered that there are very few things in this collection which were not written under the age of five-and-twenty: so that my youth may be made (as it never fails to be in executions) a case of compassion. That I was never so concerned about my works as to vindicate them in print; believing, if any thing was good, it would defend itself, and what was bad could never be defended. That I used no artifice to raise or continue a reputation, depreciated no dead author I was obliged to, bribed no living one with unjust praise, insulted no adversary with ill language: or, when I could not attack a rival's works, encouraged reports against his morals. To conclude, if this volume perish, let it serve as a warning to the critics, not to take too much pains for the future to destroy such things as will die of themselves; and a *memento mori* to some of my vain cotemporaries the poets, to teach them that, when real merit is wanting, it avails nothing to have been encouraged by the great, commended by the eminent, and favoured by the public in general.

November 10, 1716.

VARIATIONS IN THE AUTHOR'S MANUSCRIPT PREFACE.

After the words 'severely remarked on, ' p. 2, l. 41, it followed thus—For my part, I confess, had I seen things in this view at first, the public had never been troubled either with my writings, or with this apology for them. I am sensible how difficult it is to speak of one's self with decency: but when a man must speak of himself, the best way is to speak truth of himself, or, he may depend upon it, others will do it for him. I'll therefore make this preface a general confession of all my thoughts of my own poetry, resolving with the same freedom to expose myself, as it is in the power of any other to expose them. In the first place, I thank God and nature that I was born with a love to poetry; for nothing more conduces to fill up all the intervals of our time, or, if rightly used, to make the whole course of life entertaining: *Cantantes licet usque* (*minus via laedet*). 'Tis a vast happiness to possess the pleasures of the head, the only pleasures in which a man is sufficient to himself, and the only part of him which, to his satisfaction, he can employ all day long. The Muses are *amicae omnium horarum*; and, like our gay acquaintance, the best company in the world as long as one expects no real service from them. I confess there was a time when I was in love with myself, and my first productions were the children of Self-Love upon Innocence. I had made an epic poem, and panegyrics on all the princes in Europe, and thought myself the greatest genius that ever was. I can't but regret those delightful visions of my childhood, which, like the fine colours we see when our eyes are shut, are vanished for ever. Many trials and sad experience have so undeceived me by degrees, that I am utterly at a loss at what rate to value myself. As for fame, I shall be glad of any I can get, and not repine at any I miss; and as for vanity, I have enough to keep me from hanging myself, or even from wishing those hanged who would take it away. It was this that made me write. The sense of my faults made me correct.

After the words 'angry to find us so, ' p. 3, l. 36, occurred the following—In the first place I own that I have used my best endeavours to the finishing these pieces. That I made what advantage I could of the judgment of authors dead and living; and that I omitted no means in my power to be informed of my errors by my friends and by my enemies. And that I expect no favour on account of my youth, business, want of health, or any such idle excuses. But the true reason they are not yet more correct is owing to the consideration how short a time they and I have to live. A man that can expect but sixty years may be ashamed to employ thirty in measuring syllables and bringing sense and rhyme together. To spend our youth in pursuit of riches or fame, in hopes to enjoy them when we are old; and when we are old, we find it is too late to enjoy any thing. I therefore hope the wits will pardon me, if I reserve some of my time to save my soul; and that some wise men will be of my opinion, even if I should think a part of it better spent in the enjoyments of life than in pleasing the critics.

PASTORALS,

WITH A DISCOURSE ON PASTORAL POETRY. [3]

WRITTEN IN THE YEAR MDCCIV.

Rura mihi et rigui placeant in vallibus amnes,
Flumina amem, sylvasque, inglorius!

VIRG.

There are not, I believe, a greater number of any sort of verses than of those which are called Pastorals; nor a smaller, than of those which are truly so. It therefore seems necessary to give some account of this kind of poem; and it is my design to comprise in this short paper the substance of those numerous dissertations the critics have made on the subject, without omitting any of their rules in my own favour. You will also find some points reconciled, about which they seem to differ, and a few remarks which, I think, have escaped their observation.

The original of poetry is ascribed to that age which succeeded the creation of the world: and as the keeping of flocks seems to have been the first employment of mankind, the most ancient sort of poetry was probably *pastoral*. It is natural to imagine, that the leisure of those ancient shepherds admitting and inviting some diversion, none was so proper to that solitary and sedentary life as singing; and that in their songs they took occasion to celebrate their own felicity. From hence a poem was invented, and afterwards improved to a perfect image of that happy time; which, by giving us an esteem for the virtues of a former age, might recommend them to the present. And since the life of shepherds was attended with more tranquility than any other rural employment, the poets chose to introduce their persons, from whom it received the name of " pastoral. "

A pastoral is an imitation of the action of a shepherd, or one considered under that character. The form of this imitation is dramatic, or narrative, or mixed of both; the fable simple, the manners not too polite nor too rustic: the thoughts are plain, yet admit a little quickness and passion, but that short and flowing: the expression humble, yet as pure as the language will afford; neat, but not florid; easy and yet lively. In short, the fable, manners, thoughts, and expressions are full of the greatest simplicity in nature.

The complete character of this poem consists in simplicity, brevity, and delicacy; the two first of which render an eclogue natural, and the last delightful.

If we would copy nature, it may be useful to take this idea along with us, that pastoral is an image of what they call the Golden Age. So that we are not to describe our shepherds as shepherds at this day really are, but as they may be conceived then to have been, when the best of men followed the employment. To carry this resemblance yet further, it would not be amiss to give these shepherds some skill in astronomy, as far as it may be useful to that sort of life. And an air of piety to the gods should shine through the poem, which so visibly appears in all the works of antiquity: and it ought to preserve some relish of the old way of writing; the connexion should be loose, the narrations and descriptions short, and the periods concise. Yet it is not sufficient, that the sentences only be brief, the whole eclogue should be so too. For we cannot suppose poetry in those days to have been the business of men, but their recreation at vacant hours.

But with respect to the present age, nothing more conduces to make these composures natural than when some knowledge in rural affairs is discovered. This may be made to appear rather done by chance than on design, and sometimes is best shown by inference; lest by too much study to seem natural, we destroy that easy simplicity from whence arises the delight. For what is inviting in this sort of poetry, proceeds not so much from the idea of that business, as of the tranquility of a country life.

We must therefore use some illusion to render a pastoral delightful; and this consists in exposing the best side only of a shepherd's life, and in concealing its miseries. Nor is it enough to introduce shepherds discoursing together in a natural way; but a regard must be had to the subject—that it contain some particular beauty in itself, and that it be different in every eclogue. Besides, in each of them a designed scene or prospect is to be presented to our view, which should likewise have its variety. This variety is obtained in a great degree by frequent comparisons, drawn from the most agreeable objects of the country; by interrogations to things inanimate; by beautiful digressions, but those short; sometimes by insisting a little on circumstances; and lastly, by elegant turns on the words, which render the numbers extremely sweet and pleasing. As for the numbers themselves, though they are properly of the heroic measure, they should be the smoothest, the most easy and flowing imaginable.

It is by rules like these that we ought to judge of pastorals. And since the instructions given for any art are to be delivered as that art is in perfection, they must of necessity be derived from those in whom it is acknowledged so to be. It is therefore from the practice of Theocritus and Virgil (the only undisputed authors of pastoral) that the critics have drawn the foregoing notions concerning it.

Theocritus excels all others in nature and simplicity. The subjects of his 'Idyllia' are purely pastoral; but he is not so exact in his persons, having introduced reapers and fishermen as well as shepherds. He is apt to be too long in his descriptions, of which that of the cup in the first pastoral is a remarkable instance. In the manners he seems a little defective, for his swains are sometimes abusive and immodest, and perhaps too much inclining to rusticity; for instance, in his fourth and fifth 'Idyllia. ' But 'tis enough that all others learnt their excellencies from him, and that his dialect alone has a secret charm in it, which no other could ever attain.

Virgil, who copies Theocritus, refines upon his original: and in all points where judgment is principally concerned, he is much superior to his master.

Though some of his subjects are not pastoral in themselves, but only seem to be such, they have a wonderful variety in them, which the Greek was a stranger to. He exceeds him in regularity and brevity, and falls short of him in nothing but simplicity and propriety of style; the first of which perhaps was the fault of his age, and the last of his language.

Among the moderns, their success has been greatest who have most endeavoured to make these ancients their pattern. The most considerable genius appears in the famous Tasso, and our Spenser. Tasso in his 'Aminta' has as far excelled all the pastoral writers, as in his 'Gierusalemme' he has outdone the epic poets of his country. But as this piece seems to have been the original of a new sort of poem — the pastoral comedy — in Italy, it cannot so well be considered as a copy of the ancients. Spenser's Calendar, in Mr Dryden's opinion, is the most complete work of this kind which any nation has produced ever since the time of Virgil. Not but that he may be thought imperfect in some few points. His Eclogues are somewhat too long, if we compare them with the ancients. He is sometimes too allegorical, and treats of matters of religion in a pastoral style, as the Mantuan had done before him. He has employed the lyric measure, which is contrary to the practice of the old poets. His stanza is not still the same, nor always well chosen. This last may be the reason his expression is sometimes not concise enough: for the Tetrastic has obliged him to extend his sense to the length of four lines, which would have been more closely confined in the couplet.

In the manners, thoughts, and characters, he comes near to Theocritus himself; though, notwithstanding all the care he has taken, he is certainly inferior in his dialect: for the Doric had its beauty and propriety in the time of Theocritus; it was used in part of Greece, and frequent in the mouths of many of the greatest persons: whereas the old English and country phrases of Spenser were either entirely obsolete, or spoken only by people of the lowest condition. As there is a difference betwixt simplicity and rusticity, so the expression of simple thoughts should be plain, but not clownish. The addition he has made of a Calendar to his Eclogues, is very beautiful; since by this, besides the general moral of innocence and simplicity, which is common to other authors of pastoral, he has one peculiar to himself—he compares human life to the several seasons, and at once exposes to his readers a view of the great and little worlds, in their various changes and aspects. Yet the scrupulous division of his pastorals into months has obliged him either to repeat the same description, in other words, for three months together; or, when it was exhausted before, entirely to omit it: whence it comes to pass that some of his Eclogues (as the sixth, eighth, and tenth, for example) have nothing but their titles to distinguish them. The reason is evident—because the year has not that variety in it to furnish every month with a particular description, as it may every season.

Of the following eclogues I shall only say, that these four comprehend all the subjects which the critics upon Theocritus and Virgil will allow to be fit for pastoral: that they have as much variety of description, in respect of the several seasons, as Spenser's: that, in order to add to this variety, the several times of the day are observed, the rural employments in each season or time of day, and the rural scenes or places proper to such employments; not without some regard to the several ages of man, and the different passions proper to each age.

But after all, if they have any merit, it is to be attributed to some good old authors, whose works as I had leisure to study, so I hope I have not wanted care to imitate.

SPRING.

THE FIRST PASTORAL, OR DAMON.

TO SIR WILLIAM TRUMBULL. [4]

First in these fields I try the sylvan strains,
Nor blush to sport on Windsor's blissful plains:
Fair Thames, flow gently from thy sacred spring,
While on thy banks Sicilian Muses sing;
Let vernal airs through trembling osiers play,
And Albion's cliffs resound the rural lay.

You that, too wise for pride, too good for power,
Enjoy the glory to be great no more,
And, carrying with you all the world can boast,
To all the world illustriously are lost!   10
Oh, let my Muse her slender reed inspire,
Till in your native shades you tune the lyre:
So when the nightingale to rest removes,
The thrush may chant to the forsaken groves,
But, charm'd to silence, listens while she sings,
And all the aerial audience clap their wings.

Soon as the flocks shook off the nightly dews,
Two swains, whom Love kept wakeful, and the Muse,
Pour'd o'er the whitening vale their fleecy care,
Fresh as the morn, and as the season fair: 20
The dawn now blushing on the mountain's side,
Thus Daphnis spoke, and Strephou thus replied.

DAPHNIS.

Hear how the birds, on every bloomy spray,
With joyous music wake the dawning day!
Why sit we mute when early linnets sing,
When warbling Philomel salutes the spring?
Why sit we sad, when Phosphor[5] shines so clear,
And lavish Nature paints the purple year?

STREPHON.

Sing then, and Damon shall attend the strain,
While yon slow oxen turn the furrow'd plain. 30
Here the bright crocus and blue violet glow;
Here western winds on breathing roses blow.
I'll stake yon lamb, that near the fountain plays,
And from the brink his dancing shade surveys.

DAPHNIS.

And I this bowl, where wanton ivy twines,
And swelling clusters bend the curling vines:
Four Figures rising from the work appear,
The various Seasons of the rolling year;
And what is that, which binds the radiant sky,
Where twelve fair signs in beauteous order lie? 40

DAMON.

Then sing by turns, by turns the Muses sing;
Now hawthorns blossom, now the daisies spring;
Now leaves the trees, and flowers adorn the ground:
Begin, the vales shall every note rebound.

STREPHON.

Inspire me, Phoebus, in my Delia's praise,
With Waller's strains, or Granville's moving lays!
A milk-white bull shall at your altars stand,
That threats a fight, and spurns the rising sand.

DAPHNIS.

O Love! for Sylvia let me gain the prize,
And make my tongue victorious as her eyes; 50
No lambs or sheep for victims I'll impart,
Thy victim, Love, shall be the shepherd's heart.

STREPHON.

Me gentle Delia beckons from the plain,
Then hid in shades, eludes her eager swain;
But feigns a laugh, to see me search around,
And by that laugh the willing fair is found.

DAPHNIS.

The sprightly Sylvia trips along the green,
She runs, but hopes she does not run unseen;
While a kind glance at her pursuer flies,
How much at variance are her feet and eyes!   60

STREPHON.

O'er golden sands let rich Pactolus flow,
And trees weep amber on the banks of Po;
Blest Thames's shores the brightest beauties yield,
Feed here, my lambs, I'll seek no distant field.

DAPHNIS.

Celestial Venus haunts Idalia's groves;
Diana Cynthus, Ceres Hybla loves;
If Windsor-shades delight the matchless maid,
Cynthus and Hybla yield to Windsor-shade.

STREPHON.

All nature mourns, the skies relent in showers,
Hush'd are the birds, and closed the drooping flowers;   70
If Delia smile, the flowers begin to spring,
The skies to brighten, and the birds to sing.

DAPHNIS.

All nature laughs, the groves are fresh and fair,
The sun's mild lustre warms the vital air;
If Sylvia smiles, new glories gild the shore,
And vanquish'd Nature seems to charm no more.

STREPHON.

In spring the fields, in autumn hills I love,
At morn the plains, at noon the shady grove,
But Delia always; absent from her sight,
Nor plains at morn, nor groves at noon delight.   80

DAPHNIS.

Sylvia's like autumn ripe, yet mild as May,
More bright than noon, yet fresh as early day;
Even spring displeases, when she shines not here;
But, blest with her, 'tis spring throughout the year.

STREPHON.

Say, Daphnis, say, in what glad soil appears,
A wondrous tree[6] that sacred monarchs bears?
Tell me but this, and I'll disclaim the prize,
And give the conquest to thy Sylvia's eyes.

DAPHNIS.

Nay, tell me first, in what more happy fields
The thistle[7] springs, to which the lily[8] yields?   90
And then a nobler prize I will resign;
For Sylvia, charming Sylvia shall be thine.

DAMON.

Cease to contend, for, Daphnis, I decree,
The bowl to Strephon, and the lamb to thee:
Blest swains, whose nymphs in every grace excel;
Blest nymphs, whose swains those graces sing so well!
Now rise, and haste to yonder woodbine bowers,
A soft retreat from sudden vernal showers;
The turf with rural dainties shall be crown'd.
While opening blooms diffuse their sweets around.   100
For see! the gath'ring flocks to shelter tend,
And from the Pleiads fruitful showers descend.

*   *   *   *   *

VARIATIONS

VER. 36. And clusters lurk beneath the curling vines.

VER. 49-52. Originally thus in the MS.—

Pan, let my numbers equal Strephon's lays,
Of Parian stone thy statue will I raise;
But if I conquer and augment my fold,

Thy Parian statue shall be changed to gold.

VER. 61-64. It stood thus at first—

Let rich Iberia golden fleeces boast,
Her purple wool the proud Assyrian coast,
Blest Thames's shores, &c.

VER. 61-68 Originally thus in the MS.—

Go, flowery wreath, and let my Sylvia know,
Compared to thine how bright her beauties show;
Then die; and dying teach the lovely maid
How soon the brightest beauties are decay'd.

DAPHNIS.

Go, tuneful bird, that pleased the woods so long,
Of Amaryllis learn a sweeter song;
To Heaven arising then her notes convey,
For Heaven alone is worthy such a lay.

VER 69-73. These verses were thus at first—

All nature mourns, the birds their songs deny,
Nor wasted brooks the thirsty flowers supply;
If Delia smile, the flowers begin to spring,
The brooks to murmur, and the birds to sing.

VER. 99, 100, was originally—

The turf with country dainties shall be spread,
And trees with twining branches shade your head.

* * * * *

SUMMER,

THE SECOND PASTORAL, OR ALEXIS.

TO DR GARTH.

A shepherd's boy (he seeks no better name)
Led forth his flocks along the silver Thame,
Where dancing sunbeams on the waters play'd,
And verdant alders form'd a quivering shade.
Soft as he mourn'd, the streams forgot to flow,
The flocks around a dumb compassion show:
The Naiads wept in every watery bower,
And Jove consented in a silent shower.

Accept, O Garth[9] the Muse's early lays,
That adds this wreath of ivy to thy bays;   10
Hear what from love unpractised hearts endure:
From love, the sole disease thou canst not cure.

Ye shady beeches, and ye cooling streams,
Defence from Phoebus', not from Cupid's beams,
To you I mourn, nor to the deaf I sing,
'The woods shall answer, and their echo ring.'[10]
The hills and rocks attend my doleful lay;
Why art thou prouder and more hard than they?
The bleating sheep with my complaints agree,
They parch'd with heat, and I inflamed by thee.   20
The sultry Sirius burns the thirsty plains,
While in thy heart eternal winter reigns.

Where stray ye, Muses, in what lawn or grove,
While your Alexis pines in hopeless love?
In those fair fields where sacred Isis glides,
Or else where Cam his winding vales divides?
As in the crystal spring I view my face,
Fresh rising blushes paint the watery glass;
But since those graces please thy eyes no more,
I shun the fountains which I sought before.   30
Once I was skill'd in every herb that grew,
And every plant that drinks the morning dew;
Ah, wretched shepherd, what avails thy art,

To cure thy lambs, but not to heal thy heart!
Let other swains attend the rural care,
Feed fairer flocks, or richer fleeces shear:
But nigh yon mountain let me tune my lays,
Embrace my love, and bind my brows with bays.
That flute is mine which Colin's tuneful breath
Inspired when living, and bequeath'd in death; 40
He said, 'Alexis, take this pipe—the same
That taught the groves my Rosalinda's name:'
But now the reeds shall hang on yonder tree,
For ever silent, since despised by thee.
Oh! were I made by some transforming power
The captive bird that sings within thy bower!
Then might my voice thy listening ears employ,
And I those kisses he receives, enjoy.

And yet my numbers please the rural throng,
Rough Satyrs dance, and Pan applauds the song: 50
The Nymphs, forsaking every cave and spring,
Their early fruit, and milk-white turtles bring;
Each amorous nymph prefers her gifts in vain.
On you their gifts are all bestow'd again.
For you the swains the fairest flowers design,
And in one garland all their beauties join;
Accept the wreath which you deserve alone,
In whom all beauties are comprised in one.

See what delights in sylvan scenes appear!
Descending gods have found Elysium here. 60
In woods bright Venus with Adonis stray'd,
And chaste Diana haunts the forest shade.
Come, lovely nymph, and bless the silent hours,
When swains from shearing seek their nightly bowers,
When weary reapers quit the sultry field,
And crown'd with corn their thanks to Ceres yield;
This harmless grove no lurking viper hides,
But in my breast the serpent love abides.
Here bees from blossoms sip the rosy dew,
But your Alexis knows no sweets but you. 70
Oh, deign to visit our forsaken seats,
The mossy fountains, and the green retreats!
Where'er you walk, cool gales shall fan the glade,
Trees, where you sit, shall crowd into a shade:

Where'er you tread, the blushing flowers shall rise,
And all things flourish where you turn your eyes.
Oh, how I long with you to pass my days,
Invoke the Muses, and resound your praise!
Your praise the birds shall chant in every grove,
And winds shall waft it to the Powers above.   80
But would you sing, and rival Orpheus' strain,
The wondering forests soon should dance again,
The moving mountains hear the powerful call,
And headlong streams hang listening in their fall!

But see, the shepherds shun the noonday heat,
The lowing herds to murmuring brooks retreat,
To closer shades the panting flocks remove;
Ye gods! and is there no relief for love?
But soon the sun with milder rays descends
To the cool ocean, where his journey ends: 90
On me Love's fiercer flames for ever prey,
By night he scorches, as he burns by day.

* * * * *

VARIATIONS.

VER. 1-4 were thus printed in the first edition—

A faithful swain, whom Love had taught to sing, Bewail'd his fate beside a silver spring; Where gentle Thames his winding waters leads Through verdant forests, and through flowery meads.

VER. 3, 4. Originally thus in the MS. —

There to the winds he plain'd his hapless love, And Amaryllis fill'd the vocal grove.

VER. 27-29—

Oft in the crystal spring I cast a view, And equall'd Hylas, if the glass be true; But since those graces meet my eyes no more I shun, &c.

VER. 79, 80—

Your praise the tuneful birds to heaven shall bear, And listening wolves grow milder as they hear.

VER. 91—

Me love inflames, nor will his fires allay.

AUTUMN.

THE THIRD PASTORAL, Or HYLAS AND AEGON.

TO MR WYCHERLEY. [11]

Beneath the shade a spreading beech displays,
Hylas and AEgon sung their rural lays;
This mourn'd a faithless, that an absent love.
And Delia's name and Doris' fill'd the grove.
Ye Mantuan nymphs, your sacred succour bring;
Hylas and AEgon's rural lays I sing.

Thou, whom the Nine with Plautus' wit inspire,
The art of Terence, and Menander's fire;
Whose sense instructs us, and whose humour charms,
Whose judgment sways us, and whose spirit warms! 10
Oh, skill'd in Nature! see the hearts of swains,
Their artless passions, and their tender pains.

Now setting Phoebus shone serenely bright,
And fleecy clouds were streak'd with purple light;
When tuneful Hylas, with melodious moan,
Taught rocks to weep, and made the mountains groan.

Go, gentle gales, and bear my sighs away!
To Delia's ear the tender notes convey.
As some sad turtle his lost love deplores,
And with deep murmurs fills the sounding shores, 20
Thus, far from Delia, to the winds I mourn,
Alike unheard, unpitied, and forlorn.

Go, gentle gales, and bear my sighs along!
For her, the feather'd choirs neglect their song:
For her, the limes their pleasing shades deny;
For her, the lilies hang their heads and die.
Ye flowers that droop, forsaken by the spring,
Ye birds that, left by summer, cease to sing,
Ye trees that fade when autumn-heats remove,
Say, is not absence death to those who love? 30

Go, gentle gales, and bear my sighs away!

Cursed be the fields that cause my Delia's stay;
Fade every blossom, wither every tree,
Die every flower, and perish all but she.

What have I said? Where'er my Delia flies,
Let spring attend, and sudden flowers arise;
Let opening roses knotted oaks adorn,
And liquid amber drop from every thorn.

Go, gentle gales, and bear my sighs along!
The birds shall cease to tune their evening song,   40
The winds to breathe, the waving woods to move,
And streams to murmur, ere I cease to love.
Not bubbling fountains to the thirsty swain,
Not balmy sleep to labourers faint with pain,
Not showers to larks, or sunshine to the bee,
Are half so charming as thy sight to me.
Go, gentle gales, and bear my sighs away!
Come, Delia, come; ah, why this long delay?
Through rocks and caves the name of Delia sounds,
Delia, each care and echoing rock rebounds.   50
Ye Powers, what pleasing frenzy soothes my mind!
Do lovers dream, or is my Delia kind?
She comes, my Delia comes!—Now cease, my lay,
And cease, ye gales, to bear my sighs away!

Next AEgon sung, while Windsor groves admired;
Rehearse, ye Muses, what yourselves inspired.

Resound, ye hills, resound my mournful strain!
Of perjured Doris, dying I complain:
Here where the mountains, lessening as they rise,
Lose the low vales, and steal into the skies: 60
While labouring oxen, spent with toil and heat,
In their loose traces from the field retreat:
While curling smokes from village-tops are seen,
And the fleet shades glide o'er the dusky green.

Resound, ye hills, resound my mournful lay!
Beneath yon poplar oft we pass'd the day:
Oft on the rind I carved her amorous vows,
While she with garlands hung the bending boughs:
The garlands fade, the vows are worn away;

So dies her love, and so my hopes decay. 70

Resound, ye hills, resound my mournful strain!
Now bright Arcturus glads the teeming grain,
Now golden fruits on loaded branches shine,
And grateful clusters swell with floods of wine;
Now blushing berries paint the yellow grove;
Just gods! shall all things yield returns but love?

Resound, ye hills, resound my mournful lay!
The shepherds cry, 'Thy flocks are left a prey'—
Ah! what avails it me, the flocks to keep,
Who lost my heart—while I preserved my sheep. 80
Pan came, and ask'd, what magic caused my smart,
Or what ill eyes malignant glances dart?
What eyes but hers, alas, have power to move?
And is there magic but what dwells in love?

Resound, ye hills, resound my mournful strains!
I'll fly from shepherds, flocks, and flowery plains.
From shepherds, flocks, and plains, I may remove,
Forsake mankind, and all the world—but Love!
I know thee, Love! on foreign mountains bred,
Wolves gave thee suck, and savage tigers fed. 90
Thou wert from Etna's burning entrails torn,
Got by fierce whirlwinds, and in thunder born!

Resound, ye hills, resound my mournful lay!
Farewell, ye woods; adieu, the light of day!
One leap from yonder cliff shall end my pains;
No more, ye hills, no more resound my strains!

Thus sung the shepherds till the approach of night,
The skies yet blushing with departing light,
When falling dews with spangles deck'd the glade,
And the low sun had lengthen'd every shade. 100

* * * * *

VARIATIONS.

VER. 48-51—Originally thus in the MS. —

With him through Libya's burning plains I'll go, On Alpine mountains tread the eternal snow; Yet feel no heat but what our loves impart, And dread no coldness but in Thyrsis' heart.

WINTER.

THE FOURTH PASTORAL, OR DAPHNE.

TO THE MEMORY OF MRS TEMPEST. [12]

LYCIDAS.

Thyrsis, the music of that murmuring spring
Is not so mournful as the strains you sing;
Nor rivers winding through the vales below,
So sweetly warble, or so smoothly flow.
Now sleeping flocks on their soft fleeces lie,
The moon, serene in glory, mounts the sky,
While silent birds forget their tuneful lays,
Oh sing of Daphne's fate, and Daphne's praise!

THYRSIS.

Behold the groves that shine with silver frost,
Their beauty wither'd, and their verdure lost.   10
Here shall I try the sweet Alexis' strain,
That call'd the listening Dryads to the plain?
Thames heard the numbers as he flow'd along,
And bade his willows learn the moving song.

LYCIDAS.

So may kind rains their vital moisture yield
And swell the future harvest of the field.
Begin; this charge the dying Daphne gave,
And said, 'Ye shepherds, sing around my grave!'
Sing, while beside the shaded tomb I mourn,
And with fresh bays her rural shrine adorn.   20

THYRSIS.

Ye gentle Muses, leave your crystal spring,
Let nymphs and sylvans cypress garlands bring;
Ye weeping Loves, the stream with myrtles hide,
And break your bows, as when Adonis died;
And with your golden darts, now useless grown,

Inscribe a verse on this relenting stone:
'Let Nature change, let Heaven and Earth deplore,
Fair Daphne's dead, and Love is now no more!'
'Tis done, and Nature's various charms decay;
See gloomy clouds obscure the cheerful day! 30
Now hung with pearls the dropping trees appear,
Their faded honours scatter'd on her bier.
See where, on earth, the flowery glories lie,
With her they flourish'd, and with her they die.
Ah, what avail the beauties Nature wore,
Fair Daphne's dead, and Beauty is no more!

For her the flocks refuse their verdant food,
The thirsty heifers shun the gliding flood,
The silver swans her hapless fate bemoan,
In notes more sad than when they sing their own; 40
In hollow caves sweet Echo silent lies,
Silent, or only to her name replies;
Her name with pleasure once she taught the shore;
Now Daphne's dead, and Pleasure is no more!

No grateful dews descend from evening skies,
Nor morning odours from the flowers arise;
No rich perfumes refresh the fruitful field,
Nor fragrant herbs their native incense yield.
The balmy zephyrs, silent since her death,
Lament the ceasing of a sweeter breath; 50
Th' industrious bees neglect their golden store;
Fair Daphne's dead, and Sweetness is no more!

No more the mounting larks, while Daphne sings,
Shall, listening in mid air, suspend their wings;
No more the birds shall imitate her lays,
Or, hush'd with wonder, hearken from the sprays:
No more the streams their murmurs shall forbear,
A sweeter music than their own to hear;
But tell the reeds, and tell the vocal shore,
Fair Daphne's dead, and Music is no more! 60

Her fate is whisper'd by the gentle breeze,
And told in sighs to all the trembling trees;
The trembling trees, in every plain and wood,
Her fate remurmur to the silver flood;

The silver flood, so lately calm, appears
Swell'd with new passion, and o'erflows with tears;
The winds and trees and floods her death deplore,
Daphne, our grief, our glory now no more!

But see! where Daphne wondering mounts on high
Above the clouds, above the starry sky!   70
Eternal beauties grace the shining scene,
Fields ever fresh, and groves for ever green!
There while you rest in amaranthine bowers,
Or from those meads select unfading flowers,
Behold us kindly, who your name implore,
Daphne, our goddess, and our grief no more!

LYCIDAS.

How all things listen, while thy Muse complains!
Such silence waits on Philomela's strains,
In some still evening, when the whispering breeze
Pants on the leaves, and dies upon the trees.   80
To thee, bright goddess, oft a lamb shall bleed,
If teeming ewes increase my fleecy breed.
While plants their shade, or flowers their odours give,
Thy name, thy honour, and thy praise shall live!

THYRSIS.

But see, Orion sheds unwholesome dews;
Arise, the pines a noxious shade diffuse;
Sharp Boreas blows, and Nature feels decay,
Time conquers all, and we must Time obey.
Adieu, ye vales, ye mountains, streams, and groves;
Adieu, ye shepherds, rural lays, and loves;   90
Adieu, my flocks; farewell, ye sylvan crew;
Daphne, farewell; and all the world, adieu!

   * * * * *

VARIATIONS.

VER. 29, 30—Originally thus in the MS. —

'Tis done, and Nature's changed since you are gone; Behold, the clouds have put their mourning on.

VER. 83, 84. Originally thus in the MS. —

While vapours rise, and driving snows descend, Thy honour, name, and praise shall never end.

MESSIAH.

A SACRED ECLOGUE, IN IMITATION OF VIRGIL'S 'POLLIO.'

ADVERTISEMENT.

In reading several passages of the Prophet Isaiah, which foretell the coming of Christ and the felicities attending it, I could not but observe a remarkable parity between many of the thoughts, and those in the 'Pollio' of Virgil. This will not seem surprising, when we reflect, that the eclogue was taken from a Sibylline prophecy on the same subject. One may judge that Virgil did not copy it line by line, but selected such ideas as best agreed with the nature of pastoral poetry, and disposed them in that manner which served most to beautify his piece. I have endeavoured the same in this imitation of him, though without admitting anything of my own; since it was written with this particular view, that the reader, by comparing the several thoughts, might see how far the images and descriptions of the prophet are superior to those of the poet. But as I fear I have prejudiced them by my management, I shall subjoin the passages of Isaiah and those of Virgil, under the same disadvantage of a literal translation.

Ye Nymphs of Solyma! begin the song:
To heavenly themes sublimer strains belong.
The mossy fountains, and the sylvan shades,
The dreams of Pindus and the Aonian maids,
Delight no more—O Thou my voice inspire
Who touch'd Isaiah's hallow'd lips with fire!

Rapt into future times, the bard begun:
A virgin shall conceive, a virgin bear a son!
From Jesse's root behold the branch arise,
Whose sacred flower with fragrance fills the skies: 10
The ethereal Spirit o'er its leaves shall move,
And on its top descends the mystic Dove.
Ye Heavens! from high the dewy nectar pour,
And in soft silence shed the kindly shower!
The sick and weak the healing plant shall aid,
From storms a shelter, and from heat a shade.
All crimes shall cease, and ancient fraud shall fail;
Returning Justice lift aloft her scale;

Peace o'er the world her olive wand extend,
And white-robed Innocence from heaven descend.   20
Swift fly the years, and rise the expected morn!
Oh spring to light, auspicious Babe, be born!
See, Nature hastes her earliest wreaths to bring,
With all the incense of the breathing spring!
See lofty Lebanon his head advance,
See nodding forests on the mountains dance:
See spicy clouds from lowly Saron rise,
And Carmel's flowery top perfumes the skies!
Hark! a glad voice the lonely desert cheers;
'Prepare the way! a God, a God appears:'   30
'A God, a God!' the vocal hills reply,
The rocks proclaim the approaching Deity.
Lo, Earth receives him from the bending skies!
Sink down, ye mountains, and ye valleys, rise;
With heads declined, ye cedars, homage pay;
Be smooth, ye rocks, ye rapid floods, give way!
The Saviour comes! by ancient bards foretold:
Hear him, ye deaf, and all ye blind, behold!
He from thick films shall purge the visual ray,
And on the sightless eyeball pour the day: 40
'Tis he the obstructed paths of sound shall clear,
And bid new music charm th' unfolding ear:
The dumb shall sing, the lame his crutch forego,
And leap exulting like the bounding roe.
No sigh, no murmur the wide world shall hear,
From every face he wipes off every tear.
In adamantine chains shall Death be bound,
And Hell's grim tyrant feel th' eternal wound.
As the good shepherd tends his fleecy care,
Seeks freshest pasture and the purest air,   50
Explores the lost, the wandering sheep directs,
By day o'ersees them, and by night protects,
The tender lambs he raises in his arms,
Feeds from his hand, and in his bosom warms;
Thus shall mankind his guardian care engage,
The promised Father of the future age.
No more shall nation against nation rise,
Nor ardent warriors meet with hateful eyes,
Nor fields with gleaming steel be cover'd o'er,
The brazen trumpets kindle rage no more;   60
But useless lances into scythes shall bend,

And the broad falchion in a ploughshare end.
Then palaces shall rise; the joyful son
Shall finish what his short-lived sire begun;
Their vines a shadow to their race shall yield,
And the same hand that sow'd, shall reap the field;
The swain in barren deserts with surprise
See lilies spring, and sudden verdure rise;
And start, amidst the thirsty wilds, to hear
New falls of water murmuring in his ear. 70
On rifted rocks, the dragons' late abodes,
The green reed trembles, and the bulrush nods,
Waste sandy valleys, once perplex'd with thorn,
The spiry fir, and shapely box adorn:
To leafless shrubs the flowering palms succeed,
And odorous myrtle to the noisome weed.
The lambs with wolves shall graze the verdant mead,
And boys in flowery bands the tiger lead;
The steer and lion at one crib shall meet,
And harmless serpents lick the pilgrim's feet. 80
The smiling infant in his hand shall take
The crested basilisk and speckled snake,
Pleased, the green lustre of the scales survey,
And with their forky tongue shall innocently play.
Rise, crown'd with light, imperial Salem, rise!
Exalt thy towery head, and lift thy eyes!
See, a long race thy spacious courts adorn;
See future sons, and daughters yet unborn,
In crowding ranks on every side arise,
Demanding life, impatient for the skies! 90
See barbarous nations at thy gates attend,
Walk in thy light and in thy temple bend;
See thy bright altars throng'd with prostrate kings,
And heap'd with products of Sabean springs!
For thee Idume's spicy forests blow,
And seeds of gold in Ophir's mountains glow.
See Heaven its sparkling portals wide display,
And break upon thee in a flood of day!
No more the rising sun shall gild the morn,
Nor evening Cynthia fill her silver horn; 100
But lost, dissolved in thy superior rays,
One tide of glory, one unclouded blaze
O'erflow thy courts: The Light himself shall shine
Reveal'd, and God's eternal day be thine!

The seas shall waste, the skies in smoke decay,
Rocks fall to dust, and mountains melt away;
But fix'd his word, his saving power remains;
Thy realm for ever lasts, thy own MESSIAH reigns!

AN ESSAY ON CRITICISM.

WRITTEN IN THE YEAR MDCCIX.

PART I.

Introduction. —That 'tis as great a fault to judge ill, as to write ill, and a more dangerous one to the public, ver. 1. That a true taste is as rare to be found as a true genius, ver. 9-18. That most men are born with some taste, but spoiled by false education, ver. 19-25. The multitude of critics, and causes of them, ver. 26-45. That we are to study our own taste, and know the limits of it, ver. 46-67. Nature the best guide of judgment, ver. 68-87. Improved by art and rules, which are but methodised nature, ver. 88. Rules derived from the practice of the ancient poets, ver. 88-110. That therefore the ancients are necessary to be studied by a critic, particularly Homer and Virgil, ver. 120-138. Of licences, and the use of them by the ancients, ver. 140-180. Reverence due to the ancients, and praise of them, ver. 181, &c.

PART II.

Causes hindering a true judgment—(1.) pride, ver. 208; (2.) imperfect learning, ver. 215; (3.) judging by parts and not by the whole, ver. 233-288. —Critics in wit, language, versification only, ver. 288, 305, 339, &c. ; (4.) being too hard to please, or too apt to admire, ver. 384; (5.) partiality—too much love to a sect—to the ancients or moderns, ver. 394; (6.) prejudice or prevention, ver. 408; (7.) singularity, ver. 424; (8.) in constancy, ver. 430; (9.) party spirit, ver. 452, &c. ; (10.) envy, ver. 466; against envy, and in praise of good-nature, ver. 508, &c. When severity is chiefly to be used by critics, ver. 526, &c.

PART III.

Rules for the conduct of manners in a critic—(1.) candour, ver. 503; modesty, ver. 566; good-breeding, ver. 572; sincerity, and freedom of advice, ver. 578; (2.) when one's counsel is to be restrained, ver. 584. Character of an incorrigible poet, ver. 600. And of an impertinent critic, ver. 610, &c. Character of a good critic, ver. 629. The history of criticism, and characters of the best critics—Aristotle, ver. 645; Horace, ver. 653; Dionysius, ver. 665; Petronius, ver. 667; Quintillian, ver. 670; Longinus, ver. 675. Of the decay of criticism, and its revival. Erasmus, ver. 693; Vida, ver. 705; Boileau, ver. 714; Lord Roscommon, &c., ver. 725. CONCLUSION.

PART FIRST.

'Tis hard to say, if greater want of skill
Appear in writing or in judging ill;
But, of the two, less dangerous is the offence
To tire our patience, than mislead our sense.
Some few in that, but numbers err in this;
Ten censure wrong for one who writes amiss;
A fool might once himself alone expose,
Now one in verse makes many more in prose.

'Tis with our judgments as our watches, none
Go just alike, yet each believes his own.   10
In poets as true genius is but rare,
True taste as seldom, is the critic's share;
Both must alike from Heaven derive their light,
These born to judge, as well as those to write.
Let such teach others who themselves excel.
And censure freely who have written well.
Authors are partial to their wit, 'tis true,
But are not critics to their judgment too?

Yet if we look more closely, we shall find
Most have the seeds of judgment in their mind: 20
Nature affords at least a glimmering light;
The lines, though touch'd but faintly, are drawn right.
But as the slightest sketch, if justly traced,
Is by ill colouring but the more disgraced,
So by false learning is good sense defaced:
Some are bewilder'd in the maze of schools,
And some made coxcombs Nature meant but fools.
In search of wit these lose their common sense,
And then turn critics in their own defence:
Each burns alike, who can, or cannot write,   30
Or with a rival's, or an eunuch's spite.
All fools have still an itching to deride,
And fain would be upon the laughing side;
If Maevius scribble in Apollo's spite,
There are who judge still worse than he can write.

Some have at first for wits, then poets pass'd,
Turn'd critics next, and proved plain fools at last.

Some neither can for wits nor critics pass,
As heavy mules are neither horse nor ass.
Those half-learn'd witlings, numerous in our isle, 40
As half-form'd insects on the banks of Nile;
Unfinished things, one knows not what to call,
Their generation's so equivocal:
To tell 'em would a hundred tongues require,
Or one vain wit's, that might a hundred tire.

But you who seek to give and merit fame,
And justly bear a critic's noble name,
Be sure yourself and your own reach to know,
How far your genius, taste, and learning go;
Launch not beyond your depth, but be discreet, 50
And mark that point where sense and dulness meet.

Nature to all things fix'd the limits fit,
And wisely curb'd proud man's pretending wit.
As on the land while here the ocean gains,
In other parts it leaves wide sandy plains;
Thus in the soul while memory prevails,
The solid power of understanding fails;
Where beams of warm imagination play,
The memory's soft figures melt away.
One science only will one genius fit, 60
So vast is art, so narrow human wit:
Not only bounded to peculiar arts,
But oft in those confined to single parts.
Like kings, we lose the conquests gain'd before,
By vain ambition still to make them more;
Each might his several province well command,
Would all but stoop to what they understand.

First follow Nature, and your judgment frame
By her just standard, which is still the same:
Unerring Nature, still divinely bright, 70
One clear, unchanged, and universal light,
Life, force, and beauty, must to all impart,
At once the source, and end, and test of Art.
Art from that fund each just supply provides,
Works without show, and without pomp presides;
In some fair body thus the informing soul
With spirits feeds, with vigour fills the whole,

Each motion guides, and every nerve sustains,
Itself unseen, but in the effects, remains.
Some, to whom Heaven in wit has been profuse,   80
Want as much more to turn it to its use;
For wit and judgment often are at strife,
Though meant each other's aid, like man and wife,
'Tis more to guide than spur the Muse's steed,
Restrain his fury, than provoke his speed;
The winged courser, like a generous horse,
Shows most true mettle when you check his course.

Those rules, of old discover'd, not devised,
Are Nature still, but Nature methodised;
Nature, like liberty, is but restrain'd   90
By the same laws which first herself ordain'd.
Hear how learn'd Greece her useful rules indites,
When to repress, and when indulge our flights:
High on Parnassus' top her sons she show'd,
And pointed out those arduous paths they trod;
Held from afar, aloft, the immortal prize,
And urged the rest by equal steps to rise.
Just precepts thus from great examples given,
She drew from them what they derived from Heaven.
The generous critic fann'd the poet's fire,   100
And taught the world with reason to admire.
Then Criticism the Muse's handmaid proved,
To dress her charms, and make her more beloved:
But following wits from that intention stray'd,
Who could not win the mistress, woo'd the maid;
Against the poets their own arms they turn'd,
Sure to hate most the men from whom they learn'd.
So modern 'pothecaries, taught the art,
By doctor's bills to play the doctor's part,
Bold in the practice of mistaken rules,   110
Prescribe, apply, and call their masters fools.
Some on the leaves of ancient authors prey,
Nor time nor moths e'er spoil'd so much as they.
Some drily plain, without invention's aid,
Write dull receipts how poems may be made.
These leave the sense, their learning to display,
And those explain the meaning quite away.

You then, whose judgment the right course would steer,

Know well each ancient's proper character;
His fable, subject, scope in every page;   120
Religion, country, genius of his age;
Without all these at once before your eyes,
Cavil you may, but never criticise.
Be Homer's works your study and delight,
Read them by day, and meditate by night;
Thence form your judgment, thence your maxims bring,
And trace the Muses upward to their spring.
Still with itself compared, his text peruse;
And let your comment be the Mantuan Muse.
When first young Maro in his boundless mind,   130
A work t' outlast immortal Rome design'd,
Perhaps he seem'd above the critic's law,
And but from Nature's fountains scorn'd to draw:
But when t' examine every part he came,
Nature and Homer were, he found, the same.
Convinced, amazed, he checks the bold design,
And rules as strict his labour'd work confine,
As if the Stagyrite[13] o'erlook'd each line.
Learn hence for ancient rules a just esteem;
To copy nature is to copy them.   140
Some beauties yet no precepts can declare,
For there's a happiness as well as care.
Music resembles poetry, in each
Are nameless graces which no methods teach,
And which a master-hand alone can reach.
If, where the rules not far enough extend,
(Since rules were made but to promote their end)
Some lucky license answer to the full
The intent proposed, that license is a rule;
Thus Pegasus, a nearer way to take,   150
May boldly deviate from the common track;
Great wits sometimes may gloriously offend,
And rise to faults true critics dare not mend,
From vulgar bounds with brave disorder part,
And snatch a grace beyond the reach of art,
Which, without passing through the judgment, gains
The heart, and all its end at once attains.
In prospects thus, some objects please our eyes,
Which out of nature's common order rise,
The shapeless rock, or hanging precipice.   160
But though the ancients thus their rules invade,

(As kings dispense with laws themselves have made)
Moderns, beware! or if you must offend
Against the precept, ne'er transgress its end;
Let it be seldom, and compell'd by need,
And have at least their precedent to plead.
The critic else proceeds without remorse,
Seizes your fame, and puts his laws in force.

I know there are, to whose presumptuous thoughts,
Those freer beauties, even in them, seem faults.   170
Some figures monstrous and misshaped appear,
Consider'd singly, or beheld too near,
Which, but proportion'd to their light, or place,
Due distance reconciles to form and grace.
A prudent chief not always must display
His powers in equal ranks, and fair array,
But with the occasion and the place comply,
Conceal his force, nay, seem sometimes to fly.
Those oft are stratagems which errors seem,
Nor is it Homer nods, but we that dream.   180

Still green with bays each ancient altar stands,
Above the reach of sacrilegious hands;
Secure from flames, from envy's fiercer rage,
Destructive war, and all-involving age.
See from each clime the learn'd their incense bring!
Hear in all tongues consenting paeans ring!
In praise so just let every voice be join'd,
And fill the general chorus of mankind.
Hail, Bards triumphant! born in happier days;
Immortal heirs of universal praise!   190
Whose honours with increase of ages grow,
As streams roll down, enlarging as they flow;
Nations unborn your mighty names shall sound,
And worlds applaud that must not yet be found!
Oh may some spark of your celestial fire,
The last, the meanest of your sons inspire,
(That on weak wings, from far, pursues your flights,
Glows while he reads, but trembles as he writes)
To teach vain wits a science little known,
T' admire superior sense, and doubt their own!   200

* * * * *

VARIATIONS.

Between ver. 25 and 26 were these lines, since omitted by the author:—

Many are spoil'd by that pedantic throng, Who with great pains teach youth to reason wrong. Tutors, like virtuosos, oft inclined By strange transfusion to improve the mind, Draw off the sense we have, to pour in new; Which yet, with all their skill, they ne'er could do.

VER. 80,81: —

There are whom Heaven has bless'd with store of wit, Yet want as much again to manage it.

VER. 123. The author after this verse originally inserted the following, which he has however omitted in all the editions: —

Zoilus, had these been known, without a name Had died, and Perault ne'er been damn'd to fame; The sense of sound antiquity had reign'd, And sacred Homer yet been unprofaned. None e'er had thought his comprehensive mind To modern customs, modern rules confined; Who for all ages writ, and all mankind.

VER. 130, 131: —

When first young Maro sung of kings and wars, Ere warning Phoebus touch'd his trembling ears

PART SECOND.

Of all the causes which conspire to blind
Man's erring judgment, and misguide the mind,
What the weak head with strongest bias rules,
Is PRIDE, the never-failing vice of fools.
Whatever Nature has in worth denied,
She gives in large recruits of needless pride;
For as in bodies, thus in souls, we find
What wants in blood and spirits, swell'd with wind:
Pride, where wit fails, steps in to our defence,
And fills up all the mighty void of sense: 210
If once right reason drives that cloud away,
Truth breaks upon us with resistless day.
Trust not yourself; but your defects to know,
Make use of every friend—and every foe.

A little learning is a dangerous thing;
Drink deep, or taste not the Pierian spring:
There shallow draughts intoxicate the brain,
And drinking largely sobers us again.
Fired at first sight with what the Muse imparts,
In fearless youth we tempt the heights of arts, 220
While from the bounded level of our mind,
Short views we take, nor see the lengths behind;
But, more advanced, behold with strange surprise,
New distant scenes of endless science rise!
So, pleased at first the towering Alps we try,
Mount o'er the vales, and seem to tread the sky,
The eternal snows appear already past,
And the first clouds and mountains seem the last:
But, those attain'd, we tremble to survey
The growing labours of the lengthen'd way, 230
The increasing prospect tires our wandering eyes,
Hills peep o'er hills, and Alps on Alps arise!

A perfect judge will read each work of wit
With the same spirit that its author writ:
Survey the WHOLE, nor seek slight faults to find
Where nature moves, and rapture warms the mind;
Nor lose, for that malignant dull delight,

The generous pleasure to be charm'd with wit.
But in such lays as neither ebb nor flow,
Correctly cold, and regularly low,   240
That, shunning faults, one quiet tenor keep,
We cannot blame indeed—but we may sleep.
In wit, as nature, what affects our hearts
Is not the exactness of peculiar parts;
'Tis not a lip, or eye, we beauty call,
But the joint force and full result of all.
Thus when we view some well-proportion'd dome,
(The world's just wonder, and even thine, O Rome!)
No single parts unequally surprise,
All comes united to th' admiring eyes;   250
No monstrous height, or breadth, or length appear;
The whole at once is bold, and regular.

Whoever thinks a faultless piece to see,
Thinks what ne'er was, nor is, nor e'er shall be.
In every work regard the writer's end,
Since none can compass more than they intend;
And if the means be just, the conduct true,
Applause, in spite of trivial faults, is due.
As men of breeding, sometimes men of wit,
To avoid great errors, must the less commit: 260
Neglect the rules each verbal critic lays,
For not to know some trifles is a praise.
Most critics, fond of some subservient art,
Still make the whole depend upon a part:
They talk of principles, but notions prize,
And all to one loved folly sacrifice.

Once on a time, La Mancha's knight,[14] they say,
A certain bard encountering on the way,
Discoursed in terms as just, with looks as sage,
As e'er could Dennis, of the Grecian stage;   270
Concluding all were desperate sots and fools,
Who durst depart from Aristotle's rules.
Our author, happy in a judge so nice,
Produced his play, and begg'd the knight's advice;
Made him observe the subject, and the plot,
The Manners, Passions, Unities; what not?
All which, exact to rule, were brought about,
Were but a combat in the lists left out.

'What! leave the combat out?' exclaims the knight.
'Yes, or we must renounce the Stagyrite.' 280
'Not so, by Heaven!' (he answers in a rage);
'Knights, squires, and steeds must enter on the stage.'
'So vast a throng the stage can ne'er contain.'
'Then build a new, or act it in a plain.'

Thus critics, of less judgment than caprice,
Curious, not knowing, not exact but nice,
Form short ideas, and offend in arts
(As most in manners) by a love to parts.

Some to conceit alone their taste confine,
And glittering thoughts struck out at every line; 290
Pleased with a work where nothing's just or fit;
One glaring chaos and wild heap of wit.
Poets, like painters, thus, unskill'd to trace
The naked nature and the living grace,
With gold and jewels cover every part,
And hide with ornaments their want of art.
True wit is nature to advantage dress'd;
What oft was thought, but ne'er so well express'd;
Something, whose truth convinced at sight we find,
That gives us back the image of our mind. 300
As shades more sweetly recommend the light,
So modest plainness sets off sprightly wit.
For works may have more wit than does 'em good,
As bodies perish through excess of blood.

Others for language all their care express,
And value books, as women men, for dress:
Their praise is still—'The style is excellent;'
The sense, they humbly take upon content.
Words are like leaves, and where they most abound,
Much fruit of sense beneath is rarely found. 310
False eloquence, like the prismatic glass,
Its gaudy colours spreads on every place;
The face of Nature we no more survey,
All glares alike, without distinction gay;
But true expression, like the unchanging sun,
Clears, and improves whate'er it shines upon;
It gilds all objects, but it alters none.
Expression is the dress of thought, and still

Appears more decent, as more suitable;
A vile conceit in pompous words express'd,   320
Is like a clown in regal purple dress'd:
For different styles with different subjects sort,
As several garbs with country, town, and court.
Some by old words to fame have made pretence,
Ancients in phrase, mere moderns in their sense;
Such labour'd nothings, in so strange a style,
Amaze the unlearn'd, and make the learned smile.
Unlucky, as Fungoso[15] in the play,
These sparks with awkward vanity display
What the fine gentleman wore yesterday;   330
And but so mimic ancient wits at best,
As apes our grandsires, in their doublets dress'd.
In words, as fashions, the same rule will hold;
Alike fantastic, if too new, or old:
Be not the first by whom the new are tried,
Nor yet the last to lay the old aside.

But most by numbers judge a poet's song;
And smooth or rough, with them, is right or wrong:
In the bright Muse, though thousand charms conspire,
Her voice is all these tuneful fools admire;   340
Who haunt Parnassus but to please their ear,
Not mend their minds; as some to church repair,
Not for the doctrine, but the music there.
These equal syllables alone require,
Though oft the ear the open vowels tire;
While expletives their feeble aid do join,
And ten low words oft creep in one dull line:
While they ring round the same unvaried chimes,
With sure returns of still expected rhymes;
Where'er you find 'the cooling western breeze,'   350
In the next line, it 'whispers through the trees:'
If crystal streams 'with pleasing murmurs creep,'
The reader's threaten'd (not in vain) with 'sleep:'
Then, at the last and only couplet fraught
With some unmeaning thing they call a thought,
A needless Alexandrine ends the song
That, like a wounded snake, drags its slow length along.
Leave such to tune their own dull rhymes, and know
What's roundly smooth, or languishingly slow;
And praise the easy vigour of a line,   360

Where Denham's strength, and Waller's sweetness join.
True ease in writing comes from art, not chance,
As those move easiest who have learn'd to dance.
'Tis not enough no harshness gives offence,
The sound must seem an echo to the sense;
Soft is the strain when Zephyr gently blows,
And the smooth stream in smoother numbers flows:
But when loud surges lash the sounding shore,
The hoarse, rough verse should like the torrent roar.
When Ajax strives some rock's vast weight to throw,   370
The line too labours, and the words move slow;
Not so, when swift Camilla scours the plain,
Flies o'er the unbending corn, and skims along the main.
Hear how Timotheus' varied lays surprise,
And bid alternate passions fall and rise!
While, at each change, the son of Libyan Jove
Now burns with glory, and then melts with love;
Now his fierce eyes with sparkling fury glow,
Now sighs steal out, and tears begin to flow:
Persians and Greeks like turns of nature found,   380
And the world's victor stood subdued by sound!
The power of music all our hearts allow,
And what Timotheus[16] was, is Dryden now.

Avoid extremes; and shun the fault of such
Who still are pleased, too little or too much.
At every trifle scorn to take offence:
That always shows great pride or little sense;
Those heads, as stomachs, are not sure the best
Which nauseate all, and nothing can digest.
Yet let not each gay turn thy rapture move,   390
For fools admire, but men of sense approve:
As things seem large which we through mists descry,
Dulness is ever apt to magnify.

Some, foreign writers, some, our own despise;
The ancients only, or the moderns prize.
Thus wit, like faith, by each man is applied
To one small sect, and all are damn'd beside.
Meanly they seek the blessing to confine,
And force that sun but on a part to shine,
Which not alone the southern wit sublimes,   400
But ripens spirits in cold northern climes;

Which from the first has shone on ages past,
Enlights the present, and shall warm the last;
Though each may feel increases and decays,
And see now clearer and now darker days.
Regard not then if wit be old or new,
But blame the false, and value still the true.

Some ne'er advance a judgment of their own,
But catch the spreading notion of the town;
They reason and conclude by precedent,   410
And own stale nonsense which they ne'er invent.
Some judge of authors' names, not works, and then
Nor praise nor blame the writings, but the men.
Of all this servile herd, the worst is he
That in proud dulness joins with quality;
A constant critic at the great man's board,
To fetch and carry nonsense for my lord.
What woful stuff this madrigal would be,
In some starved hackney sonnetteer, or me?
But let a lord once own the happy lines   420
How the wit brightens! how the style refines!
Before his sacred name flies every fault,
And each exalted stanza teems with thought!

The vulgar thus through imitation err;
As oft the learn'd by being singular:
So much they scorn the crowd, that if the throng
By chance go right, they purposely go wrong:
So schismatics the plain believers quit,
And are but damn'd for having too much wit.
Some praise at morning what they blame at night,   430
But always think the last opinion right.
A Muse by these is like a mistress used,
This hour she's idolised, the next abused;
While their weak heads, like towns unfortified,
'Twixt sense and nonsense daily change their side.
Ask them the cause; they're wiser still, they say;
And still to-morrow's wiser than to-day.
We think our fathers fools, so wise we grow;
Our wiser sons, no doubt, will think us so.
Once school-divines this zealous isle o'erspread;   440
Who knew most sentences, was deepest read;
Faith, Gospel, all, seem'd made to be disputed,

And none had sense enough to be confuted:
Scotists and Thomists[17] now in peace remain,
Amidst their kindred cobwebs in Duck-lane.[18]
If Faith itself has different dresses worn,
What wonder modes in wit should take their turn?
Oft, leaving what is natural and fit,
The current folly proves the ready wit,
And authors think their reputation safe   450
Which lives as long as fools are pleased to laugh.

Some valuing those of their own side or mind,
Still make themselves the measure of mankind:
Fondly we think we honour merit then,
When we but praise ourselves in other men.
Parties in wit attend on those of state,
And public faction doubles private hate.
Pride, malice, folly, against Dryden rose,
In various shapes of parsons, critics, beaux;
But sense survived, when merry jests were past;   460
For rising merit will buoy up at last.
Might he return, and bless once more our eyes,
New Blackmores and new Milbourns[19] must arise:
Nay, should great Homer lift his awful head,
Zoilus again would start up from the dead.
Envy will Merit, as its shade, pursue,
But like a shadow, proves the substance true;
For envied wit, like Sol eclipsed, makes known
The opposing body's grossness, not its own.
When first that sun too powerful beams displays,   470
It draws up vapours which obscure its rays;
But even those clouds at last adorn its way,
Reflect new glories, and augment the day.[20]

Be thou the first true merit to befriend;
His praise is lost, who stays till all commend.
Short is the date, alas! of modern rhymes,
And 'tis but just to let them live betimes.
No longer now that golden age appears,
When patriarch-wits survived a thousand years:
Now length of fame (our second life) is lost,   480
And bare threescore is all even that can boast;
Our sons their fathers' failing language see,
And such as Chaucer is, shall Dryden be.

So when the faithful pencil has design'd
Some bright idea of the master's mind,
Where a new world leaps out at his command,
And ready Nature waits upon his hand;
When the ripe colours soften and unite,
And sweetly melt into just shade and light;
When mellowing years their full perfection give,   490
And each bold figure just begins to live,
The treacherous colours the fair art betray,
And all the bright creation fades away!

Unhappy wit, like most mistaken things,
Atones not for that envy which it brings.
In youth alone its empty praise we boast,
But soon the short-lived vanity is lost:
Like some fair flower the early spring supplies,
That gaily blooms, but even in blooming dies.
What is this wit, which must our cares employ?   500
The owner's wife, that other men enjoy;
Then most our trouble still when most admired,
And still the more we give, the more required;
Whose fame with pains we guard, but lose with ease,
Sure some to vex, but never all to please;
'Tis what the vicious fear, the virtuous shun,
By fools 'tis hated, and by knaves undone!

If wit so much from ignorance undergo,
Ah, let not learning too commence its foe!
Of old, those met rewards who could excel,   510
And such were praised who but endeavour'd well:
Though triumphs were to generals only due,
Crowns were reserved to grace the soldiers too.
Now, they who reach Parnassus' lofty crown,
Employ their pains to spurn some others down;
And while self-love each jealous writer rules,
Contending wits become the sport of fools:
But still the worst with most regret commend,
For each ill author is as bad a friend.   520
To what base ends, and by what abject ways,
Are mortals urged through sacred lust of praise!
Ah, ne'er so dire a thirst of glory boast,
Nor in the critic let the man be lost.
Good-nature and good-sense must ever join;

To err is human—to forgive, divine.

But if in noble minds some dregs remain,
Not yet purged off, of spleen and sour disdain;
Discharge that rage on more provoking crimes,
Nor fear a dearth in these flagitious times.   530
No pardon vile obscenity should find,
Though wit and art conspire to move your mind;
But dulness with obscenity must prove
As shameful sure as impotence in love.
In the fat age of pleasure, wealth, and ease,
Sprung the rank weed, and thrived with large increase:
When love was all an easy monarch's care;[21]
Seldom at council, never in a war:
Jilts ruled the state, and statesmen farces writ;
Nay, wits had pensions, and young lords had wit;   540
The fair sat panting at a courtier's play,
And not a mask went unimproved away:
The modest fan was lifted up no more,
And virgins smiled at what they blush'd before.
The following license of a foreign reign
Did all the dregs of bold Socinus drain;
Then unbelieving priests reform'd the nation,
And taught more pleasant methods of salvation;
Where Heaven's free subjects might their rights dispute,
Lest God himself should seem too absolute: 550
Pulpits their sacred satire learn'd to spare,
And vice admired to find a flatterer there!
Encouraged thus, wit's Titans braved the skies,
And the press groan'd with licensed blasphemies.
These monsters, critics! with your darts engage,
Here point your thunder, and exhaust your rage!
Yet shun their fault, who, scandalously nice,
Will needs mistake an author into vice;
All seems infected that the infected spy,
As all looks yellow to the jaundiced eye.   560

* * * * *

VARIATIONS.

VER. 225-228: —

So pleased at first the towering Alps to try, Fill'd with ideas of fair Italy, The traveller beholds with cheerful eyes The lessening vales, and seems to tread the skies.

VER. 447. Between this and ver. 448: —

The rhyming clowns that gladded Shakspeare's age, No more with crambo entertain the stage. Who now in anagrams their patron praise, Or sing their mistress in acrostic lays? Even pulpits pleased with merry puns of yore; Now all are banish'd to the Hibernian shore! Thus leaving what was natural and fit, The current folly proved their ready wit; And authors thought their reputation safe, Which lived as long as fools were pleased to laugh.

PART THIRD.

Learn, then, what MORALS critics ought to show,
For 'tis but half a judge's task to know.
'Tis not enough, taste, judgment, learning join;
In all you speak, let truth and candour shine:
That not alone what to your sense is due
All may allow; but seek your friendship too.

Be silent always when you doubt your sense;
And speak, though sure, with seeming diffidence:
Some positive, persisting fops we know,
Who, if once wrong, will needs be always so;   570
But you, with pleasure own your errors past,
And make each day a critique on the last.

'Tis not enough your counsel still be true;
Blunt truths more mischief than nice falsehoods do;
Men must be taught as if you taught them not,
And things unknown proposed as things forgot.
Without good-breeding, truth is disapproved;
That only makes superior sense beloved.

Be niggards of advice on no pretence;
For the worst avarice is that of sense.   580
With mean complaisance ne'er betray your trust,
Nor be so civil as to prove unjust.
Fear not the anger of the wise to raise;
Those best can bear reproof, who merit praise.

'Twere well might critics still this freedom take,
But Appius[22] reddens at each word you speak,
And stares tremendous, with a threatening eye,
Like some fierce tyrant in old tapestry.
Fear most to tax an Honourable fool,
Whose right it is, uncensured, to be dull;   590
Such, without wit, are poets when they please,
As without learning they can take degrees.
Leave dangerous truths to unsuccessful satires,
And flattery to fulsome dedicators,
Whom, when they praise, the world believes no more,
Than when they promise to give scribbling o'er.

'Tis best sometimes your censure to restrain,
And charitably let the dull be vain:
Your silence there is better than your spite,
For who can rail so long as they can write?   600
Still humming on, their drowsy course they keep,
And lash'd so long, like tops, are lash'd asleep.
False steps but help them to renew the race,
As, after stumbling, jades will mend their pace.
What crowds of these, impenitently bold,
In sounds and jingling syllables grown old,
Still run on poets, in a raging vein,
Even to the dregs and squeezings of the brain,
Strain out the last dull droppings of their sense,
And rhyme with all the rage of impotence!   610

Such shameless bards we have; and yet 'tis true,
There are as mad, abandon'd critics too.
The bookful blockhead, ignorantly read,
With loads of learned lumber in his head,
With his own tongue still edifies his ears,
And always listening to himself appears.
All books he reads, and all he reads assails,
From Dryden's Fables down to D'Urfey's Tales.
With him, most authors steal their works, or buy;
Garth did not write[23] his own Dispensary.   620
Name a new play, and he's the poet's friend,
Nay, show'd his faults—but when would poets mend?
No place so sacred from such fops is barr'd,
Nor is Paul's church more safe than Paul's churchyard:
Nay, fly to altars; there they'll talk you dead:
For fools rush in where angels fear to tread.
Distrustful sense with modest caution speaks,
It still looks home, and short excursions makes;
But rattling nonsense in full volleys breaks,
And, never shock'd, and never turn'd aside,   630
Bursts out, resistless, with a thundering tide.

But where's the man, who counsel can bestow,
Still pleased to teach, and yet not proud to know?
Unbiass'd, or by favour, or by spite;
Not dully prepossess'd, nor blindly right;
Though learn'd, well-bred; and though well-bred, sincere;
Modestly bold, and humanly severe:

Who to a friend his faults can freely show,
And gladly praise the merit of a foe?
Bless'd with a taste exact, yet unconfined; 640
A knowledge both of books and human kind;
Generous converse; a soul exempt from pride;
And love to praise, with reason on his side?

Such once were critics; such the happy few,
Athens and Rome in better ages knew.
The mighty Stagyrite first left the shore,
Spread all his sails, and durst the deeps explore;
He steer'd securely, and discover'd far,
Led by the light of the Maeonian star.[24]
Poets, a race long unconfined, and free, 650
Still fond and proud of savage liberty,
Received his laws; and stood convinced 'twas fit,
Who conquer'd Nature, should preside o'er Wit.

Horace still charms with graceful negligence,
And without method talks us into sense,
Will, like a friend, familiarly convey
The truest notions in the easiest way.
He who, supreme in judgment, as in wit,
Might boldly censure, as he boldly writ,
Yet judged with coolness, though he sung with fire;
His precepts teach but what his works inspire. 660
Our critics take a contrary extreme,
They judge with fury, but they write with phlegm:
Nor suffers Horace more in wrong translations
By wits, than critics in as wrong quotations.

See Dionysius[25] Homer's thoughts refine,
And call new beauties forth from every line!

Fancy and art in gay Petronius please,
The scholar's learning, with the courtier's ease.

In grave Quintilian's copious work we find 670
The justest rules and clearest method join'd:
Thus useful arms in magazines we place,
All ranged in order, and disposed with grace,
But less to please the eye, than arm the hand,
Still fit for use, and ready at command.

Thee, bold Longinus! all the Nine inspire,
And bless their critic with a poet's fire.
An ardent judge, who, zealous in his trust,
With warmth gives sentence, yet is always just;
Whose own example strengthens all his laws;   680
And is himself that Great Sublime he draws.

Thus long succeeding critics justly reign'd,
Licence repress'd, and useful laws ordain'd.
Learning and Rome alike in empire grew;
And arts still follow'd where her eagles flew;
From the same foes, at last, both felt their doom,
And the same age saw Learning fall, and Rome.
With Tyranny then Superstition join'd,
As that the body, this enslaved the mind;
Much was believed, but little understood,   690
And to be dull was construed to be good;
A second deluge Learning thus o'errun,
And the Monks finish'd what the Goths begun.

At length Erasmus, that great injured name,
(The glory of the priesthood, and the shame!)
Stemm'd the wild torrent of a barbarous age,
And drove those holy Vandals off the stage.

But see! each Muse, in Leo's golden days,
Starts from her trance, and trims her wither'd bays,
Rome's ancient Genius, o'er its ruins spread,   700
Shakes off the dust, and rears his reverend head.
Then Sculpture and her sister-arts revive;
Stones leap'd to form, and rocks began to live;
With sweeter notes each rising temple rung:
A Raphael painted, and a Vida sung:
Immortal Vida! on whose honour'd brow
The poet's bays and critic's ivy grow;
Cremona now shall ever boast thy name,
As next in place to Mantua,[26] next in fame!

But soon by impious arms from Latium chased,   710
Their ancient bounds the banish'd Muses pass'd;
Thence Arts o'er all the northern world advance,
But critic-learning flourish'd most in France:

The rules a nation, born to serve, obeys;
And Boileau still in right of Horace sways.
But we, brave Britons, foreign laws despised,
And kept unconquer'd and uncivilised;
Fierce for the liberties of wit, and bold,
We still defied the Romans, as of old.
Yet some there were, among the sounder few   720
Of those who less presumed, and better knew,
Who durst assert the juster ancient cause,
And here restored Wit's fundamental laws.
Such was the Muse,[27] whose rules and practice tell,
'Nature's chief masterpiece is writing well.'
Such was Roscommon, not more learn'd than good,
With manners generous as his noble blood;
To him the wit of Greece and Rome was known,
And every author's merit, but his own.
Such late was Walsh—the Muse's judge and friend,   730
Who justly knew to blame or to commend;
To failings mild, but zealous for desert;
The clearest head, and the sincerest heart.
This humble praise, lamented Shade! receive,
This praise at least a grateful Muse may give:
The Muse, whose early voice you taught to sing,
Prescribed her heights, and pruned her tender wing,
(Her guide now lost) no more attempts to rise,
But in low numbers short excursions tries:
Content, if hence the unlearn'd their wants may view, 740
The learn'd reflect on what before they knew:
Careless of censure, nor too fond of fame;
Still pleased to praise, yet not afraid to blame;
Averse alike to flatter, or offend;
Not free from faults, nor yet too vain to mend.

* * * * *

VARIATIONS.

VER. 624. Between this and ver. 625: —

In vain you shrug, and sweat, and strive to fly; These know no manners but of poetry. They'll stop a hungry chaplain in his grace, To treat of unities of time and place.

Between ver. 647 and 648, were the following lines, afterwards suppressed by the author: —

That bold Columbus of the realms of wit, Whose first discovery's not exceeded yet. Led by the light of the Maeonian star, He steer'd securely, and discover'd far. He, when all Nature was subdued before, Like his great pupil, sigh'd, and long'd for more: Fancy's wild regions yet unvanquish'd lay, A boundless empire, and that own'd no sway. Poets, &c.

Between ver. 691 and 692, the author omitted these two: —

Vain wits and critics were no more allow'd, When none but saints had licence to be proud.

THE RAPE OF THE LOCK:

AN HEROI-COMICAL POEM.

WRITTEN IN THE YEAR MDCCXII.

'Nolueram, Belinda, tuos violare capillos;
Sed juvat, hoc precibus me tribuisse tuis. '

MART.

TO MRS ARABELLA FERMOR.

Madam, —It will be in vain to deny that I have some regard for this piece, since I dedicate it to you. Yet you may bear me witness, it was intended only to divert a few young ladies, who have good sense and good-humour enough to laugh not only at their sex's little unguarded follies, but at their own. But as it was communicated with the air of a secret, it soon found its way into the world. An imperfect copy having been offered to a bookseller, you had the good-nature for my sake to consent to the publication of one more correct: this I was forced to, before I had executed half my design, for the machinery was entirely wanting to complete it.

The machinery, Madam, is a term invented by the critics, to signify that part which the deities, angels, or demons are made to act in a poem: for the ancient poets are in one respect like many modern ladies: let an action be never so trivial in itself, they always make it appear of the utmost importance. These machines I determined to raise on a very new and odd foundation—the Rosicrucian doctrine of spirits.

I know how disagreeable it is to make use of hard words before a lady; but 'tis so much the concern of a poet to have his works understood, and particularly by your sex, that you must give me leave to explain two or three difficult terms.

The Rosicrucians are a people I must bring you acquainted with. The best account I know of them is in a French book called 'Le Comte de Gabalis, ' which both in its title and size is so like a novel, that many of the fair sex have read it for one by mistake. According to these gentlemen, the four elements are inhabited by spirits, which they call

Sylphs, Gnomes, Nymphs, and *Salamanders*. The Gnomes, or Demons of Earth, delight in mischief; but the Sylphs, whose habitation is in the air, are the best-conditioned creatures imaginable. For they say, any mortals may enjoy the most intimate familiarities with these gentle spirits, upon a condition very easy to all true adepts—an inviolate preservation of chastity.

As to the following cantos, all the passages of them are as fabulous as the vision at the beginning, or the transformation at the end; (except the loss of your hair, which I always mention with reverence). The human persons are as fictitious as the airy ones; and the character of Belinda, as it is now managed, resembles you in nothing but in beauty.

If this poem had as many graces as there are in your person, or in your mind, yet I could never hope it should pass through the world half so uncensured as you have done. But let its fortune be what it will, mine is happy enough to have given me this occasion of assuring you that I am, with the truest esteem, Madam, your most obedient, humble servant,

A. POPE.

CANTO I.

What dire offence from amorous causes springs,
What mighty contests rise from trivial things,
I sing—This verse to Caryll,[28] Muse! is due:
This, even Belinda may vouchsafe to view:
Slight is the subject, but not so the praise,
If she inspire, and he approve my lays.

Say what strange motive, Goddess! could compel
A well-bred lord t'assault a gentle belle?
Oh, say what stranger cause, yet unexplored,
Could make a gentle belle reject a lord?   10
In tasks so bold, can little men engage,
And in soft bosoms dwells such mighty rage?

Sol through white curtains shot a timorous ray,
And oped those eyes that must eclipse the day:
Now lap-dogs give themselves the rousing shake,
And sleepless lovers, just at twelve, awake:
Thrice rung the bell, the slipper knock'd the ground,
And the press'd watch return'd a silver sound.
Belinda still her downy pillow press'd,
Her guardian Sylph[29] prolong'd the balmy rest: 20
'Twas he had summon'd to her silent bed
The morning-dream that hover'd o'er her head,
A youth more glittering than a birth-night beau,
(That even in slumber caused her cheek to glow),
Seem'd to her ear his willing lips to lay,
And thus in whispers said, or seem'd to say:

'Fairest of mortals, thou distinguish'd care
Of thousand bright inhabitants of air!
If e'er one vision touch thy infant thought,
Of all the nurse and all the priest have taught;   30
Of airy elves by moonlight shadows seen,
The silver token, and the circled green,
Or virgins visited by angel-powers,
With golden crowns and wreaths of heavenly flowers;
Hear and believe! thy own importance know,
Nor bound thy narrow views to things below.
Some secret truths, from learned pride conceal'd,
To maids alone and children are reveal'd:

What though no credit doubting wits may give?
The fair and innocent shall still believe.   40
Know then, unnumber'd spirits round thee fly,
The light militia of the lower sky:
These, though unseen, are ever on the wing,
Hang o'er the box, and hover round the ring.
Think what an equipage thou hast in air,
And view with scorn two pages and a chair.
As now your own, our beings were of old,
And once enclosed in woman's beauteous mould;
Thence, by a soft transition, we repair
From earthly vehicles to these of air.   50
Think not, when woman's transient breath is fled,
That all her vanities at once are dead;
Succeeding vanities she still regards,
And though she plays no more, o'erlooks the cards.
Her joy in gilded chariots, when alive,
And love of ombre, after death survive.
For when the fair in all their pride expire,
To their first elements their souls retire:
The sprites of fiery termagants in flame
Mount up, and take a Salamander's name.   60
Soft yielding minds to water glide away,
And sip, with Nymphs, their elemental tea.
The graver prude sinks downward to a Gnome,
In search of mischief still on earth to roam.
The light coquettes in Sylphs aloft repair,
And sport and flutter in the fields of air.

'Know further yet; whoever fair and chaste
Rejects mankind, is by some Sylph embraced:
For spirits, freed from mortal laws, with ease
Assume what sexes and what shapes they please.   70
What guards the purity of melting maids,
In courtly balls, and midnight masquerades,
Safe from the treacherous friend, the daring spark,
The glance by day, the whisper in the dark,
When kind occasion prompts their warm desires,
When music softens, and when dancing fires?
'Tis but their Sylph, the wise celestials know,
Though honour is the word with men below.

'Some nymphs there are, too conscious of their face,

For life predestined to the Gnomes' embrace.   80
These swell their prospects, and exalt their pride,
When offers are disdain'd, and love denied;
Then gay ideas crowd the vacant brain,
While peers, and dukes, and all their sweeping train,
And garters, stars, and coronets appear,
And in soft sounds, 'Your Grace' salutes their ear.
'Tis these that early taint the female soul,
Instruct the eyes of young coquettes to roll,
Teach infant cheeks a bidden blush to know,
And little hearts to flutter at a beau.   90

'Oft, when the world imagine women stray,
The Sylphs through mystic mazes guide their way,
Through all the giddy circle they pursue,
And old impertinence expel by new.
What tender maid but must a victim fall
To one man's treat, but for another's ball?
When Florio speaks, what virgin could withstand,
If gentle Damon did not squeeze her hand?
With varying vanities, from every part,
They shift the moving toyshop of their heart,   100
Where wigs with wigs, with sword-knots sword-knots strive,
Beaux banish beaux, and coaches coaches drive.
This erring mortals levity may call,
Oh, blind to truth! the Sylphs contrive it all.

'Of these am I, who thy protection claim,
A watchful sprite, and Ariel is my name.
Late, as I ranged the crystal wilds of air,
In the clear mirror of thy ruling star
I saw, alas! some dread event impend,
Ere to the main this morning sun descend,   110
But heaven reveals not what, or how, or where:
Warn'd by the Sylph, oh, pious maid, beware!
This to disclose is all thy guardian can:
Beware of all, but most beware of man!'

He said; when Shock, who thought she slept too long,
Leap'd up, and waked his mistress with his tongue.
'Twas then, Belinda, if report say true,
Thy eyes first open'd on a billet-doux;
Wounds, charms, and ardours, were no sooner read,

But all the vision vanish'd from thy head.   120

And now, unveil'd, the toilet stands display'd,
Each silver vase in mystic order laid.
First, robed in white, the nymph intent adores,
With head uncover'd, the cosmetic powers.
A heavenly image in the glass appears,
To that she bends, to that her eyes she rears;
The inferior priestess, at her altar's side,
Trembling, begins the sacred rites of pride.
Unnumber'd treasures ope at once, and here
The various offerings of the world appear;   130
From each she nicely culls with curious toil,
And decks the goddess with the glittering spoil.
This casket India's glowing gems unlocks,
And all Arabia breathes from yonder box.
The tortoise here, and elephant unite,
Transform'd to combs, the speckled and the white.
Here files of pins extend their shining rows,
Puffs, powders, patches, Bibles, billet-doux.
Now awful beauty puts on all its arms;
The fair each moment rises in her charms,   140
Repairs her smiles, awakens every grace,
And calls forth all the wonders of her face;
Sees by degrees a purer blush arise,
And keener lightnings quicken in her eyes.
The busy Sylphs surround their darling care,
These set the head, and those divide the hair,
Some fold the sleeve, whilst others plait the gown:
And Betty's praised for labours not her own.

* * * * *

VARIATIONS.

VER. 11,12. It was in the first editions: —

And dwells such rage in softest bosoms then, And lodge such daring souls in little men?

VER. 13-18 Stood thus in the first edition: —

Sol through white curtains did his beams display, And op'd those eyes which brighter shone than they; Shock just had given himself the rousing shake, And nymphs prepared their chocolate to take; Thrice the wrought slipper knock'd against the ground, And striking watches the tenth hour resound.

CANTO II.

Not with more glories, in the ethereal plain,
The sun first rises o'er the purpled main,
Than, issuing forth, the rival of his beams
Launched on the bosom of the silver Thames.
Fair nymphs and well-dress'd youths around her shone,
But every eye was fix'd on her alone.
On her white breast a sparkling cross she wore,
Which Jews might kiss, and infidels adore.
Her lively looks a sprightly mind disclose,
Quick as her eyes, and as unfix'd as those: 10
Favours to none, to all she smiles extends;
Oft she rejects, but never once offends.
Bright as the sun, her eyes the gazers strike,
And, like the sun, they shine on all alike.
Yet graceful ease, and sweetness void of pride
Might hide her faults, if belles had faults to hide:
If to her share some female errors fall,
Look on her face, and you'll forget 'em all.

This nymph, to the destruction of mankind,
Nourish'd two locks, which graceful hung behind   20
In equal curls, and well conspired to deck
With shining ringlets the smooth ivory neck.
Love in these labyrinths his slaves detains,
And mighty hearts are held in slender chains.
With hairy springes we the birds betray,
Slight lines of hair surprise the finny prey,
Fair tresses man's imperial race ensnare,
And beauty draws us with a single hair.

The adventurous Baron[30] the bright locks admired;
He saw, he wished, and to the prize aspired.   30
Resolved to win, he meditates the way,
By force to ravish, or by fraud betray;
For when success a lover's toil attends,
Few ask if fraud or force attain'd his ends.

For this, ere Phoebus rose, he had implored
Propitious Heaven, and every power adored,
But chiefly Love—to Love an altar built,

Of twelve vast French romances, neatly gilt.
There lay three garters, half a pair of gloves;
And all the trophies of his former loves; 40
With tender billet-doux he lights the pyre,
And breathes three amorous sighs to raise the fire.
Then prostrate falls, and begs with ardent eyes
Soon to obtain, and long possess the prize:
The powers gave ear, and granted half his prayer,
The rest, the winds dispersed in empty air.

But now secure the painted vessel glides,
The sunbeams trembling on the floating tides:
While melting music steals upon the sky,
And soften'd sounds along the waters die; 50
Smooth flow the waves, the zephyrs gently play,
Belinda smiled, and all the world was gay.
All but the Sylph—with careful thoughts oppress'd,
The impending woe sat heavy on his breast.
He summons straight his denizens of air;
The lucid squadrons round the sails repair;
Soft o'er the shrouds aerial whispers breathe,
That seem'd but zephyrs to the train beneath.
Some to the sun their insect-wings unfold,
Waft on the breeze, or sink in clouds of gold; 60
Transparent forms, too fine for mortal sight,
Their fluid bodies half dissolved in light.
Loose to the wind their airy garments flew,
Thin glittering textures of the filmy dew,
Dipp'd in the richest tincture of the skies,
Where light disports in ever-mingling dyes;
While every beam new transient colours flings,
Colours that change whene'er they wave their wings.
Amid the circle, on the gilded mast,
Superior by the head, was Ariel placed; 70
His purple pinions opening to the sun,
He raised his azure wand, and thus begun:

'Ye Sylphs and Sylphids, to your chief give ear,
Fays, fairies, genii, elves, and demons hear!
Ye know the spheres, and various tasks assign'd
By laws eternal to the aerial kind.
Some in the fields of purest ether play,
And bask and whiten in the blaze of day:

Some guide the course of wandering orbs on high,
Or roll the planets through the boundless sky: 80
Some, less refined, beneath the moon's pale light
Pursue the stars that shoot athwart the night,
Or suck the mists in grosser air below,
Or dip their pinions in the painted bow,
Or brew fierce tempests on the wintry main,
Or o'er the glebe distil the kindly rain.
Others on earth o'er human race preside,
Watch all their ways, and all their actions guide:
Of these the chief the care of nations own,
And guard with arms divine the British throne.[31] 90

'Our humbler province is to tend the fair,
Not a less pleasing, though less glorious care;
To save the powder from too rude a gale,
Nor let the imprison'd essences exhale;
To draw fresh colours from the vernal flowers;
To steal from rainbows, ere they drop in showers,
A brighter wash; to curl their waving hairs,
Assist their blushes, and inspire their airs;
Nay, oft, in dreams, invention we bestow,
To change a flounce, or add a furbelow. 100

'This day, black omens threat the brightest fair
That e'er deserved a watchful spirit's care;
Some dire disaster, or by force, or flight;
But what, or where, the Fates have wrapt in night.
Whether the nymph shall break Diana's law,
Or some frail China jar receive a flaw;
Or stain her honour, or her new brocade;
Forget her prayers, or miss a masquerade;
Or lose her heart, or necklace, at a ball;
Or whether Heaven has doom'd that Shock must fall, 110
Haste then, ye spirits! to your charge repair:
The fluttering fan be Zephyretta's care;
The drops to thee, Brillante, we consign;
And, Momentilla, let the watch be thine;
Do thou, Crispissa, tend her favourite lock;
Ariel himself shall be the guard of Shock.

'To fifty chosen Sylphs, of special note,
We trust the important charge, the petticoat:

Oft have we known that sevenfold fence to fail,
Though stiff with hoops, and arm'd with ribs of whale;   120
Form a strong line about the silver bound,
And guard the wide circumference around.

'Whatever spirit, careless of his charge,
His post neglects, or leaves the fair at large,
Shall feel sharp vengeance soon o'ertake his sins,
Be stopp'd in vials, or transfix'd with pins;
Or plunged in lakes of bitter washes lie,
Or wedged whole ages in a bodkin's eye:
Gums and pomatums shall his flight restrain,
While, clogg'd, he beats his silken wings in vain;   130
Or alum styptics with contracting power
Shrink his thin essence like a rivell'd flower:
Or, as Ixion fix'd, the wretch shall feel
The giddy motion of the whirling mill,
In fumes of burning chocolate shall glow,
And tremble at the sea that froths below!'

He spoke; the spirits from the sails descend;
Some, orb in orb, around the nymph extend;
Some thread the mazy ringlets of her hair;
Some hang upon the pendants of her ear;   140
With beating hearts the dire event they wait,
Anxious, and trembling for the birth of Fate.

* * * * *

VARIATION.

VER. 4. From hence the poem continues, in the first edition, to ver. 46: —

The rest the winds dispersed in empty air;

all after, to the end of this canto, being additional.

CANTO III.

Close by those meads, for ever crown'd with flowers,
Where Thames with pride surveys his rising towers,
There stands a structure of majestic frame,
Which from the neighb'ring Hampton takes its name.
Here Britain's statesmen oft the fall foredoom
Of foreign tyrants, and of nymphs at home;
Here thou, great Anna! whom three realms obey,
Dost sometimes counsel take — and sometimes tea.

Hither the heroes and the nymphs resort,
To taste awhile the pleasures of a court;   10
In various talk the instructive hours they pass'd,
Who gave the ball, or paid the visit last;
One speaks the glory of the British Queen,
And one describes a charming Indian screen;
A third interprets motions, looks, and eyes;
At every word a reputation dies.
Snuff, or the fan, supply each pause of chat,
With singing, laughing, ogling, and all that.

Meanwhile, declining from the noon of day,
The sun obliquely shoots his burning ray;   20
The hungry judges soon the sentence sign,
And wretches hang that jurymen may dine;
The merchant from the Exchange returns in peace,
And the long labours of the toilet cease.
Belinda now, whom thirst of fame invites,
Burns to encounter two adventurous knights,
At ombre singly to decide their doom,
And swells her breast with conquests yet to come.
Straight the three bands prepare in arras to join,
Each band the number of the sacred Nine.   30
Soon as she spreads her hand, the aerial guard
Descend, and sit on each important card:
First Ariel perch'd upon a Matadore,
Then each, according to the rank they bore;
For Sylphs, yet mindful of their ancient race,
Are, as when women, wondrous fond of place.

Behold, four Kings in majesty revered,

With hoary whiskers and a forky beard;
And four fair Queens, whose hands sustain a flower,
Th' expressive emblem of their softer power;   40
Four Knaves in garbs succinct, a trusty band,
Caps on their heads, and halberts in their hand;
And particolour'd troops, a shining train,
Draw forth to combat on the velvet plain.

The skilful nymph reviews her force with care:
'Let Spades be Trumps!' she said, and Trumps they were.

Now move to war her sable Matadores,
In show like leaders of the swarthy Moors.
Spadillio first, unconquerable lord!
Led off two captive Trumps, and swept the board.   50
As many more Manillio forced to yield,
And march'd a victor from the verdant field.
Him Basto follow'd, but his fate more hard
Gain'd but one Trump and one plebeian card.
With his broad sabre next, a chief in years,
The hoary Majesty of Spades appears,
Puts forth one manly leg, to sight reveal'd,
The rest, his many-colour'd robe conceal'd.
The rebel Knave, who dares his prince engage,
Proves the just victim of his royal rage.   60
Even mighty Pam, that Kings and Queens o'erthrew
And mow'd down armies in the fights of Loo,
Sad chance of war! now destitute of aid,
Falls undistinguish'd by the victor Spade!

Thus far both armies to Belinda yield;
Now to the Baron fate inclines the field.
His warlike Amazon her host invades,
The imperial consort of the crown of Spades.
The Club's black tyrant first her victim died,
Spite of his haughty mien, and barbarous pride: 70
What boots the regal circle on his head,
His giant limbs in state unwieldy spread;
That long behind he trails his pompous robe,
And, of all monarchs, only grasps the globe?

The Baron now his Diamonds pours apace;
The embroider'd King who shows but half his face,

And his refulgent Queen, with powers combined,
Of broken troops an easy conquest find.
Clubs, Diamonds, Hearts, in wild disorder seen,
With throngs promiscuous strew the level green.   80
Thus when dispersed a routed army runs,
Of Asia's troops, and Afric's sable sons,
With like confusion different nations fly,
Of various habit and of various dye;
The pierced battalions disunited fall
In heaps on heaps; one fate o'erwhelms them all.

The Knave of Diamonds tries his wily arts,
And wins (oh shameful chance!) the Queen of Hearts.
At this, the blood the virgin's cheek forsook,
A livid paleness spreads o'er all her look;   90
She sees, and trembles at the approaching ill,
Just in the jaws of ruin, and Codille.
And now, (as oft in some distemper'd state)
On one nice trick depends the general fate,
An Ace of Hearts steps forth: the King unseen
Lurk'd in her hand, and mourn'd his captive Queen:
He springs to vengeance with an eager pace,
And falls like thunder on the prostrate Ace.
The nymph, exulting, fills with shouts the sky;
The walls, the woods, and long canals reply.   100

O thoughtless mortals! ever blind to fate,
Too soon dejected, and too soon elate.
Sudden these honours shall be snatch'd away,
And cursed for ever this victorious day.

For lo! the board with cups and spoons is crown'd,
The berries crackle, and the mill turns round;
On shining altars of Japan they raise
The silver lamp; the fiery spirits blaze:
From silver spouts the grateful liquors glide,
While China's earth receives the smoking tide: 110
At once they gratify their scent and taste,
And frequent cups prolong the rich repast.
Straight hover round the fair her airy band;
Some, as she sipp'd, the fuming liquor fann'd,
Some o'er her lap their careful plumes display'd,
Trembling, and conscious of the rich brocade.

Coffee (which makes the politician wise,
And see through all things with his half-shut eyes)
Sent up in vapours to the Baron's brain
New stratagems, the radiant lock to gain.　　　120
Ah, cease, rash youth! desist ere 'tis too late,
Fear the just gods, and think of Scylla's fate!
Changed to a bird, and sent to flit in air,
She dearly pays for Nisus' injured hair!

But when to mischief mortals bend their will,
How soon they find fit instruments of ill!
Just then, Clarissa drew with tempting grace
A two-edged weapon from her shining case:
So ladies in romance assist their knight,
Present the spear, and arm him for the fight,　　　130
He takes the gift with reverence, and extends
The little engine on his fingers' ends:
This just behind Belinda's neck he spread,
As o'er the fragrant steams she bends her head.
Swift to the lock a thousand sprites repair,
A thousand wings, by turns, blow back the hair;
And thrice they twitch'd the diamond in her ear;
Thrice she look'd back, and thrice the foe drew near.
Just in that instant, anxious Ariel sought
The close recesses of the virgin's thought;　　　140
As on the nosegay in her breast reclined,
He watch'd the ideas rising in her mind,
Sudden he view'd, in spite of all her art,
An earthly lover lurking at her heart.
Amazed, confused, he found his power expired,
Resign'd to fate, and with a sigh retired.

The Peer now spreads the glittering forfex wide,
To inclose the lock; now joins it to divide.
Even then, before the fatal engine closed,
A wretched Sylph too fondly interposed;　　　150
Fate urged the shears, and cut the Sylph in twain,
(But airy substance soon unites again)
The meeting points the sacred hair dissever
From the fair head, for ever, and for ever!

Then flash'd the living lightning from her eyes,
And screams of horror rend the affrighted skies.

Not louder shrieks to pitying heaven are cast,
When husbands, or when lapdogs breathe their last;
Or when rich China vessels, fallen from high,
In glittering dust and painted fragments lie!   160

'Let wreaths of triumph now my temples twine,
(The victor cried) the glorious prize is mine!
While fish in streams, or birds delight in air,
Or in a coach-and-six the British fair,
As long as Atalantis[32] shall be read,
Or the small pillow grace a lady's bed,
While visits shall be paid on solemn days,
When numerous wax-lights in bright order blaze,
While nymphs take treats, or assignations give,
So long my honour, name, and praise shall live!'   170

What Time would spare, from steel receives its date,
And monuments, like men, submit to fate!
Steel could the labour of the gods destroy,
And strike to dust the imperial towers of Troy;
Steel could the works of mortal pride confound,
And hew triumphal arches to the ground.
What wonder then, fair nymph! thy hairs should feel,
The conquering force of unresisted steel?

* * * * *

VARIATIONS.

VER. 1. The first edition continues from this line to ver. 24 of this canto.

VER. 12. Originally in the first edition: —

In various talk the cheerful hours they pass'd, Of who was bit, or who capotted last.

VER. 24. All that follows of the game at ombre, was added since the first edition, till ver. 105, which connected thus: —

Sudden the board with cups and spoons is crown'd.

VER. 105. From hence, the first edition continues to ver 134.

VER. 134. In the first edition it was thus: —

As o'er the fragrant stream she bends her head. First he expands the glittering forfex wide To inclose the lock; then joins it to divide: The meeting points the sacred hair dissever, From the fair head for ever and for ever.

Ver. 154. All that is between was added afterwards.

CANTO IV.

But anxious cares the pensive nymph oppress'd,
And secret passions labour'd in her breast.
Not youthful kings in battle seized alive,
Not scornful virgins who their charms survive,
Not ardent lovers robb'd of all their bliss,
Not ancient ladies when refused a kiss,
Not tyrants fierce that unrepenting die,
Not Cynthia when her manteau's pinn'd awry,
E'er felt such rage, resentment, and despair,
As thou, sad virgin! for thy ravish'd hair. 10

For, that sad moment, when the Sylphs withdrew,
And Ariel weeping from Belinda flew,
Umbriel, a dusky, melancholy sprite,
As ever sullied the fair face of light,
Down to the central earth, his proper scene,
Repair'd, to search the gloomy cave of Spleen.

Swift on his sooty pinions flits the Gnome,
And in a vapour reach'd the dismal dome.
No cheerful breeze this sullen region knows,
The dreaded east is all the wind that blows; 20
Here in a grotto, shelter'd close from air,
And screened in shades from day's detested glare,
She sighs for ever on her pensive bed,
Pain at her side, and Megrim at her head.

Two handmaids wait the throne: alike in place,
But differing far in figure and in face.
Here stood Ill-nature like an ancient maid,
Her wrinkled form in black and white array'd;
With store of prayers for mornings, nights, and noons
Her hand is fill'd; her bosom with lampoons. 30

There Affectation, with a sickly mien,
Shows in her cheek the roses of eighteen;
Practised to lisp, and hang the head aside,
Faints into airs, and languishes with pride;
On the rich quilt sinks with becoming woe,
Wrapp'd in a gown, for sickness, and for show.

The fair ones feel such maladies as these,
When each new night-dress gives a new disease.

A constant vapour o'er the palace flies,
Strange phantoms rising as the mists arise; 40
Dreadful, as hermits' dreams in haunted shades,
Or bright, as visions of expiring maids.
Now glaring fiends, and snakes on rolling spires,
Pale spectres, gaping tombs, and purple fires:
Now lakes of liquid gold, Elysian scenes,
And crystal domes, and angels in machines.
Unnumber'd throngs on every side are seen
Of bodies changed to various forms by Spleen.
Here living teapots stand, one arm held out,
One bent; the handle this, and that the spout: 50
A pipkin there, like Homer's tripod walks;
Here sighs a jar, and there a goose-pie talks;
Men prove with child, as powerful fancy works,
And maids turn'd bottles, call aloud for corks.

Safe pass'd the Gnome through this fantastic band,
A branch of healing spleenwort in his hand.
Then thus address'd the power—'Hail, wayward Queen!
Who rule the sex to fifty from fifteen:
Parent of vapours and of female wit,
Who give the hysteric, or poetic fit, 60
On various tempers act by various ways,
Make some take physic, others scribble plays;
Who cause the proud their visits to delay,
And send the godly in a pet to pray;
A nymph there is, that all thy power disdains,
And thousands more in equal mirth maintains.
But oh! if e'er thy Gnome could spoil a grace,
Or raise a pimple on a beauteous face,
Like citron-waters matrons' cheeks inflame,
Or change complexions at a losing game; 70
If e'er with airy horns I planted heads,
Or rumpled petticoats, or tumbled beds,
Or caused suspicion when no soul was rude,
Or discomposed the head-dress of a prude,
Or e'er to costive lapdog gave disease,
Which not the tears of brightest eyes could ease:
Hear me, and touch Belinda with chagrin,

That single act gives half the world the spleen.'

The goddess with a discontented air
Seems to reject him, though she grants his prayer. 80
A wondrous bag with both her hands she binds,
Like that where once Ulysses held the winds;[33]
There she collects the force of female lungs,
Sighs, sobs, and passions, and the war of tongues.
A vial next she fills with fainting fears,
Soft sorrows, melting griefs, and flowing tears.
The Gnome rejoicing bears her gifts away,
Spreads his black wings, and slowly mounts to day.

Sunk in Thalestris'[34] arms the nymph he found,
Her eyes dejected and her hair unbound. 90
Full o'er their heads the swelling bag he rent,
And all the furies issued at the vent.
Belinda burns with more than mortal ire,
And fierce Thalestris fans the rising fire.
'O wretched maid!' she spread her hands, and cried,
(While Hampton's echoes 'wretched maid!' replied)
'Was it for this you took such constant care
The bodkin, comb, and essence to prepare?
For this your locks in paper durance bound,
For this with torturing irons wreath'd around? 100
For this with fillets strain'd your tender head,
And bravely bore the double loads of lead?
Gods! shall the ravisher display your hair,
While the fops envy, and the ladies stare?
Honour forbid! at whose unrivall'd shrine
Ease, pleasure, virtue, all our sex resign.
Methinks already I your tears survey,
Already hear the horrid things they say,
Already see you a degraded toast,
And all your honour in a whisper lost! 110
How shall I, then, your helpless fame defend?
'Twill then be infamy to seem your friend!
And shall this prize, the inestimable prize,
Exposed through crystal to the gazing eyes,
And heighten'd by the diamond's circling rays,
On that rapacious hand for ever blaze?
Sooner shall grass in Hyde-park Circus grow,
And wits take lodgings in the sound of Bow;

Sooner let earth, air, sea to chaos fall,
Men, monkeys, lapdogs, parrots, perish all!'   120

She said; then raging to Sir Plume[35] repairs,
And bids her beau demand the precious hairs:
(Sir Plume of amber snuff-box justly vain,
And the nice conduct of a clouded cane.)
With earnest eyes, and round, unthinking face,
He first the snuff-box open'd, then the case,
And thus broke out—'My Lord, why, what the devil?
Z—ds! damn the lock! 'fore Gad, you must be civil!
Plague on't! 'tis past a jest—nay, prithee, pox!
Give her the hair'—he spoke, and rapp'd his box.   130

'It grieves me much' (replied the Peer again)
Who speaks so well should ever speak in vain;
'But by this lock, this sacred lock I swear,
(Which never more shall join its parted hair;
Which never more its honours shall renew,
Clipp'd from the lovely head where late it grew)
That while my nostrils draw the vital air,
This hand, which won it, shall for ever wear.'
He spoke, and, speaking, in proud triumph spread
The long-contended honours of her head.   140

But Umbriel, hateful Gnome! forbears not so;
He breaks the vial whence the sorrows flow.
Then see! the nymph in beauteous grief appears,
Her eyes half-languishing, half-drown'd in tears;
On her heaved bosom hung her drooping head,
Which, with a sigh, she raised; and thus she said:

'For ever cursed be this detested day,
Which snatch'd my best, my favourite curl away!
Happy! ah, ten times happy had I been,
If Hampton Court these eyes had never seen!   150
Yet am not I the first mistaken maid,
By love of courts to numerous ills betray'd.
Oh, had I rather unadmired remain'd
In some lone isle, or distant northern land;
Where the gilt chariot never marks the way,
Where none learn ombre, none e'er taste bohea!
There kept my charms conceal'd from mortal eye,

Like roses that in deserts bloom and die.
What moved my mind with youthful lords to roam?
Oh, had I stay'd, and said my prayers at home!   160
'Twas this the morning omens seem'd to tell:
Thrice from my trembling hand the patch-box fell;
The tottering china shook without a wind,
Nay, Poll sat mute, and Shock was most unkind!
A Sylph too warn'd me of the threats of Fate,
In mystic visions, now believed too late.
See the poor remnants of these slighted hairs!
My hands shall rend what ev'n thy rapine spares:
These in two sable ringlets taught to break,
Once gave new beauties to the snowy neck;   170
The sister-lock now sits uncouth, alone,
And in its fellow's fate foresees its own;
Uncurl'd it hangs, the fatal shears demands,
And tempts, once more, thy sacrilegious hands.
Oh hadst thou, cruel! been content to seize
Hairs less in sight, or any hairs but these!'

* * * * *

VARIATION.

VER. 11. All the lines from hence to the 94th verse, that describe the house of Spleen, are not in the first edition; instead of them followed only these: —

While her rack'd soul repose and peace requires, The fierce Thalestris fans the rising fires.

And continued at the 94th verse of this canto.

CANTO V.

She said: the pitying audience melt in tears;
But Fate and Jove had stopp'd the Baron's ears.
In vain Thalestris with reproach assails,
For who can move when fair Belinda fails?
Not half so fix'd the Trojan could remain,
While Anna begg'd and Dido raged in vain.
Then grave Clarissa graceful waved her fan;
Silence ensued, and thus the nymph began:

'Say, why are beauties praised and honour'd most,
The wise man's passion, and the vain man's toast?   10
Why deck'd with all that land and sea afford?
Why angels call'd, and angel-like adored?
Why round our coaches crowd the white-gloved beaux?
Why bows the side-box from its inmost rows?
How vain are all these glories, all our pains,
Unless good sense preserve what beauty gains:
That men may say, when we the front-box grace,
Behold the first in virtue as in face!
Oh! if to dance all night, and dress all day,
Charm'd the small-pox, or chased old-age away;   20
Who would not scorn what housewife's cares produce,
Or who would learn one earthly thing of use?
To patch, nay ogle, might become a saint,
Nor could it, sure, be such a sin to paint.
But since, alas! frail beauty must decay,
Curl'd or uncurl'd, since locks will turn to gray;
Since painted, or not painted, all shall fade,
And she who scorns a man, must die a maid;
What then remains, but well our power to use,
And keep good-humour still, whate'er we lose?   30
And trust me, dear! good-humour can prevail,
When airs, and flights, and screams, and scolding fail.
Beauties in vain their pretty eyes may roll;
Charms strike the sight, but merit wins the soul.'

So spoke the dame, but no applause ensued;
Belinda frown'd, Thalestris call'd her prude.
'To arms, to arms!' the fierce virago cries,
And swift as lightning to the combat flies.

All side in parties, and begin the attack;
Fans clap, silks rustle, and tough whalebones crack;   40
Heroes' and heroines' shouts confusedly rise,
And bass and treble voices strike the skies.
No common weapons in their hands are found,
Like gods they fight, nor dread a mortal wound.

So when bold Homer makes the gods engage,
And heavenly breasts with human passions rage;
'Gainst Pallas, Mars; Latona, Hermes arms,
And all Olympus rings with loud alarms:
Jove's thunder roars, heaven trembles all around,
Blue Neptune storms, the bellowing deeps resound: 50
Earth shakes her nodding towers, the ground gives way,
And the pale ghosts start at the flash of day!

Triumphant Umbriel on a sconce's height
Clapp'd his glad wings, and sat to view the fight;
Propp'd on their bodkin spears, the sprites survey
The growing combat, or assist the fray.

While through the press enraged Thalestris flies,
And scatters death around from both her eyes,
A beau and witling perish'd in the throng,
One died in metaphor, and one in song.   60
'O cruel nymph! a living death I bear,'
Cried Dapperwit, and sunk beside his chair.
A mournful glance Sir Fopling upwards cast,
'Those eyes are made so killing!'—was his last.
Thus on Maeander's[36] flowery margin lies
The expiring swan, and as he sings he dies.

When bold Sir Plume had drawn Clarissa down,
Chloe stepped in, and kill'd him with a frown;
She smiled to see the doughty hero slain,
But, at her smile, the beau revived again.   70

Now Jove suspends his golden scales in air,
Weighs the men's wits against the lady's hair;
The doubtful beam long nods from side to side;
At length the wits mount up, the hairs subside.

See fierce Belinda on the Baron flies,

With more than usual lightning in her eyes:
Nor fear'd the chief th' unequal fight to try,
Who sought no more than on his foe to die.
But this bold lord, with manly strength endued,
She with one finger and a thumb subdued: 80
Just where the breath of life his nostrils drew,
A charge of snuff the wily virgin threw;
The Gnomes direct, to every atom just,
The pungent grains of titillating dust.
Sudden, with starting tears each eye o'erflows,
And the high dome re-echoes to his nose.
'Now meet thy fate!' incensed Belinda cried,
And drew a deadly bodkin from her side,
(The same, his ancient personage to deck,
Her great-great-grandsire wore about his neck, 90
In three seal-rings; which after, melted down,
Form'd a vast buckle for his widow's gown:
Her infant grandame's whistle next it grew,
The bells she jingled, and the whistle blew;
Then in a bodkin graced her mother's hairs,
Which long she wore, and now Belinda wears.)
'Boast not my fall,' (he cried) 'insulting foe!
Thou by some other shalt be laid as low.
Nor think, to die dejects my lofty mind: 100
All that I dread is leaving you behind!
Rather than so, ah! let me still survive,
And burn in Cupid's flames,—but burn alive.'

'Restore the lock!' she cries; and all around
'Restore the lock!' the vaulted roofs rebound.
Not fierce Othello in so loud a strain
Roar'd for the handkerchief that caused his pain.
But see how oft ambitious aims are cross'd,
And chiefs contend till all the prize is lost!
The lock, obtain'd with guilt, and kept with pain,
In every place is sought, but sought in vain: 110
With such a prize no mortal must be blest,
So Heaven decrees! with Heaven who can contest?

Some thought it mounted to the lunar sphere,
Since all things lost on earth are treasured there.
There heroes' wits are kept in ponderous vases,
And beaux' in snuff-boxes and tweezer-cases.

There broken vows, and death-bed alms are found,
And lovers' hearts with ends of ribbon bound,
The courtier's promises, and sick man's prayers,
The smiles of harlots, and the tears of heirs,　　120
Cages for gnats, and chains to yoke a flea,
Dried butterflies, and tomes of casuistry.

But trust the Muse—she saw it upward rise,
Though mark'd by none but quick, poetic eyes:
(So Rome's great founder to the heavens withdrew,
To Proculus alone confess'd in view)
A sudden star, it shot through liquid air,
And drew behind a radiant trail of hair.
Not Berenice's locks first rose so bright,
The heaven's bespangling with dishevell'd light.　　130
The Sylphs behold it kindling as it flies,
And, pleased, pursue its progress through the skies.

This the beau-monde shall from the Mall survey,
And hail with music its propitious ray.
This the bless'd lover shall for Venus take,
And send up vows from Rosamonda's lake.
This Partridge[37] soon shall view in cloudless skies,
When next he looks through Galileo's eyes;
And hence th' egregious wizard shall foredoom
The fate of Louis, and the fall of Rome.　　140

Then cease, bright nymph! to mourn thy ravish'd hair,
Which adds new glory to the shining sphere!
Not all the tresses that fair head can boast,
Shall draw such envy as the lock you lost.
For, after all the murders of your eye,
When, after millions slain, yourself shall die;
When those fair suns shall set, as set they must,
And all those tresses shall be laid in dust,
This lock the Muse shall consecrate to fame,
And 'midst the stars inscribe Belinda's name.　　150

* * * * *

WINDSOR-FOREST. [38]

TO THE RIGHT HONOURABLE GEORGE LORD LANSDOWNE.

'Non injussa cano: te nostrae, Vare, myricae,
Te nemus omne canet; nee Phoebo gratior ulla est,
Quam sibi quae Vari praescripsit pagina nomen.'

    VIRG.

Thy forests, Windsor! and thy green retreats,
At once the Monarch's and the Muse's seats,
Invite my lays. Be present, sylvan Maids!
Unlock your springs, and open all your shades.
Granville commands; your aid, O Muses, bring!
What Muse for Granville can refuse to sing?

The groves of Eden, vanish'd now so long,
Live in description, and look green in song:
These, were my breast inspired with equal flame,
Like them in beauty, should be like in fame.   10
Here hills and vales, the woodland and the plain,
Here earth and water seem to strive again;
Not chaos-like, together crush'd and bruised,
But, as the world, harmoniously confused;
Where order in variety we see,
And where, though all things differ, all agree.
Here waving groves a chequer'd scene display,
And part admit, and part exclude the day;
As some coy nymph her lover's warm address
Nor quite indulges, nor can quite repress.   20
There, interspersed in lawns and opening glades,
Thin trees arise that shun each other's shades.
Here in full light the russet plains extend:
There, wrapt in clouds the bluish hills ascend.
Ev'n the wild heath displays her purple dyes,
And 'midst the desert fruitful fields arise,
That crown'd with tufted trees and springing corn,
Like verdant isles the sable waste adorn.
Let India boast her plants, nor envy we
The weeping amber or the balmy tree,   30

While by our oaks the precious loads are born,
And realms commanded which those trees adorn.
Not proud Olympus yields a nobler sight,
Though gods assembled grace his towering height.
Than what more humble mountains offer here,
Where, in their blessings, all those gods appear.
See Pan with flocks, with fruits Pomona crown'd,
Here blushing Flora paints the enamell'd ground,
Here Ceres' gifts in waving prospect stand,
And nodding tempt the joyful reaper's hand;   40
Rich industry sits smiling on the plains,
And peace and plenty tell a Stuart[39] reigns.

Not thus the land appear'd in ages past,
A dreary desert, and a gloomy waste,
To savage beasts and savage laws[40] a prey,
And kings more furious and severe than they;
Who claim'd the skies, dispeopled air and floods,
The lonely lords of empty wilds and woods:
Cities laid waste, they storm'd the dens and caves,
(For wiser brutes were backward to be slaves).   50
What could be free, when lawless beasts obey'd,
And even the elements a tyrant sway'd?
In vain kind seasons swell'd the teeming grain,
Soft showers distill'd, and suns grew warm in vain;
The swain with tears his frustrate labour yields,
And famish'd dies amidst his ripen'd fields.
What wonder, then, a beast or subject slain
Were equal crimes in a despotic reign?
Both doom'd alike, for sportive tyrants bled,
But while the subject starved, the beast was fed.   60
Proud Nimrod first the bloody chase began,
A mighty hunter, and his prey was man:
Our haughty Norman boasts that barbarous name,
And makes his trembling slaves the royal game.
The fields are ravish'd[41] from the industrious swains,
From men their cities, and from gods their fanes:
The levell'd towns with weeds lie cover'd o'er;
The hollow winds through naked temples roar;
Round broken columns clasping ivy twined;
O'er heaps of ruin stalk'd the stately hind;   70
The fox obscene to gaping tombs retires,
And savage howlings fill the sacred choirs.

Awed by his Nobles, by his Commons cursed,
The oppressor ruled tyrannic where he durst,
Stretch'd o'er the poor and Church his iron rod,
And served alike his vassals and his God.
Whom even the Saxon spared, and bloody Dane,
The wanton victims of his sport remain.
But see, the man who spacious regions gave
A waste for beasts, himself denied a grave![42]   80
Stretch'd on the lawn, his second hope[43] survey,
At once the chaser, and at once the prey:
Lo Rufus, tugging at the deadly dart,
Bleeds in the forest like a wounded hart.
Succeeding monarchs heard the subjects' cries,
Nor saw displeased the peaceful cottage rise.
Then gathering flocks on unknown mountains fed,
O'er sandy wilds were yellow harvests spread,
The forests wonder'd at the unusual grain,
And secret transport touch'd the conscious swain.   90
Fair Liberty, Britannia's goddess, rears
Her cheerful head, and leads the golden years.

Ye vigorous swains! while youth ferments your blood,
And purer spirits swell the sprightly flood,
Now range the hills, the gameful woods beset,
Wind the shrill horn, or spread the waving net.
When milder autumn summer's heat succeeds,
And in the new-shorn field the partridge feeds,
Before his lord the ready spaniel bounds,
Panting with hope, he tries the furrow'd grounds;   100
But when the tainted gales the game betray,
Couch'd close he lies, and meditates the prey:
Secure they trust the unfaithful field beset,
Till hovering o'er 'em sweeps the swelling net.
Thus (if small things we may with great compare)
When Albion sends her eager sons to war,
Some thoughtless town, with ease and plenty blest,
Near, and more near, the closing lines invest;
Sudden they seize the amazed, defenceless prize,
And high in air Britannia's standard flies.   110

See! from the brake the whirring pheasant springs,
And mounts exulting on triumphant wings:
Short is his joy; he feels the fiery wound,

Flutters in blood, and panting beats the ground.
Ah! what avail his glossy, varying dyes,
His purple crest, and scarlet-circled eyes,
The vivid green his shining plumes unfold,
His painted wings, and breast that flames with gold?

Nor yet, when moist Arcturus clouds the sky,
The woods and fields their pleasing toils deny.   120
To plains with well-breath'd beagles we repair,
And trace the mazes of the circling hare;
(Beasts, urged by us, their fellow-beasts pursue,
And learn of man each other to undo.)
With slaughtering gun the unwearied fowler roves,
When frosts have whiten'd all the naked groves;
Where doves in flocks the leafless trees o'ershade,
And lonely woodcocks haunt the watery glade.
He lifts the tube, and levels with his eye;
Straight a short thunder breaks the frozen sky;   130
Oft, as in airy rings they skim the heath,
The clamorous lapwings feel the leaden death:
Oft, as the mounting larks their notes prepare,
They fall, and leave their little lives in air.

In genial spring, beneath the quivering shade,
Where cooling vapours breathe along the mead,
The patient fisher takes his silent stand,
Intent, his angle trembling in his hand:
With looks unmoved, he hopes the scaly breed,
And eyes the dancing cork, and bending reed.   140
Our plenteous streams a various race supply,
The bright-eyed perch with fins of Tyrian dye,
The silver eel, in shining volumes roll'd,
The yellow carp, in scales bedropp'd with gold,
Swift trouts, diversified with crimson stains,
And pikes, the tyrants of the watery plains.

Now Cancer glows with Phoebus' fiery car:
The youth rush eager to the sylvan war,
Swarm o'er the lawns, the forest walks surround,
Rouse the fleet hart, and cheer the opening hound.   150
The impatient courser pants in every vein,
And pawing, seems to beat the distant plain:
Hills, vales, and floods appear already cross'd,

And ere he starts, a thousand steps are lost.
See the bold youth strain up the threatening steep,
Rush through the thickets, down the valleys sweep,
Hang o'er their coursers' heads with eager speed,
And earth rolls back beneath the flying steed.
Let old Arcadia boast her ample plain,
The immortal huntress, and her virgin-train;   160
Nor envy, Windsor! since thy shades have seen
As bright a goddess, and as chaste a queen,[44]
Whose care, like hers, protects the sylvan reign,
The earth's fair light, and empress of the main.

Here too, 'tis sung, of old Diana stray'd,
And Cynthus' top forsook for Windsor shade;
Here was she seen o'er airy wastes to rove,
Seek the clear spring, or haunt the pathless grove;
Here, arm'd with silver bows, in early dawn,
Her buskin'd virgins traced the dewy lawn.   170

Above the rest a rural nymph was famed,
Thy offspring, Thames! the fair Lodona named;
(Lodona's fate, in long oblivion cast,
The Muse shall sing, and what she sings shall last).
Scarce could the goddess from her nymph be known,
But by the crescent and the golden zone.
She scorn'd the praise of beauty, and the care;
A belt her waist, a fillet binds her hair;
A painted quiver on her shoulder sounds,
And with her dart the flying deer she wounds.
It chanced, as eager of the chase, the maid
Beyond the forest's verdant limits stray'd,   180
Pan saw and loved, and, burning with desire,
Pursued her flight, her flight increased his fire.
Not half so swift the trembling doves can fly,
When the fierce eagle cleaves the liquid sky;
Not half so swiftly the fierce eagle moves,
When through the clouds he drives the trembling doves;
As from the god she flew with furious pace,
Or as the god, more furious, urged the chase.
Now fainting, sinking, pale the nymph appears;
Now close behind, his sounding steps she hears;   190
And now his shadow reach'd her as she run,
His shadow lengthen'd by the setting sun;

And now his shorter breath, with sultry air,
Pants on her neck, and fans her parting hair.
In vain on father Thames she calls for aid,
Nor could Diana help her injured maid.
Faint, breathless, thus she pray'd, nor pray'd in vain:
'Ah, Cynthia! ah—though banish'd from thy train,
Let me, oh! let me, to the shades repair,
My native shades—there weep, and murmur there.'   200
She said, and melting as in tears she lay,
In a soft, silver stream dissolved away.
The silver stream her virgin coldness keeps,
For ever murmurs, and for ever weeps;
Still bears the name[45] the hapless virgin bore,
And bathes the forest where she ranged before.
In her chaste current oft the goddess laves,
And with celestial tears augments the waves.
Oft in her glass the musing shepherd spies
The headlong mountains and the downward skies,   210
The watery landscape of the pendent woods,
And absent trees that tremble in the floods;
In the clear azure gleam the flocks are seen,
And floating forests paint the waves with green,
Through the fair scene roll slow the lingering streams,
Then foaming pour along, and rush into the Thames.

Thou, too, great Father of the British floods!
With joyful pride survey'st our lofty woods;
Where towering oaks their growing honours rear,
And future navies on thy shores appear.   220
Not Neptune's self from all her streams receives
A wealthier tribute, than to thine he gives.
No seas so rich, so gay no banks appear,
No lake so gentle, and no spring so clear.
Nor Po so swells the fabling poet's lays,
While led along the skies his current strays,
As thine, which visits Windsor's famed abodes,
To grace the mansion of our earthly gods:
Nor all his stars above a lustre show,
Like the bright beauties on thy banks below;   230
Where Jove, subdued by mortal passion still,
Might change Olympus for a nobler hill.

Happy the man whom this bright court approves,

His sovereign favours, and his country loves:
Happy next him who to these shades retires,
Whom Nature charms, and whom the Muse inspires:
Whom humbler joys of home-felt quiet please,
Successive study, exercise, and ease.
He gathers health from herbs the forest yields,
And of their fragrant physic spoils the fields: 240
With chemic art exalts the mineral powers,
And draws the aromatic souls of flowers:
Now marks the course of rolling orbs on high;
O'er figured worlds now travels with his eye;
Of ancient writ unlocks the learned store,
Consults the dead, and lives past ages o'er:
Or wandering thoughtful in the silent wood,
Attends the duties of the wise and good,
To observe a mean, be to himself a friend,
To follow nature, and regard his end;   250
Or looks on Heaven with more than mortal eyes,
Bids his free soul expatiate in the skies,
Amid her kindred stars familiar roam,
Survey the region, and confess her home!
Such was the life great Scipio once admired,
Thus Atticus, and Trumbull[46] thus retired.

Ye sacred Nine! that all my soul possess,
Whose raptures fire me, and whose visions bless,
Bear me, oh, bear me to sequester'd scenes,
The bowery mazes, and surrounding greens: 260
To Thames's banks which fragrant breezes fill,
Or where ye Muses sport on Cooper's Hill.[47]
(On Cooper's Hill eternal wreaths shall grow,
While lasts the mountain, or while Thames shall flow.)
I seem through consecrated walks to rove,
I hear soft music die along the grove:
Led by the sound, I roam from shade to shade,
By godlike poets venerable made:
Here his first lays majestic Denham sung;
There the last numbers flow'd from Cowley's tongue.[48] 270
Oh early lost! what tears the river shed,
When the sad pomp along his banks was led!
His drooping swans on every note expire,
And on his willows hung each Muse's lyre.

Since fate relentless stopp'd their heavenly voice,
No more the forests ring, or groves rejoice;
Who now shall charm the shades, where Cowley strung
His living harp, and lofty Denham sung?
But hark! the groves rejoice, the forest rings!
Are these revived? or is it Granville sings? 280
'Tis yours, my lord, to bless our soft retreats,
And call the Muses to their ancient seats;
To paint anew the flowery sylvan scenes,
To crown the forest with immortal greens,
Make Windsor hills in lofty numbers rise,
And lift her turrets nearer to the skies;
To sing those honours you deserve to wear,
And add new lustre to her silver star.

Here noble Surrey[49] felt the sacred rage,
Surrey, the Granville of a former age: 290
Matchless his pen, victorious was his lance,
Bold in the lists, and graceful in the dance:
In the same shades the Cupids tuned his lyre,
To the same notes, of love and soft desire:
Fair Geraldine, bright object of his vow,
Then fill'd the groves, as heavenly Mira now.

Oh, wouldst thou sing what heroes Windsor bore,
What kings first breathed upon her winding shore,
Or raise old warriors, whose adored remains
In weeping vaults her hallow'd earth contains! 300
With Edward's acts[50] adorn the shining page,
Stretch his long triumphs down through every age,
Draw monarchs chain'd, and Cressy's glorious field,
The lilies blazing on the regal shield:
Then, from her roofs when Verrio's colours fall,
And leave inanimate the naked wall,
Still in thy song should vanquish'd France appear,
And bleed for ever under Britain's spear.

Let softer strains ill-fated Henry mourn,[51]
And palms eternal flourish round his urn. 310
Here o'er the martyr-king the marble weeps,
And, fast beside him, once-fear'd Edward sleeps.[52]
Whom not the extended Albion could contain,
From old Belerium to the northern main,

The grave unites; where ev'n the great find rest,
And blended lie the oppressor and the oppress'd!

Make sacred Charles' tomb for ever known,
(Obscure the place, and uninscribed the stone)
Oh fact accursed! what tears has Albion shed,
Heavens, what new wounds! and how her old have bled! 320
She saw her sons with purple deaths expire,
Her sacred domes involved in rolling fire,
A dreadful series of intestine wars,
Inglorious triumphs and dishonest scars.
At length great Anna said—'Let discord cease!'
She said, the world obey'd, and all was peace!

In that blest moment, from his oozy bed
Old Father Thames advanced his reverend head;
His tresses dropp'd with dews, and o'er the stream
His shining horns diffused a golden gleam: 330
Graved on his urn appear'd the moon, that guides
His swelling waters, and alternate tides;
The figured streams in waves of silver roll'd,
And on their banks Augusta[53] rose in gold.
Around his throne the sea-born brothers stood,
Who swell with tributary urns his flood;
First the famed authors of his ancient name,
The winding Isis and the fruitful Thame:
The Kennet swift, for silver eels renown'd;
The Loddon slow, with verdant alders crown'd; 340
Cole, whose dark streams his flowery islands lave;
And chalky Wey, that rolls a milky wave;
The blue, transparent Vandalis appears;
The gulfy Lee his sedgy tresses rears;
And sullen Mole, that hides his diving flood;
And silent Darent, stain'd with Danish blood.

High in the midst, upon his urn reclined,
(His sea-green mantle waving with the wind)
The god appear'd: he turn'd his azure eyes
Where Windsor-domes and pompous turrets rise; 350
Then bow'd and spoke; the winds forget to roar,
And the hush'd waves glide softly to the shore.

Hail, sacred Peace! hail, long-expected days,

That Thames's glory to the stars shall raise!
Though Tiber's streams immortal Rome behold,
Though foaming Hermus swells with tides of gold,
From heaven itself though sevenfold Nilus flows,
And harvests on a hundred realms bestows;
These now no more shall be the Muse's themes,
Lost in my fame, as in the sea their streams.   360
Let Volga's banks with iron squadrons shine,
And groves of lances glitter on the Rhine,
Let barbarous Ganges arm a servile train;
Be mine the blessings of a peaceful reign.
No more my sons shall dye with British blood
Red Iber's sands, or Ister's foaming flood:
Safe on my shore each unmolested swain
Shall tend the flocks, or reap the bearded grain;
The shady empire shall retain no trace
Of war or blood, but in the sylvan chase;   370
The trumpet sleep, while cheerful horns are blown,
And arms employ'd on birds and beasts alone.
Behold! the ascending villas on my side,
Project long shadows o'er the crystal tide,
Behold! Augusta's glittering spires increase,
And temples rise,[54] the beauteous works of Peace.
I see, I see, where two fair cities bend
Their ample bow, a new Whitehall ascend!
There mighty nations shall inquire their doom,
The world's great oracle in times to come;   380
There kings shall sue, and suppliant states be seen
Once more to bend before a British queen.

Thy trees, fair Windsor! now shall leave their woods,
And half thy forests rush into the floods,
Bear Britain's thunder, and her cross display,
To the bright regions of the rising day;
Tempt icy seas, where scarce the waters roll,
Where clearer flames glow round the frozen pole;
Or under southern skies exalt their sails,
Led by new stars, and borne by spicy gales!   390
For me the balm shall bleed, and amber flow,
The coral redden, and the ruby glow,
The pearly shell its lucid globe infold,
And Phoebus warm the ripening ore to gold.
The time shall come when, free as seas or wind,

Unbounded Thames shall flow for all mankind,
Whole nations enter with each swelling tide,
And seas but join the regions they divide;
Earth's distant ends our glory shall behold,
And the new world launch forth to seek the old.   400
Then ships of uncouth form shall stem the tide,
And feather'd people crowd my wealthy side,
And naked youths and painted chiefs admire
Our speech, our colour, and our strange attire!
O stretch thy reign, fair Peace! from shore to shore,
Till conquest cease, and slavery be no more;
Till the freed Indians in their native groves
Reap their own fruits, and woo their sable loves,
Peru once more a race of kings behold,
And other Mexicos be roof'd with gold.   410
Exiled by thee from earth to deepest hell,
In brazen bonds, shall barbarous Discord dwell;
Gigantic Pride, pale Terror, gloomy Care,
And mad Ambition shall attend her there:
There purple Vengeance bathed in gore retires,
Her weapons blunted, and extinct her fires:
There hateful Envy her own snakes shall feel,
And Persecution mourn her broken wheel:
There Faction roar, Rebellion bite her chain,
And gasping Furies thirst for blood in vain.   420

Here cease thy flight, nor with unhallow'd lays
Touch the fair fame of Albion's golden days:
The thoughts of gods let Granville's verse recite,
And bring the scenes of opening fate to light.
My humble Muse, in unambitious strains,
Paints the green forests and the flowery plains,
Where Peace descending bids her olives spring,
And scatters blessings from her dove-like wing.
Ev'n I more sweetly pass my careless days,
Pleased in the silent shade with empty praise;   430
Enough for me, that to the listening swains
First in these fields I sung the sylvan strains.

* * * * *

VARIATIONS.

VER. 3-6, originally thus: —

  Chaste Goddess of the woods,
Nymphs of the vales, and Naiads of the floods,
Lead me through arching bowers, and glimmering glades.
Unlock your springs, &c.

VER. 25-28. Originally thus: —

Why should I sing our better suns or air,
Whose vital draughts prevent the leech's care,
While through fresh fields the enlivening odours breathe,
Or spread with vernal blooms the purple heath?

VER. 49, 50. Originally thus in the MS. —

From towns laid waste, to dens and caves they ran
(For who first stoop'd to be a slave was man.)

VER. 57, 58: —

No wonder savages or subjects slain—
But subjects starved while savages were fed.

VER. 91-94: —

Oh may no more a foreign master's rage,
With wrongs yet legal, curse a future age!
Still spread, fair Liberty! thy heavenly wings,
Breathe plenty on the fields, and fragrance on the springs.

VER. 97-100: —

When yellow autumn summer's heat succeeds,
And into wine the purple harvest bleeds,
The partridge feeding in the new-shorn fields,
Both morning sports and evening pleasures yields.

VER. 107-110. It stood thus in the first editions: —

Pleased, in the General's sight, the host lie down

Sudden before some unsuspecting town;
The young, the old, one instant makes our prize,
And o'er their captive heads Britannia's standard flies.

VER. 126—

O'er rustling leaves around the naked groves.

VER. 129—

The fowler lifts his levell'd tube on high.

VER. 233-236—

Happy the man, who to the shades retires,
But doubly happy, if the Muse inspires!
Blest whom the sweets of home-felt quiet please;
But far more blest, who study joins with ease.

VER. 231, 232. It stood thus in the MS. —

And force great Jove, if Jove's a lover still,
To change Olympus, &c.

VER. 265-268. It stood thus in the MS. —

Methinks around your holy scenes I rove,
And hear your music echoing through the grove:
With transport visit each inspiring shade
By god-like poets venerable made.

VER. 273, 274—

What sighs, what murmurs fill'd the vocal shore!
His tuneful swans were heard to sing no more.

VER. 288. All the lines that follow were not added to the poem till the year 1710. What immediately followed this, and made the conclusion, were these: —

My humble Muse in unambitious strains
Paints the green forests and the flowery plains;
Where I obscurely pass my careless days,

Pleased in the silent shade with empty praise,
Enough for me that to the listening swains
First in these fields I sung the sylvan strains.

VER. 305, 306. Originally thus in the MS. —

When brass decays, when trophies lie o'erthrown,
And mouldering into dust drops the proud stone.

VER. 319-322. Originally thus in the MS. —

Oh fact accurst! oh sacrilegious brood,
Sworn to rebellion, principled in blood!
Since that dire morn what tears has Albion shed,
Gods! what new wounds, &c.

VER. 325, 326. Thus in the MS. —

Till Anna rose and bade the Furies cease; '
Let there be peace'—she said, and all was peace.

Between VER. 328 and 329, originally stood these lines—

From shore to shore exulting shouts he heard,
O'er all his banks a lambent light appear'd,
With sparkling flames heaven's glowing concave shone,
Fictitious stars, and glories not her own.
He saw, and gently rose above the stream;
His shining horns diffuse a golden gleam:
With pearl and gold his towery front was dress'd,
The tributes of the distant East and West.

VER. 361-364. Originally thus in the MS. —

Let Venice boast her towers amidst the main,
Where the rough Adrian swells and roars in vain;
Here not a town, but spacious realm shall have
A sure foundation on the rolling wave.

VER. 383-387 were originally thus—

Now shall our fleets the bloody cross display
To the rich regions of the rising day,

Or those green isles, where headlong Titan steeps
His hissing axle in the Atlantic deeps:
Tempt icy seas, &c.

ODE ON ST CECILIA'S DAY,

MDCCVIII.

1 Descend, ye Nine! descend and sing;
　　The breathing instruments inspire,
　Wake into voice each silent string,
　　And sweep the sounding lyre;
　　In a sadly-pleasing strain
　　Let the warbling lute complain:
　　　Let the loud trumpet sound,
　　　Till the roofs all around
　　　The shrill echoes rebound:
　While in more lengthen'd notes and slow,
　The deep, majestic, solemn organs blow.
　　　Hark! the numbers soft and clear,
　　　Gently steal upon the ear;
　　　Now louder, and yet louder rise,
　　　And fill with spreading sounds the skies;
　Exulting in triumph now swell the bold notes,
　In broken air, trembling, the wild music floats;
　　　Till, by degrees, remote and small,
　　　　The strains decay,
　　　　And melt away,
　　　In a dying, dying fall.

2 By Music, minds an equal temper know,
　Nor swell too high, nor sink too low.
　If in the breast tumultuous joys arise,
　Music her soft, assuasive voice applies;
　　Or, when the soul is press'd with cares,
　　Exalts her in enlivening airs.
　Warriors she fires with animated sounds;
　Pours balm into the bleeding lover's wounds;
　　　Melancholy lifts her head,
　　　Morpheus rouses from his bed,
　　　Sloth unfolds her arms and wakes,
　　　Listening Envy drops her snakes;
　Intestine war no more our passions wage,
　And giddy factions hear away their rage.

3 But when our country's cause provokes to arms,
　How martial music every bosom warms!
　So when the first bold vessel dared the seas,
　High on the stern the Thracian raised his strain,
　　While Argo saw her kindred trees
　　Descend from Pelion to the main.
　　Transported demigods stood round,
　　And men grew heroes at the sound,
　　Inflamed with glory's charms:
　Each chief his sevenfold shield display'd,
　And half unsheath'd the shining blade:
　And seas, and rocks, and skies rebound,
　'To arms, to arms, to arms!'

4 But when through all the infernal bounds,
　Which flaming Phlegethon surrounds,
　　Love, strong as death, the poet led
　　To the pale nations of the dead,
　What sounds were heard,
　What scenes appear'd,
　　O'er all the dreary coasts!
　　　Dreadful gleams,
　　　Dismal screams,
　　　Fires that glow,
　　　Shrieks of woe,
　　　Sullen moans,
　　　Hollow groans,
　　And cries of tortured ghosts!
　But, hark! he strikes the golden lyre;
　And see! the tortured ghosts respire,
　　　See, shady forms advance!
　　Thy stone, O Sisyphus! stands still,
　　Ixion rests upon his wheel.
　　　And the pale spectres dance!
　The Furies sink upon their iron beds,
　And snakes uncurl'd hang listening round their heads.

5　'By the streams that ever flow,
　　By the fragrant winds that blow
　　　O'er the Elysian flowers;
　　By those happy souls who dwell
　　In yellow meads of asphodel,
　　　Or amaranthine bowers;

By the hero's armed shades,
Glittering through the gloomy glades;
By the youths that died for love,
Wandering in the myrtle grove,
Restore, restore Eurydice to life:
Oh take the husband, or return the wife!'
   He sung, and hell consented
     To hear the poet's prayer:
   Stern Proserpine relented,
     And gave him back the fair.
     Thus song could prevail
     O'er death and o'er hell,
A conquest how hard and how glorious!
   Though fate had fast bound her
   With Styx nine times round her,
Yet Music and Love were victorious.

6 But soon, too soon, the lover turns his eyes:
Again she falls, again she dies, she dies!
How wilt thou now the fatal sisters move?
No crime was thine, if 'tis no crime to love.
   Now under hanging mountains,
   Beside the falls of fountains,
   Or where Hebrus wanders,
   Rolling in meanders,
     All alone,
     Unheard, unknown,
     He makes his moan;
     And calls her ghost,
   For ever, ever, ever lost!
   Now with Furies surrounded,
   Despairing, confounded,
   He trembles, he glows,
   Amidst Rhodope's snows:
See, wild as the winds, o'er the desert he flies;
Hark! Haemus resounds with the bacchanals' cries—
       Ah see, he dies!
Yet even in death Eurydice he sung,
Eurydice still trembled on his tongue,
     Eurydice the woods,
     Eurydice the floods,
Eurydice the rocks and hollow mountains rung.

7   Music the fiercest grief can charm,
      And Fate's severest rage disarm:
      Music can soften pain to ease,
      And make despair and madness please:
      Our joys below it can improve,
      And antedate the bliss above.
   This the divine Cecilia found,
And to her Maker's praise confined the sound.
When the full organ joins the tuneful choir,
   The immortal powers incline their ear;
Borne on the swelling notes our souls aspire,
While solemn airs improve the sacred fire;
   And angels lean from heaven to hear.
Of Orpheus now no more let poets tell,
To bright Cecilia greater power is given;
   His numbers raised a shade from hell,
     Hers lift the soul to heaven.

TWO CHORUSES TO THE TRAGEDY OF BRUTUS.

CHORUS OF ATHENIANS.

STROPHE I.

Ye shades, where sacred truth is sought;
Groves, where immortal sages taught:
   Where heavenly visions Plato fired,
   And Epicurus' lay inspired;
   In vain your guiltless laurels stood
   Unspotted long with human blood.
War, horrid war, your thoughtful walks invades,
And steel now glitters in the Muses' shades.

ANTISTROPHE I.

   O heaven-born sisters! source of art!
   Who charm the sense, or mend the heart;
   Who lead fair Virtue's train along,
   Moral truth, and mystic song!
   To what new clime, what distant sky,
   Forsaken, friendless, shall ye fly?
Say, will ye bless the bleak Atlantic shore,
Or bid the furious Gaul be rude no more?

STROPHE II.

   When Athens sinks by fates unjust,
   When wild barbarians spurn her dust;
   Perhaps even Britain's utmost shore
   Shall cease to blush with strangers' gore,
   See Arts her savage sons control,
   And Athens rising near the pole!
Till some new tyrant lifts his purple hand,
And civil madness tears them from the land.

ANTISTROPHE II.

   Ye gods! what justice rules the ball?
   Freedom and Arts together fall;
   Fools grant whate'er Ambition craves,

And men, once ignorant, are slaves.
Oh, cursed effects of civil hate,
In every age, in every state!
Still, when the lust of tyrant power succeeds,
Some Athens perishes, some Tully bleeds.

CHORUS OF YOUTHS AND VIRGINS.

SEMICHORUS.

O tyrant Love! hast thou possess'd
The prudent, learn'd, and virtuous breast?
Wisdom and wit in vain reclaim,
And arts but soften us to feel thy flame.
  Love, soft intruder, enters here,
  But entering learns to be sincere.
  Marcus with blushes owns he loves,
  And Brutus tenderly reproves.
    Why, Virtue, dost thou blame desire,
      Which Nature has impress'd
    Why, Nature, dost thou soonest fire
      The mild and generous breast?

CHORUS.

  Love's purer flames the gods approve;
  The gods and Brutus bend to love:
  Brutus for absent Portia sighs,
And sterner Cassius melts at Junia's eyes.
What is loose love? a transient gust,
Spent in a sudden storm of lust,
A vapour fed from wild desire,
A wandering, self-consuming fire.
  But Hymen's kinder flames unite,
    And burn for ever one;
  Chaste as cold Cynthia's virgin light,
    Productive as the sun.

SEMICHORUS.

  Oh source of every social tie,
  United wish, and mutual joy!
  What various joys on one attend,

As son, as father, brother, husband, friend!
  Whether his hoary sire he spies,
  While thousand grateful thoughts arise;
  Or meets his spouse's fonder eye;
  Or views his smiling progeny;
    What tender passions take their turns,
    What home-felt raptures move?
    His heart now melts, now leaps, now burns,
    With reverence, hope, and love.

CHORUS.

Hence, guilty joys, distastes, surmises,
Hence, false tears, deceits, disguises,
Dangers, doubts, delays, surprises,
  Fires that scorch, yet dare not shine!
Purest love's unwasting treasure,
Constant faith, fair hope, long leisure,
Days of ease, and nights of pleasure;
  Sacred Hymen! these are thine.

TO THE

AUTHOR OF A POEM ENTITLED SUCCESSIO.[55]

Begone, ye critics, and restrain your spite,
Codrus writes on, and will for ever write.
The heaviest Muse the swiftest course has gone,
As clocks run fastest when most lead is on;
What though no bees around your cradle flew,
Nor on your lips distill'd the golden dew,
Yet have we oft discover'd in their stead
A swarm of drones that buzz'd about your head.
When you, like Orpheus, strike the warbling lyre,
Attentive blocks stand round you and admire.
Wit pass'd through thee no longer is the same,
As meat digested takes a different name,
But sense must sure thy safest plunder be,
Since no reprisals can be made on thee.
Thus thou may'st rise, and in thy daring flight
(Though ne'er so weighty) reach a wondrous height.
So, forced from engines, lead itself can fly,
And ponderous slugs move nimbly through the sky.
Sure Bavius copied Maevius to the full,
And Chaerilus taught Codrus to be dull;
Therefore, dear friend, at my advice give o'er
This needless labour; and contend no more
To prove a *dull succession* to be true,
Since 'tis enough we find it so in you.

* * * * *

ODE ON SOLITUDE.[56]

1 Happy the man, whose wish and care
   A few paternal acres bound,
  Content to breathe his native air
     In his own ground.

2 Whose herds with milk, whose fields with bread,
   Whose flocks supply him with attire,
  Whose trees in summer yield him shade,
     In winter fire.

3 Blest, who can unconcern'dly find
   Hours, days, and years slide soft away,
  In health of body, peace of mind,
     Quiet by day;

4 Sound sleep by night; study and ease,
   Together mix'd; sweet recreation;
  And innocence, which most does please,
     With meditation.

5 Thus let me live, unseen, unknown,
   Thus unlamented let me die,
  Steal from the world, and not a stone
     Tell where I lie.

    *   *   *   *   *

THE DYING CHRISTIAN TO HIS SOUL.[57]

1 Vital spark of heavenly flame!
   Quit, oh quit this mortal frame:
   Trembling, hoping, lingering, flying,
   Oh the pain, the bliss of dying!
   Cease, fond Nature, cease thy strife,
   And let me languish into life!

2 Hark! they whisper; angels say,
   'Sister Spirit, come away!'
   What is this absorbs me quite?
   Steals my senses, shuts my sight,
   Drowns my spirits, draws my breath?
   Tell me, my soul, can this be Death?

3 The world recedes; it disappears!
   Heaven opens on my eyes! my ears
   With sounds seraphic ring!
   Lend, lend your wings! I mount! I fly!
   O Grave! where is thy victory?
   O Death! where is thy sting?

   *   *   *   *   *

ELEGY TO THE MEMORY OF AN UNFORTUNATE LADY[58]

What beckoning ghost, along the moonlight shade
Invites my steps, and points to yonder glade?
'Tis she!—but why that bleeding bosom gored,
Why dimly gleams the visionary sword?
Oh, ever beauteous, ever friendly! tell,
Is it, in heaven, a crime to love too well?
To bear too tender, or too firm a heart,
To act a lover's or a Roman's part?
Is there no bright reversion in the sky,
For those who greatly think, or bravely die?   10

Why bade ye else, ye Powers! her soul aspire
Above the vulgar flight of low desire?
Ambition first sprung from your blest abodes;
The glorious fault of angels and of gods:
Thence to their images on earth it flows,
And in the breasts of kings and heroes glows.
Most souls, 'tis true, but peep out once an age,
Dull, sullen prisoners in the body's cage:
Dim lights of life, that burn a length of years
Useless, unseen, as lamps in sepulchres;   20
Like Eastern kings a lazy state they keep,
And, close confined to their own palace, sleep.

From these perhaps (ere Nature bade her die)
Fate snatch'd her early to the pitying sky.
As into air the purer spirits flow,
And separate from their kindred dregs below;
So flew the soul to its congenial place,
Nor left one virtue to redeem her race.

But thou, false guardian of a charge too good,
Thou, mean deserter of thy brother's blood!   30
See on these ruby lips the trembling breath,
These cheeks, now fading at the blast of death;
Cold is that breast which warm'd the world before,
And those love-darting eyes must roll no more.
Thus, if Eternal Justice rules the ball,
Thus shall your wives, and thus your children fall:

On all the line a sudden vengeance waits,
And frequent hearses shall besiege your gates.
There passengers shall stand, and pointing say,
(While the long funerals blacken all the way)   40
'Lo, these were they, whose souls the Furies steel'd,
And cursed with hearts unknowing how to yield.'
Thus unlamented pass the proud away,
The gaze of fools, and pageant of a day!
So perish all, whose breast ne'er learn'd to glow
For others' good, or melt at others' woe.

What can atone (O ever-injured Shade!)
Thy fate unpitied, and thy rites unpaid?
No friend's complaint, no kind domestic tear
Pleased thy pale ghost, or graced thy mournful bier,   50
By foreign hands thy dying eyes were closed,
By foreign hands thy decent limbs composed,
By foreign hands thy humble grave adorn'd,
By strangers honour'd, and by strangers mourn'd!
What, though no friends in sable weeds appear,
Grieve for an hour, perhaps, then mourn a year,
And bear about the mockery of woe
To midnight dances, and the public show?
What, though no weeping loves thy ashes grace,
Nor polish'd marble emulate thy face?   60
What, though no sacred earth allow thee room,
Nor hallow'd dirge be mutter'd o'er thy tomb?
Yet shall thy grave with rising flowers be dress'd,
And the green turf lie lightly on thy breast:
There shall the morn her earliest tears bestow,
There the first roses of the year shall blow;
While angels with their silver wings o'ershade
The ground, now sacred by thy relics made.

So peaceful rests, without a stone, a name,
What once had beauty, titles, wealth, and fame.   70
How loved, how honour'd once, avails thee not,
To whom related, or by whom begot;
A heap of dust alone remains of thee,
'Tis all thou art, and all the proud shall be!

Poets themselves must fall, like those they sung,
Deaf the praised ear, and mute the tuneful tongue.

Even he, whose soul now melts in mournful lays,
Shall shortly want the generous tear he pays;
Then from his closing eyes thy form shall part,
And the last pang shall tear thee from his heart;   80
Life's idle business at one gasp be o'er,
The Muse forgot, and thou beloved no more!

*   *   *   *   *

PROLOGUE TO MR ADDISON'S TRAGEDY OF CATO.

To wake the soul by tender strokes of art,
To raise the genius, and to mend the heart;
To make mankind, in conscious virtue bold,
Live o'er each scene, and be what they behold:
For this the tragic Muse first trod the stage,
Commanding tears to stream through every age;
Tyrants no more their savage nature kept,
And foes to virtue wonder'd how they wept.
Our author shuns by vulgar springs to move
The hero's glory, or the virgin's love;   10
In pitying love, we but our weakness show,
And wild ambition well deserves its woe.
Here tears shall flow from a more generous cause,
Such tears as patriots shed for dying laws:
He bids your breasts with ancient ardour rise,
And calls forth Roman drops from British eyes.
Virtue confess'd in human shape he draws,
What Plato thought, and godlike Cato was:
No common object to your sight displays,
But what with pleasure[59] Heaven itself surveys,   20
A brave man struggling in the storms of fate,
And greatly falling with a falling state.
While Cato gives his little senate laws,
What bosom beats not in his country's cause?
Who sees him act, but envies every deed?
Who hears him groan, and does not wish to bleed?
Even when proud Caesar, 'midst triumphal cars,
The spoils of nations, and the pomp of wars,
Ignobly vain and impotently great,
Show'd Rome her Cato's figure drawn in state;   30
As her dead father's reverend image pass'd,
The pomp was darken'd and the day o'ercast;
The triumph ceased, tears gush'd from every eye;
The world's great victor pass'd unheeded by;
Her last good man dejected Rome adored,
And honour'd Caesar's less than Cato's sword.

Britons, attend: be worth like this approved,
And show you have the virtue to be moved.

With honest scorn the first famed Cato view'd
Rome learning arts from Greece, whom she subdued; 40
Your scene precariously subsists too long
On French translation, and Italian song.
Dare to have sense yourselves; assert the stage,
Be justly warm'd with your own native rage;
Such plays alone should win a British ear,
As Cato's self had not disdain'd to hear.

* * * * *

IMITATIONS OF ENGLISH POETS.[60]

I. CHAUCER.

Women ben full of ragerie,
Yet swinken nat sans secresie.
Thilke moral shall ye understond,
From schoole-boy's tale of fayre Irelond:
Which to the fennes hath him betake,
To filche the gray ducke fro the lake.
Right then, there passen by the way
His aunt, and eke her daughters tway.
Ducke in his trowses hath he hent,
Not to be spied of ladies gent.   10
'But ho! our nephew!' crieth one;
'Ho!' quoth another, 'Cozen John;'
And stoppen, and lough, and callen out, —
This sely clerke full low doth lout:
They asken that, and talken this,
'Lo here is Coz, and here is Miss.'
But, as he glozeth with speeches soote,
The ducke sore tickleth his erse roote:
Fore-piece and buttons all to-brest,
Forth thrust a white neck, and red crest.   20
'Te-he,' cried ladies; clerke nought spake:
Miss stared; and gray ducke crieth 'Quaake.'
'O moder, moder!' quoth the daughter,
'Be thilke same thing maids longen a'ter?
Bette is to pyne on coals and chalke,
Then trust on mon, whose yerde can talke.'

II. SPENSER.

THE ALLEY.

1 In every town, where Thamis rolls his tyde,
   A narrow pass there is, with houses low;
  Where ever and anon the stream is eyed,
   And many a boat soft sliding to and fro.
   There oft are heard the notes of infant woe,

   The short thick sob, loud scream, and shriller squall:
   How can ye, mothers, vex your children so?
   Some play, some eat, some cack against the wall,
   And as they crouchen low, for bread and butter call.

2 And on the broken pavement, here and there,
   Doth many a stinking sprat and herring lie;
  A brandy and tobacco shop is near,
   And hens, and dogs, and hogs are feeding by;
  And here a sailor's jacket hangs to dry.
  At every door are sunburnt matrons seen,
   Mending old nets to catch the scaly fry;
  Now singing shrill, and scolding oft between;
  Scolds answer foul-mouth'd scolds; bad neighbourhood, I ween.

3 The snappish cur (the passenger's annoy)
   Close at my heel with yelping treble flies;
  The whimpering girl, and hoarser-screaming boy,
   Join to the yelping treble shrilling cries;
  The scolding quean to louder notes doth rise,
  And her full pipes those shrilling cries confound;
   To her full pipes the grunting hog replies;
  The grunting hogs alarm the neighbours round,
  And curs, girls, boys, and scolds, in the deep base are drown'd.

4 Hard by a sty, beneath a roof of thatch,
   Dwelt Obloquy, who in her early days
  Baskets of fish at Billingsgate did watch,
   Cod, whiting, oyster, mack'rel, sprat, or plaice:
   There learn'd she speech from tongues that never cease.
  Slander beside her, like a magpie, chatters,
   With Envy (spitting cat!), dread foe to peace;
  Like a cursed cur, Malice before her clatters,
  And vexing every wight, tears clothes and all to tatters.

5 Her dugs were mark'd by every collier's hand,
   Her mouth was black as bull-dog's at the stall:
  She scratched, bit, and spared ne lace ne band,
   And 'bitch' and 'rogue' her answer was to all;
   Nay, even the parts of shame by name would call:
  Yea, when she passed by or lane or nook,
   Would greet the man who turn'd him to the wall,
  And by his hand obscene the porter took,

Nor ever did askance like modest virgin look.

6 Such place hath Deptford, navy-building town,
　Woolwich and Wapping, smelling strong of pitch;
Such Lambeth, envy of each band and gown,
　And Twick'nam such, which fairer scenes enrich,
　Grots, stutues, urns, and Jo—n's dog and bitch,
Ne village is without, on either side,
　All up the silver Thames, or all adown;
Ne Richmond's self, from whose tall front are eyed
Vales, spires, meandering streams, and Windsor's towery pride.

III. WALLER.

OF A LADY SINGING TO HER LUTE.

Fair charmer, cease! nor make your voice's prize,
A heart resign'd, the conquest of your eyes:
Well might, alas! that threaten'd vessel fail,
Which winds and lightning both at once assail.
We were too blest with these enchanting lays,
Which must be heavenly when an angel plays:
But killing charms your lover's death contrive,
Lest heavenly music should be heard alive.
Orpheus could charm the trees, but thus a tree,
Taught by your hand, can charm no less than he:
A poet made the silent wood pursue,
This vocal wood had drawn the poet too.

ON A FAN OF THE AUTHOR'S DESIGN,

IN WHICH WAS PAINTED THE STORY OF CEPHALUS AND PROCRIS, WITH THE MOTTO, 'AURA VENI.'

'Come, gentle Air!' the Aeolian shepherd said,
While Procris panted in the secret shade;
'Come, gentle Air!' the fairer Delia cries,
While at her feet her swain expiring lies.
Lo! the glad gales o'er all her beauties stray,
Breathe on her lips, and in her bosom play!
In Delia's hand this toy is fatal found,

Nor could that fabled dart more surely wound:
Both gifts destructive to the givers prove;
Alike both lovers fall by those they love.
Yet guiltless too this bright destroyer lives,
At random wounds, nor knows the wound she gives:
She views the story with attentive eyes,
And pities Procris, while her lover dies.

IV. COWLEY.

THE GARDEN.

Fain would my Muse the flowery treasures sing,
And humble glories of the youthful Spring;
Where opening roses breathing sweets diffuse,
And soft carnations shower their balmy dews;
Where lilies smile in virgin robes of white,
The thin undress of superficial light,
And varied tulips show so dazzling gay,
Blushing in bright diversities of day.
Each painted floweret in the lake below
Surveys its beauties, whence its beauties grow;   10
And pale Narcissus on the bank, in vain
Transformed, gazes on himself again.
Here aged trees cathedral walks compose,
And mount the hill in venerable rows:
There the green infants in their beds are laid,
The garden's hope, and its expected shade.
Here orange-trees with blooms and pendants shine,
And vernal honours to their autumn join;
Exceed their promise in the ripen'd store,   20
Yet in the rising blossom promise more.
There in bright drops the crystal fountains play,
By laurels shielded from the piercing day:
Where Daphne, now a tree, as once a maid,
Still from Apollo vindicates her shade,
Still turns her beauties from the invading beam,
Nor seeks in vain for succour to the stream.
The stream at once preserves her virgin leaves,
At once a shelter from her boughs receives,
Where summer's beauty midst of winter stays,
And winter's coolness spite of summer's rays.   30

WEEPING.

1 While Celia's tears make sorrow bright,
   Proud grief sits swelling in her eyes;
 The sun, next those the fairest light,
   Thus from the ocean first did rise:
 And thus through mists we see the sun,
 Which, else we durst not gaze upon.

2 These silver drops, like morning dew,
   Foretell the fervour of the day:
 So from one cloud soft showers we view,
   And blasting lightnings burst away.
 The stars that fall from Celia's eye,
 Declare our doom in drawing nigh.

3 The baby in that sunny sphere
   So like a Phaeton appears,
 That Heaven, the threaten'd world to spare,
   Thought fit to drown him in her tears:
 Else might the ambitious nymph aspire,
 To set, like him, Heaven too on fire.

V. EARL OF ROCHESTER.

ON SILENCE.[61]

1 Silence! coeval with eternity;
   Thou wert, ere Nature's self began to be,
 'Twas one vast Nothing all, and all slept fast in thee.

2 Thine was the sway, ere heaven was form'd, or earth,
   Ere fruitful Thought conceived Creation's birth,
 Or midwife Word gave aid, and spoke the infant forth.

3 Then various elements against thee join'd,
   In one more various animal combined,
 And framed the clamorous race of busy humankind.

4 The tongue moved gently first, and speech was low,
   Till wrangling Science taught it noise and show,
 And wicked Wit arose, thy most abusive foe.

5 But rebel Wit deserts thee oft in vain;
   Lost in the maze of words he turns again,
And seeks a surer state, and courts thy gentle reign.

6 Afflicted Sense thou kindly dost set free,
   Oppress'd with argumental tyranny,
And routed Reason finds a safe retreat in thee.

7 With thee in private modest Dulness lies,
   And in thy bosom lurks in Thought's disguise;
Thou varnisher of fools, and cheat of all the wise!

8 Yet thy indulgence is by both confess'd;
   Folly by thee lies sleeping in the breast,
And 'tis in thee at last that Wisdom seeks for rest.

9 Silence! the knave's repute, the whore's good name,
   The only honour of the wishing dame;
Thy very want of tongue makes thee a kind of fame.

10 But couldst thou seize some tongues that now are free,
   How Church and State should be obliged to thee!
At Senate, and at Bar, how welcome would'st thou be!

11 Yet Speech even there submissively withdraws
   From rights of subjects, and the poor man's cause:
Then pompous Silence reigns, and stills the noisy laws.

12 Past services of friends, good deeds of foes,
   What favourites gain, and what the nation owes,
Fly the forgetful world, and in thy arms repose.

13 The country wit, religion of the town,
   The courtier's learning, policy o' the gown,
Are best by thee express'd, and shine in thee alone.

14 The parson's cant, the lawyer's sophistry,
   Lord's quibble, critic's jest, all end in thee,
All rest in peace at last, and sleep eternally.

VI. EARL OF DORSET.

ARTEMISIA.[62]

1 Though Artemisia talks, by fits,
　Of councils, classics, fathers, wits;
　　Reads Malebranche, Boyle, and Locke:
　Yet in some things methinks she fails—
　'Twere well if she would pare her nails,
　　And wear a cleaner smock.

2 Haughty and huge as High-Dutch bride,
　Such nastiness, and so much pride
　　Are oddly join'd by fate:
　On her large squab you find her spread,
　Like a fat corpse upon a bed,
　　That lies and stinks in state.

3 She wears no colours (sign of grace)
　On any part except her face;
　　All white and black beside:
　Dauntless her look, her gesture proud,
　Her voice theatrically loud,
　　And masculine her stride.

4 So have I seen, in black and white
　A prating thing, a magpie height,
　　Majestically stalk;
　A stately, worthless animal,
　That plies the tongue, and wags the tail,
　　All flutter, pride, and talk.

PHRYNE.

1 Phryne had talents for mankind,
　Open she was, and unconfined,
　　Like some free port of trade:
　Merchants unloaded here their freight,
　And agents from each foreign state
　　Here first their entry made.

2 Her learning and good breeding such,
　Whether the Italian or the Dutch,
　　Spaniards or French came to her:
　To all obliging she'd appear,

'Twas 'Si, Signor,' 'twas 'Yaw, Mynheer,'
'Twas 'S' il vous plait, Monsieur.'

3 Obscure by birth, renown'd by crimes,
  Still changing names, religions, climes,
    At length she turns a bride:
  In diamonds, pearls, and rich brocades,
  She shines the first of batter'd jades,
    And flutters in her pride.

4 So have I known those insects fair,
  (Which curious Germans hold so rare)
    Still vary shapes and dyes;
  Still gain new titles with new forms;
  First grubs obscene, then wriggling worms,
    Then painted butterflies.

VII. DR SWIFT.

THE HAPPY LIFE OF A COUNTRY PARSON.

Parson, these things in thy possessing
Are better than the bishop's blessing:—
A wife that makes conserves; a steed
That carries double when there's need:
October store, and best Virginia,
Tithe-pig, and mortuary guinea:
Gazettes sent gratis down, and frank'd,
For which thy patron's weekly thank'd:
A large Concordance, bound long since:
Sermons to Charles the First, when prince:
A Chronicle of ancient standing;
A Chrysostom to smooth thy band in:
The Polyglot—three parts—my text,
Howbeit—likewise—now to my next:
Lo, here the Septuagint—and Paul,
To sum the whole—the close of all.
He that has these, may pass his life,
Drink with the squire, and kiss his wife;
On Sundays preach, and eat his fill;
And fast on Fridays—if he will;
Toast Church and Queen, explain the news,

Talk with churchwardens about pews,
Pray heartily for some new gift,
And shake his head at Doctor S— —t.

*   *   *   *   *

THE TEMPLE OF FAME.

WRITTEN IN THE YEAR MDCCXI.

ADVERTISEMENT.

The hint of the following piece was taken from Chaucer's 'House of Fame.' The design is in a manner entirely altered, the descriptions and most of the particular thoughts my own: yet I could not suffer it to be printed without this acknowledgment. The reader who would compare this with Chaucer, may begin with his third book of 'Fame,' there being nothing in the two first books that answers to their title. Wherever any hint is taken from him, the passage itself is set down in the marginal notes.

In that soft season, when descending showers
Call forth the greens, and wake the rising flowers;
When opening buds salute the welcome day,
And earth relenting feels the genial ray;
As balmy sleep had charm'd my cares to rest,
And love itself was banish'd from my breast,
(What time the morn mysterious visions brings,
While purer slumbers spread their golden wings),
A train of phantoms in wild order rose,
And, join'd, this intellectual scene compose.   10

I stood, methought, betwixt earth, seas, and skies;
The whole creation open to my eyes:
In air self-balanced hung the globe below,
Where mountains rise and circling oceans flow;
Here naked rocks, and empty wastes were seen,
There towery cities, and the forests green:
Here sailing ships delight the wandering eyes:
There trees, and intermingled temples rise;
Now a clear sun the shining scene displays,
The transient landscape now in clouds decays.   20

O'er the wide prospect, as I gazed around,
Sudden I heard a wild promiscuous sound,
Like broken thunders that at distance roar,

Or billows murmuring on the hollow shore:
Then gazing up, a glorious pile beheld,
Whose towering summit ambient clouds conceal'd.
High on a rock of ice the structure lay,
Steep its ascent, and slippery was the way;
The wondrous rock like Parian marble shone,
And seem'd, to distant sight, of solid stone. 30
Inscriptions here of various names I view'd,
The greater part by hostile time subdued;
Yet wide was spread their fame in ages past,
And poets once had promised they should last.
Some fresh engraved appear'd of wits renown'd;
I look'd again, nor could their trace be found.
Critics I saw, that other names deface,
And fix their own, with labour, in their place:
Their own, like others, soon their place resign'd,
Or disappear'd, and left the first behind. 40
Nor was the work impair'd by storms alone,
But felt the approaches of too warm a sun;
For Fame, impatient of extremes, decays
Not more by envy than excess of praise.
Yet part no injuries of heaven could feel,
Like crystal faithful to the graving steel:
The rock's high summit, in the temple's shade,
Nor heat could melt, nor beating storm invade.
Their names inscribed unnumber'd ages past
From time's first birth, with time itself shall last; 50
These ever new, nor subject to decays,
Spread, and grow brighter with the length of days.

So Zembla's rocks (the beauteous work of frost)
Rise white in air, and glitter o'er the coast;
Pale suns, unfelt, at distance roll away,
And on the impassive ice the lightnings play;
Eternal snows the growing mass supply,
Till the bright mountains prop the incumbent sky:
As Atlas fix'd, each hoary pile appears,
The gather'd winter of a thousand years. 60

On this foundation Fame's high temple stands.
Stupendous pile! not rear'd by mortal hands.
Whate'er proud Rome or artful Greece beheld,
Or elder Babylon, its frame excell'd.

Four faces had the dome, and every face
Of various structure, but of equal grace;
Four brazen gates, on columns lifted high,
Salute the different quarters of the sky.
Here fabled chiefs in darker ages born,
Or worthies old, whom arms or arts adorn,   70
Who cities raised, or tamed a monstrous race,
The walls in venerable order grace;
Heroes in animated marble frown,
And legislators seem to think in stone.

Westward, a sumptuous frontispiece appear'd,
On Doric pillars of white marble rear'd,
Crown'd with an architrave of antique mould,
And sculpture rising on the roughen'd gold.
In shaggy spoils here Theseus was beheld,
And Perseus dreadful with Minerva's shield: 80
There great Alcides stooping with his toil,
Rests on his club, and holds th' Hesperian spoil.
Here Orpheus sings; trees, moving to the sound,
Start from their roots, and form a shade around;
Amphion there the loud creating lyre
Strikes, and behold a sudden Thebes aspire!
Cythaeron's echoes answer to his call,
And half the mountain rolls into a wall:
There might you see the lengthening spires ascend,
The domes swell up, the widening arches bend,   90
The growing towers, like exhalations rise,
And the huge columns heave into the skies.

The eastern front was glorious to behold,
With diamond flaming, and barbaric gold.
There Ninus shone, who spread the Assyrian fame,
And the great founder of the Persian name:
There in long robes the royal Magi stand,
Grave Zoroaster waves the circling wand,
The sage Chaldeans robed in white appear'd,
And Brachmans, deep in desert woods revered.   100
These stopp'd the moon, and call'd the unbodied shades
To midnight banquets in the glimmering glades;
Made visionary fabrics round them rise,
And airy spectres skim before their eyes;
Of talismans and sigils knew the power,

And careful watch'd the planetary hour.
Superior, and alone, Confucius stood,
Who taught that useful science—to be good.

But on the south, a long majestic race
Of Egypt's priests the gilded niches grace, 110
Who measured earth, described the starry spheres,
And traced the long records of lunar years.
High on his car Sesostris struck my view,
Whom sceptred slaves in golden harness drew:
His hands a bow and pointed javelin hold;
His giant limbs are arm'd in scales of gold.
Between the statues obelisks were placed,
And the learn'd walls with hieroglyphics graced.

Of Gothic structure was the northern side,
O'erwrought with ornaments of barbarous pride. 120
There huge Colosses rose, with trophies crown'd,
And Runic characters were graved around.
There sat Zamolxis[63] with erected eyes,
And Odin here in mimic trances dies.
There on rude iron columns, smear'd with blood,
The horrid forms of Seythian heroes stood,
Druids and Bards (their once loud harps unstrung)
And youths that died to be by poets sung.
These, and a thousand more of doubtful fame,
To whom old fables gave a lasting name, 130
In ranks adorn'd the temple's outward face;
The wall, in lustre and effect like glass,
Which o'er each object casting various dyes,
Enlarges some, and others multiplies:
Nor void of emblem was the mystic wall,
For thus romantic Fame increases all.

The temple shakes, the sounding gates unfold
Wide vaults appear, and roofs of fretted gold:
Raised on a thousand pillars, wreathed around
With laurel foliage, and with eagles crown'd: 140
Of bright, transparent beryl were the walls,
The friezes gold, and gold the capitals:
As heaven with stars, the roof with jewels glows,
And ever-living lamps depend in rows.
Full in the passage of each spacious gate,

The sage historians in white garments wait;
Graved o'er their seats the form of Time was found,
His scythe reversed, and both his pinions bound.
Within stood heroes, who through loud alarms
In bloody fields pursued renown in arms.   150
High on a throne, with trophies charged, I view'd
The youth[64] that all things but himself subdued;
His feet on sceptres and tiaras trod,
And his horn'd head belied the Libyan god.
There Caesar, graced with both Minervas, shone;
Caesar, the world's great master, and his own;
Unmoved, superior still in every state,
And scarce detested in his country's fate.
But chief were those, who not for empire fought,
But with their toils their people's safety bought: 160
High o'er the rest Epaminondas stood;
Timoleon,[65] glorious in his brother's blood;
Bold Scipio, saviour of the Roman state;
Great in his triumphs, in retirement great;
And wise Aurelius, in whose well-taught mind,
With boundless power unbounded virtue join'd,
His own strict judge, and patron of mankind.

Much-suffering heroes next their honours claim,
Those of less noisy, and less guilty fame,
Fair Virtue's silent train: supreme of these   170
Here ever shines the godlike Socrates:
He whom ungrateful Athens[66] could expel,
At all times just, but when he sign'd the shell:
Here his abode the martyr'd Phocion claims,
With Agis, not the last of Spartan names:
Unconquer'd Cato shows the wound he tore,
And Brutus his ill Genius meets no more.

But in the centre of the hallow'd choir,
Six pompous columns o'er the rest aspire;
Around the shrine itself of Fame they stand,   180
Hold the chief honours, and the fane command.
High on the first, the mighty Homer shone;
Eternal adamant composed his throne;
Father of verse! in holy fillets dress'd,
His silver beard waved gently o'er his breast;
Though blind, a boldness in his looks appears;

In years he seem'd, but not impair'd by years.
The wars of Troy were round the pillar seen:
Here fierce Tydides wounds the Cyprian Queen;
Here Hector, glorious from Patroclus' fall,   190
Here dragg'd in triumph round the Trojan wall:
Motion and life did every part inspire,
Bold was the work, and proved the master's fire;
A strong expression most he seem'd to affect,
And here and there disclosed a brave neglect.

A golden column next in rank appear'd,
On which a shrine of purest gold was rear'd;
Finish'd the whole, and labour'd every part,
With patient touches of unwearied art:
The Mantuan there in sober triumph sate,   200
Composed his posture, and his look sedate;
On Homer still he fix'd a reverend eye,
Great without pride, in modest majesty.
In living sculpture on the sides were spread
The Latian wars, and haughty Turnus dead;
Eliza stretch'd upon the funeral pyre,
AEneas bending with his aged sire:
Troy flamed in burning gold, and o'er the throne,
ARMS AND THE MAN in golden cyphers shone.

Four swans sustain a car of silver bright,   210
With heads advanced, and pinions stretch'd for flight:
Here, like some furious prophet, Pindar rode,
And seem'd to labour with the inspiring god.
Across the harp a careless hand he flings,
And boldly sinks into the sounding strings.
The figured games of Greece the column grace,
Neptune and Jove survey the rapid race.
The youths hang o'er their chariots as they run;
The fiery steeds seem starting from the stone;
The champions in distorted postures threat;   220
And all appear'd irregularly great.

Here happy Horace tuned the Ausonian lyre
To sweeter sounds, and temper'd Pindar's fire:
Pleased with Alcaeus' manly rage t' infuse
The softer spirit of the Sapphic Muse.
The polish'd pillar different sculptures grace;

A work outlasting monumental brass.
Here smiling Loves and Bacchanals appear,
The Julian star, and great Augustus here;
The doves that round the infant poet spread   230
Myrtles and bays, hung hovering o'er his head.

Here in a shrine that cast a dazzling light,
Sat, fix'd in thought, the mighty Stagyrite;
His sacred head a radiant zodiac crown'd,
And various animals his side surround;
His piercing eyes, erect, appear to view
Superior worlds, and look all Nature through.

With equal rays immortal Tully shone,
The Roman rostra deck'd the Consul's throne:
Gathering his flowing robe, he seem'd to stand   240
In act to speak, and graceful stretch'd his hand.
Behind, Rome's Genius waits with civic crowns,
And the great Father of his country owns.

These massy columns in a circle rise,
O'er which a pompous dome invades the skies:
Scarce to the top I stretch'd my aching sight,
So large it spread, and swell'd to such a height.
Full in the midst, proud Fame's imperial seat
With jewels blazed, magnificently great;
The vivid emeralds there revive the eye,   250
The flaming rubies show their sanguine dye,
Bright azure rays from lively sapphires stream,
And lucid amber casts a golden gleam.
With various-colour'd light the pavement shone,
And all on fire appear'd the glowing throne;
The dome's high arch reflects the mingled blaze,
And forms a rainbow of alternate rays.
When on the goddess first I cast my sight,
Scarce seem'd her stature of a cubit's height;
But swell'd to larger size, the more I gazed,   260
Till to the roof her towering front she raised.
With her, the temple every moment grew,
And ampler vistas open'd to my view:
Upward the columns shoot, the roofs ascend,
And arches widen, and long aisles extend.
Such was her form as ancient bards have told,

Wings raise her arms, and wings her feet infold;
A thousand busy tongues the goddess bears,
A thousand open eyes, and thousand listening ears.
Beneath, in order ranged, the tuneful Nine   270
(Her virgin handmaids) still attend the shrine:
With eyes on Fame for ever fix'd, they sing;
For Fame they raise the voice, and tune the string;
With Time's first birth began the heavenly lays,
And last, eternal, through the length of days.

Around these wonders as I cast a look,
The trumpet sounded, and the temple shook,
And all the nations, summon'd at the call,
From different quarters fill the crowded hall:
Of various tongues the mingled sounds were heard   280
In various garbs promiscuous throngs appear'd;
Thick as the bees, that with the spring renew
Their flowery toils, and sip the fragrant dew,
When the wing'd colonies first tempt the sky,
O'er dusky fields and shaded waters fly,
Or settling, seize the sweets the blossoms yield,
And a low murmur runs along the field.
Millions of suppliant crowds the shrine attend,
And all degrees before the goddess bend;
The poor, the rich, the valiant, and the sage,   290
And boasting youth, and narrative old age.
Their pleas were different, their request the same:
For good and bad alike are fond of Fame.
Some she disgraced, and some with honours crown'd;
Unlike successes equal merits found.
Thus her blind sister, fickle Fortune, reigns,
And, undiscerning, scatters crowns and chains.

First at the shrine the learned world appear,
And to the goddess thus prefer their prayer:
'Long have we sought to instruct and please mankind, 300
With studies pale, with midnight vigils blind;
But thank'd by few, rewarded yet by none,
We here appeal to thy superior throne;
On wit and learning the just prize bestow,
For fame is all we must expect below.'

The goddess heard, and bade the Muses raise

The golden trumpet of eternal praise:
From pole to pole the winds diffuse the sound,
That fills the circuit of the world around;
Not all at once, as thunder breaks the cloud;   310
The notes at first were rather sweet than loud:
By just degrees they every moment rise,
Fill the wide earth, and gain upon the skies.
At every breath were balmy odours shed,
Which still grew sweeter as they wider spread;
Less fragrant scents the unfolding rose exhales,
Or spices breathing in Arabian gales.

Next these, the good and just, an awful train,
Thus on their knees address the sacred fane:
'Since living virtue is with envy cursed,   320
And the best men are treated like the worst,
Do thou, just goddess, call our merits forth,
And give each deed the exact intrinsic worth.'

'Not with bare justice shall your act be crown'd,'
(Said Fame), 'but high above desert renown'd:
Let fuller notes the applauding world amaze,
And the loud clarion labour in your praise.'

This band dismiss'd, behold, another crowd
Preferr'd the same request, and lowly bow'd;
The constant tenor of whose well-spent days   330
No less deserved a just return of praise.
But straight the direful trump of Slander sounds;
Through the big dome the doubling thunder bounds;
Loud as the burst of cannon rends the skies,
The dire report through every region flies,
In every ear incessant rumours rung,
And gathering scandals grew on every tongue.
From the black trumpet's rusty concave broke
Sulphureous flames, and clouds of rolling smoke:
The poisonous vapour blots the purple skies,   340
And withers all before it as it flies.

A troop came next, who crowns and armour wore,
And proud defiance in their looks they bore:
'For thee' (they cried), 'amidst alarms and strife,
We sail'd in tempests down the stream of life;

For thee whole nations fill'd with flames and blood,
And swam to empire through the purple flood.
Those ills we dared, thy inspiration own,
What virtue seem'd, was done for thee alone.'

'Ambitious fools!' (the Queen replied, and frown'd)   350
'Be all your acts in dark oblivion drown'd;
There sleep forgot, with mighty tyrants gone,
Your statues moulder'd, and your names unknown!'
A sudden cloud straight snatch'd them from my sight,
And each majestic phantom sunk in night.

Then came the smallest tribe I yet had seen;
Plain was their dress, and modest was their mien.
'Great idol of mankind! we neither claim
The praise of merit, nor aspire to fame;
But safe in deserts from the applause of men,   360
Would die unheard of, as we lived unseen;
'Tis all we beg thee, to conceal from sight
Those acts of goodness which themselves requite.
Oh let us still the secret joy partake,
To follow virtue even for virtue's sake.'

'And live there men, who slight immortal Fame?
Who then with incense shall adore our name?
But, mortals! know, 'tis still our greatest pride
To blaze those virtues which the good would hide.
Rise, Muses, rise! add all your tuneful breath;   370
These must not sleep in darkness and in death.'
She said: in air the trembling music floats,
And on the winds triumphant swell the notes;
So soft, though high, so loud, and yet so clear,
Even listening angels lean'd from heaven to hear:
To furthest shores the ambrosial spirit flies,
Sweet to the world, and grateful to the skies.

Next these a youthful train their vows express'd,
With feathers crown'd, with gay embroidery dress'd:
'Hither' (they cried) 'direct your eyes, and see   380
The men of pleasure, dress, and gallantry;
Ours is the place at banquets, balls, and plays,
Sprightly our nights, polite are all our days;
Courts we frequent, where 'tis our pleasing care

To pay due visits, and address the fair:
In fact, 'tis true, no nymph we could persuade,
But still in fancy vanquish'd every maid;
Of unknown duchesses lewd tales we tell,
Yet, would the world believe us, all were well.
The joy let others have, and we the name,   390
And what we want in pleasure, grant in fame.'

The Queen assents, the trumpet rends the skies,
And at each blast a lady's honour dies.

Pleased with the strange success, vast numbers press'd
Around the shrine, and made the same request:
'What! you,' (she cried) 'unlearn'd in arts to please,
Slaves to yourselves, and even fatigued with ease,
Who lose a length of undeserving days,
Would you usurp the lover's dear-bought praise?
To just contempt, ye vain pretenders, fall,   400
The people's fable and the scorn of all.'
Straight the black clarion sends a horrid sound,
Loud laughs burst out, and bitter scoffs fly round,
Whispers are heard, with taunts reviling loud,
And scornful hisses run through all the crowd.

Last, those who boast of mighty mischiefs done,
Enslave their country, or usurp a throne;
Or who their glory's dire foundation laid
On sovereigns ruin'd, or on friends betray'd;
Calm, thinking villains, whom no faith could fix,   410
Of crooked counsels, and dark politics;
Of these a gloomy tribe surround the throne,
And beg to make the immortal treasons known.
The trumpet roars, long flaky flames expire,
With sparks, that seem'd to set the world on fire.
At the dread sound, pale mortals stood aghast,
And startled Nature trembled with the blast.

This having heard and seen, some Power unknown
Straight changed the scene, and snatch'd me from the throne.
Before my view appear'd a structure fair,   420
Its site uncertain, if in earth or air;
With rapid motion turn'd the mansion round;
With ceaseless noise the ringing walls resound;

Not less in number were the spacious doors,
Than leaves on trees, or sands upon the shores;
Which still unfolded stand, by night, by day,
Pervious to winds, and open every way.
As flames by nature to the skies ascend,
As weighty bodies to the centre tend,
As to the sea returning rivers roll,   430
And the touch'd needle trembles to the pole;
Hither, as to their proper place, arise
All various sounds from earth, and seas, and skies,
Or spoke aloud, or whisper'd in the ear;
Nor ever silence, rest, or peace is here.
As on the smooth expanse of crystal lakes
The sinking stone at first a circle makes;
The trembling surface by the motion stirr'd,
Spreads in a second circle, then a third;
Wide, and more wide, the floating rings advance,   440
Fill all the watery plain, and to the margin dance:
Thus every voice and sound, when first they break,
On neighbouring air a soft impression make;
Another ambient circle then they move;
That, in its turn, impels the next above;
Through undulating air the sounds are sent,
And spread o'er all the fluid element.

There various news I heard of love and strife,
Of peace and war, health, sickness, death, and life,
Of loss and gain, of famine and of store,   450
Of storms at sea, and travels on the shore,
Of prodigies, and portents seen in air,
Of fires and plagues, and stars with blazing hair,
Of turns of fortune, changes in the state,
The falls of favourites, projects of the great,
Of old mismanagements, taxations new:
All neither wholly false, nor wholly true.

Above, below, without, within, around,
Confused, unnumber'd multitudes are found,
Who pass, repass, advance, and glide away;   460
Hosts raised by fear, and phantoms of a day:
Astrologers, that future fates foreshow;
Projectors, quacks, and lawyers not a few;
And priests, and party-zealots, numerous bands

With home-born lies, or tales from foreign lands;
Each talk'd aloud, or in some secret place,
And wild impatience stared in every face.
The flying rumours gather'd as they roll'd,
Scarce any tale was sooner heard than told;
And all who told it added something new,   470
And all who heard it made enlargements too,
In every ear it spread, on every tongue it grew.
Thus flying east and west, and north and south,
News travell'd with increase from mouth to mouth.
So from a spark, that kindled first by chance,
With gathering force the quickening flames advance;
Till to the clouds their curling heads aspire,
And towers and temples sink in floods of fire.
When thus ripe lies are to perfection sprung,
Full grown, and fit to grace a mortal tongue,   480
Through thousand vents, impatient, forth they flow,
And rush in millions on the world below.
Fame sits aloft, and points them out their course,
Their date determines, and prescribes their force:
Some to remain, and some to perish soon;
Or wane and wax alternate like the moon.
Around, a thousand winged wonders fly,
Born by the trumpet's blast, and scatter'd through the sky.

There, at one passage, oft you might survey
A lie and truth contending for the way;   490
And long 'twas doubtful, both so closely pent,
Which first should issue through the narrow vent:
At last agreed, together out they fly,
Inseparable now, the truth and lie;
The strict companions are for ever join'd,
And this or that unmix'd, no mortal e'er shall find.

While thus I stood, intent to see and hear,
One came, methought, and whisper'd in my ear:
'What could thus high thy rash ambition raise?
Art thou, fond youth, a candidate for praise?'   500

"Tis true,' said I, 'not void of hopes I came,
For who so fond as youthful bards of fame?
But few, alas! the casual blessing boast,
So hard to gain, so easy to be lost.

How vain that second life in others' breath,
The estate which wits inherit after death!
Ease, health, and life, for this they must resign,
(Unsure the tenure, but how vast the fine!)
The great man's curse, without the gains, endure,
Be envied, wretched, and be flatter'd, poor; 510
All luckless wits their enemies profess'd,
And all successful, jealous friends at best.
Nor Fame I slight, nor for her favours call;
She comes unlook'd for, if she comes at all.
But if the purchase costs so dear a price,
As soothing folly, or exalting vice;
Oh! if the Muse must flatter lawless sway,
And follow still where fortune leads the way;
Or if no basis bear my rising name,
But the fallen ruins of another's fame; 520
Then teach me, Heaven! to scorn the guilty bays,
Drive from my breast that wretched lust of praise,
Unblemish'd let me live, or die unknown;
Oh, grant an honest fame, or grant me none!'

* * * * *

ELOISA TO ABELARD.

ARGUMENT.

Abelard and Eloisa flourished in the twelfth century; they were two of the most distinguished persons of their age in learning and beauty, but for nothing more famous than for their unfortunate passion. After a long course of calamities, they retired each to a several convent, and consecrated the remainder of their days to religion. It was many years after this separation that a letter of Abelard's to a friend, which contained the history of his misfortune, fell into the hands of Eloisa. This, awakening all her tenderness, occasioned those celebrated letters (out of which the following is partly extracted) which give so lively a picture of the struggles of grace and nature, virtue and passion.

In these deep solitudes and awful cells,
Where heavenly-pensive Contemplation dwells,
And ever-musing Melancholy reigns,
What means this tumult in a vestal's veins?
Why rove my thoughts beyond this last retreat?
Why feels my heart its long-forgotten heat?
Yet, yet I love!—From Abelard it came,
And Eloisa yet must kiss the name.

Dear fatal name! rest ever unreveal'd,
Nor pass these lips in holy silence seal'd: 10
Hide it, my heart, within that close disguise
Where, mix'd with God's, his loved idea lies:
Oh write it not, my hand!—the name appears
Already written—wash it out, my tears!
In vain lost Eloisa weeps and prays,
Her heart still dictates, and her hand obeys.

Relentless walls! whose darksome round contains
Repentant sighs, and voluntary pains:
Ye rugged rocks! which holy knees have worn;
Ye grots and caverns, shagg'd with horrid thorn! 20
Shrines! where their vigils pale-eyed virgins keep,
And pitying saints, whose statues learn to weep!

Though cold like you, unmoved and silent grown,
I have not yet forgot myself to stone.
All is not Heaven's while Abelard has part,
Still rebel nature holds out half my heart;
Nor prayers nor fasts its stubborn pulse restrain,
Nor tears for ages taught to flow in vain.

Soon as thy letters trembling I unclose,
That well-known name awakens all my woes. 30
Oh, name for ever sad! for ever dear!
Still breathed in sighs, still usher'd with a tear.
I tremble too, where'er my own I find,
Some dire misfortune follows close behind.
Line after line my gushing eyes o'erflow,
Led through a sad variety of woe;
Now warm in love, now withering in my bloom,
Lost in a convent's solitary gloom!
There stern religion quench'd the unwilling flame,
There died the best of passions, Love and Fame. 40

Yet write, oh! write me all, that I may join
Griefs to thy griefs, and echo sighs to thine.
Nor foes nor fortune take this power away;
And is my Abelard less kind than they?
Tears still are mine, and those I need not spare,
Love but demands what else were shed in prayer;
No happier task these faded eyes pursue;
To read and weep is all they now can do.

Then share thy pain, allow that sad relief;
Ah, more than share it, give me all thy grief! 50
Heaven first taught letters for some wretch's aid,
Some banish'd lover, or some captive maid;
They live, they speak, they breathe what love inspires,
Warm from the soul, and faithful to its fires;
The virgin's wish without her fears impart,
Excuse the blush, and pour out all the heart,
Speed the soft intercourse from soul to soul,
And waft a sigh from Indus to the Pole.

Thou know'st how guiltless first I met thy flame,
When Love approach'd me under Friendship's name; 60
My fancy form'd thee of angelic kind,

Some emanation of the all-beauteous Mind.
Those smiling eyes, attempering every ray,
Shone sweetly lambent with celestial day.
Guiltless I gazed; Heaven listen'd while you sung;
And truths divine came mended from that tongue.
From lips like those, what precept fail'd to move?
Too soon they taught me 'twas no sin to love:
Back through the paths of pleasing sense I ran,
Nor wish'd an angel whom I loved a man.   70
Dim and remote the joys of saints I see;
Nor envy them that heaven I lose for thee.

How oft, when press'd to marriage, have I said,
Curse on all laws but those which Love has made!
Love, free as air, at sight of human ties,
Spreads his light wings, and in a moment flies.
Let wealth, let honour, wait the wedded dame,
August her deed, and sacred be her fame;   80
Before true passion all those views remove;
Fame, wealth, and honour! what are you to Love?
The jealous god, when we profane his fires,
Those restless passions in revenge inspires,
And bids them make mistaken mortals groan,
Who seek in love for aught but love alone.
Should at my feet the world's great master fall,
Himself, his throne, his world, I'd scorn them all:
Not Caesar's empress would I deign to prove;
No, make me mistress to the man I love;
If there be yet another name more free,
More fond than mistress, make me that to thee!   90
Oh, happy state! when souls each other draw,
When love is liberty, and nature law:
All then is full, possessing and possess'd,
No craving void left aching in the breast:
Even thought meets thought, ere from the lips it part,
And each warm wish springs mutual from the heart.
This, sure, is bliss (if bliss on earth there be)
And once the lot of Abelard and me.

Alas, how changed! what sudden horrors rise!
A naked lover bound and bleeding lies!   100
Where, where was Eloise? her voice, her hand,
Her poniard, had opposed the dire command.

Barbarian, stay! that bloody stroke restrain;
The crime was common, common be the pain.
I can no more; by shame, by rage suppress'd,
Let tears and burning blushes speak the rest.

Canst thou forget that sad, that solemn day,
When victims at yon altar's foot we lay?
Canst thou forget what tears that moment fell,
When, warm in youth, I bade the world farewell? 110
As with cold lips I kiss'd the sacred veil,
The shrines all trembled, and the lamps grew pale:
Heaven scarce believed the conquest it survey'd,
And saints with wonder heard the vows I made.
Yet then, to those dread altars as I drew,
Not on the cross my eyes were fix'd, but you:
Not grace, or zeal, love only was my call,
And if I lose thy love, I lose my all.
Come! with thy looks, thy words, relieve my woe;
Those still at least are left thee to bestow. 120
Still on that breast enamour'd let me lie,
Still drink delicious poison from thy eye,
Pant on thy lip, and to thy heart be press'd;
Give all thou canst—and let me dream the rest.
Ah, no! instruct me other joys to prize,
With other beauties charm my partial eyes,
Full in my view set all the bright abode,
And make my soul quit Abelard for God.

Ah, think at least thy flock deserves thy care,
Plants of thy hand, and children of thy prayer. 130
From the false world in early youth they fled,
By thee to mountains, wilds, and deserts led.
You raised these hallow'd walls; the desert smiled,
And Paradise was open'd in the wild.
No weeping orphan saw his father's stores
Our shrines irradiate, or emblaze the floors;
No silver saints, by dying misers given,
Here bribed the rage of ill-requited Heaven:
But such plain roofs as Piety could raise,
And only vocal with the Maker's praise. 140
In these lone walls, (their day's eternal bound)
These moss-grown domes with spiry turrets crown'd,
Where awful arches make a noonday night,

And the dim windows shed a solemn light;
Thy eyes diffused a reconciling ray,
And gleams of glory brighten'd all the day.
But now no face divine contentment wears,
'Tis all blank sadness, or continual tears.
See how the force of others' prayers I try,
(Oh pious fraud of amorous charity!)   150
But why should I on others' prayers depend?
Come thou, my father, brother, husband, friend!
Ah, let thy handmaid, sister, daughter move,
And all those tender names in one—thy love!
The darksome pines that, o'er yon rocks reclined,
Wave high, and murmur to the hollow wind,
The wandering streams that shine between the hills,
The grots that echo to the tinkling rills,
The dying gales that pant upon the trees,
The lakes that quiver to the curling breeze;   160
No more these scenes my meditation aid,
Or lull to rest the visionary maid.
But o'er the twilight groves and dusky caves,
Long-sounding aisles, and intermingled graves,
Black Melancholy sits, and round her throws
A death-like silence, and a dread repose:
Her gloomy presence saddens all the scene,
Shades every flower, and darkens every green,
Deepens the murmur of the falling floods,
And breathes a browner horror on the woods.   170

Yet here for ever, ever must I stay;
Sad proof how well a lover can obey!
Death, only death, can break the lasting chain;
And here, even then, shall my cold dust remain;
Here all its frailties, all its flames resign,
And wait till 'tis no sin to mix with thine.

Ah, wretch! believed the spouse of God in vain,
Confess'd within the slave of love and man.
Assist me, Heaven! but whence arose that prayer?
Sprung it from piety, or from despair?   180
Even here, where frozen chastity retires,
Love finds an altar for forbidden fires.
I ought to grieve, but cannot what I ought;
I mourn the lover, not lament the fault;

I view my crime, but kindle at the view,
Repent old pleasures, and solicit new;
Now turn'd to Heaven, I weep my past offence,
Now think of thee, and curse my innocence.
Of all affliction taught a lover yet,
'Tis sure the hardest science to forget!   190
How shall I lose the sin, yet keep the sense,
And love the offender, yet detest the offence?
How the dear object from the crime remove,
Or how distinguish penitence from love?
Unequal task! a passion to resign,
For hearts so touch'd, so pierced, so lost as mine.
Ere such a soul regains its peaceful state,
How often must it love, how often hate!
How often hope, despair, resent, regret,
Conceal, disdain,—do all things but forget!   200
But let Heaven seize it, all at once 'tis fired;
Not touch'd, but rapt; not waken'd, but inspired!
Oh come! oh teach me nature to subdue,
Renounce my love, my life, myself—and you.
Fill my fond heart with God alone, for He
Alone can rival, can succeed to thee.

How happy is the blameless Vestal's lot!
The world forgetting, by the world forgot:
Eternal sunshine of the spotless mind!
Each prayer accepted, and each wish resign'd;   210
Labour and rest, that equal periods keep;
'Obedient slumbers that can wake and weep;'
Desires composed, affections ever even;
Tears that delight, and sighs that waft to heaven.
Grace shines around her with serenest beams,
And whispering angels prompt her golden dreams.
For her the unfading rose of Eden blooms,
And wings of seraphs shed divine perfumes;
For her the spouse prepares the bridal ring,
For her white virgins hymeneals sing,   220
To sounds of heavenly harps she dies away,
And melts in visions of eternal day.

Far other dreams my erring soul employ,
Far other raptures, of unholy joy:
When at the close of each sad, sorrowing day,

Fancy restores what vengeance snatch'd away,
Then conscience sleeps, and leaving nature free,
All my loose soul unbounded springs to thee.
O curst, dear horrors of all-conscious night!
How glowing guilt exalts the keen delight! 230
Provoking demons all restraint remove,
And stir within me every source of love.
I hear thee, view thee, gaze o'er all thy charms,
And round thy phantom glue my clasping arms.
I wake:—no more I hear, no more I view,
The phantom flies me, as unkind as you.
I call aloud; it hears not what I say:
I stretch my empty arms; it glides away.
To dream once more I close my willing eyes;
Ye soft illusions, dear deceits, arise! 240
Alas, no more! methinks we wandering go
Through dreary wastes, and weep each other's woe,
Where round some mouldering tower pale ivy creeps,
And low-brow'd rocks hang nodding o'er the deeps.
Sudden you mount, you beckon from the skies;
Clouds interpose, waves roar, and winds arise.
I shriek, start up, the same sad prospect find,
And wake to all the griefs I left behind.

For thee the Fates, severely kind, ordain
A cool suspense from pleasure and from pain; 250
Thy life a long dead calm of fix'd repose;
No pulse that riots, and no blood that glows.
Still as the sea, ere winds were taught to blow,
Or moving spirit bade the waters flow;
Soft as the slumbers of a saint forgiven,
And mild as opening gleams of promised heaven.

Come, Abelard! for what hast thou to dread?
The torch of Venus burns not for the dead.
Nature stands check'd; Religion disapproves;
Even thou art cold—yet Eloisa loves. 260
Ah hopeless, lasting flames! like those that burn
To light the dead, and warm the unfruitful urn.

What scenes appear where'er I turn my view?
The dear ideas, where I fly, pursue,
Rise in the grove, before the altar rise,

Stain all my soul, and wanton in my eyes.
I waste the matin lamp in sighs for thee,
Thy image steals between my God and me,
Thy voice I seem in every hymn to hear,
With every bead I drop too soft a tear. 270
When from the censer clouds of fragrance roll,
And swelling organs lift the rising soul,
One thought of thee puts all the pomp to flight,
Priests, tapers, temples, swim before my sight:
In seas of flame my plunging soul is drown'd,
While altars blaze, and angels tremble round.

While prostrate here in humble grief I lie,
Kind, virtuous drops just gathering in my eye,
While praying, trembling, in the dust I roll,
And dawning grace is opening on my soul: 280
Come, if thou dar'st, all charming as thou art!
Oppose thyself to heaven; dispute my heart;
Come, with one glance of those deluding eyes
Blot out each bright idea of the skies;
Take back that grace, those sorrows, and those tears;
Take back my fruitless penitence and prayers;
Snatch me, just mounting, from the blest abode;
Assist the fiends, and tear me from my God!

No, fly me, fly me, far as pole from pole;
Rise Alps between us! and whole oceans roll! 290
Ah, come not, write not, think not once of me,
Nor share one pang of all I felt for thee!
Thy oaths I quit, thy memory resign;
Forget, renounce me, hate whate'er was mine.
Fair eyes, and tempting looks (which yet I view)
Long loved, adored ideas, all adieu!
O Grace serene! O Virtue heavenly fair!
Divine oblivion of low-thoughted care!
Fresh blooming Hope, gay daughter of the sky! 300
And Faith, our early immortality!
Enter, each mild, each amicable guest;
Receive, and wrap me in eternal rest!

See in her cell sad Eloisa spread,
Propp'd on some tomb, a neighbour of the dead.
In each low wind methinks a spirit calls,

And more than echoes talk along the walls.
Here, as I watch'd the dying lamps around,
From yonder shrine I heard a hollow sound.
'Come, sister, come!' (it said, or seem'd to say)
'Thy place is here, sad sister, come away! 310
Once like thyself, I trembled, wept, and pray'd,
Love's victim then, though now a sainted maid:
But all is calm in this eternal sleep;
Here Grief forgets to groan, and Love to weep,
Even Superstition loses every fear:
For God, not man, absolves our frailties here.'

I come, I come! prepare your roseate bowers,
Celestial palms, and ever-blooming flowers.
Thither, where sinners may have rest, I go,
Where flames refined in breasts seraphic glow: 320
Thou, Abelard! the last sad office pay,
And smooth my passage to the realms of day;
See my lips tremble, and my eyeballs roll,
Suck my last breath, and catch my flying soul!
Ah, no!—in sacred vestments may'st thou stand,
The hallow'd taper trembling in thy hand,
Present the cross before my lifted eye,
Teach me at once, and learn of me to die.
Ah, then thy once-loved Eloisa see!
It will be then no crime to gaze on me. 330
See from my cheek the transient roses fly!
See the last sparkle languish in my eye!
Till every motion, pulse, and breath be o'er;
And even my Abelard be loved no more.
O Death all-eloquent! you only prove
What dust we doat on when 'tis man we love.

Then too, when fate shall thy fair frame destroy,
(That cause of all my guilt, and all my joy!)
In trance ecstatic may thy pangs be drown'd,
Bright clouds descend, and angels watch thee round, 340
From opening skies may streaming glories shine,
And saints embrace thee with a love like mine.

May one kind grave[67] unite each hapless name,
And graft my love immortal on thy fame!
Then, ages hence, when all my woes are o'er,

When this rebellious heart shall beat no more;
If ever chance two wandering lovers brings
To Paraclete's white walls and silver springs,
O'er the pale marble shall they join their heads,
And drink the falling tears each other sheds;   350
Then sadly say,—with mutual pity moved,
'Oh, may we never love as these have loved!'
From the full choir when loud hosannas rise,
And swell the pomp of dreadful sacrifice,
Amid that scene, if some relenting eye
Glance on the stone where our cold relics lie,
Devotion's self shall steal a thought from heaven,
One human tear shall drop, and be forgiven.
And sure, if Fate some future bard shall join
In sad similitude of griefs to mine,   360
Condemn'd whole years in absence to deplore,
And image charms he must behold no more;
Such if there be, who love so long, so well,
Let him our sad, our tender story tell;
The well-sung woes will soothe my pensive ghost;
He best can paint them who shall feel them most.

* * * * *

EPISTLE TO ROBERT EARL OF OXFORD AND EARL MORTIMER.[68]

Such were the notes thy once-loved Poet sung,
Till Death untimely stopp'd his tuneful tongue.
Oh just beheld and lost! admired and mourn'd!
With softest manners, gentlest arts adorn'd!
Blest in each science, blest in every strain!
Dear to the Muse! to Harley dear—in vain!

For him, thou oft hast bid the world attend,
Fond to forget the statesman in the friend;
For Swift and him, despised the farce of state,
The sober follies of the wise and great;   10
Dext'rous, the craving, fawning crowd to quit,
And pleased to 'scape from Flattery to Wit.

Absent or dead, still let a friend be dear,
(A sigh the absent claims, the dead a tear,)
Recall those nights that closed thy toilsome days,
Still hear thy Parnell in his living lays,
Who, careless now of interest, fame, or fate,
Perhaps forgets that Oxford e'er was great;
Or deeming meanest what we greatest call,
Behold thee glorious only in thy fall.   20

And sure, if aught below the seats divine
Can touch immortals, 'tis a soul like thine:
A soul supreme, in each hard instance tried,
Above all pain, all passion, and all pride,
The rage of power, the blast of public breath,
The lust of lucre, and the dread of death.

In vain to deserts thy retreat is made;
The Muse attends thee to thy silent shade:
'Tis hers the brave man's latest steps to trace,
Rejudge his acts, and dignify disgrace.   30
When interest calls off all her sneaking train,
And all the obliged desert, and all the vain,
She waits, or to the scaffold, or the cell,
When the last lingering friend has bid farewell.

Even now she shades thy evening-walk with bays,
(No hireling she, no prostitute to praise),
Even now, observant of the parting ray,
Eyes the calm sunset of thy various day;
Through Fortune's cloud one truly great can see,
Nor fears to tell that Mortimer is he. 40

* * * * *

EPISTLE TO JAMES CRAGGS, ESQ.,

SECRETARY OF STATE.[69]

A soul as full of worth, as void of pride,
Which nothing seeks to show, or needs to hide,
Which nor to guilt nor fear its caution owes,
And boasts a warmth that from no passion flows.
A face untaught to feign; a judging eye,
That darts severe upon a rising lie,
And strikes a blush through frontless flattery.
All this thou wert; and being this before,
Know, kings and fortune cannot make thee more.
Then scorn to gain a friend by servile ways,
Nor wish to lose a foe these virtues raise;
But candid, free, sincere, as you began,
Proceed—a minister, but still a man.
Be not (exalted to whate'er degree)
Ashamed of any friend, not even of me:
The patriot's plain, but untrod path pursue;
If not, 'tis I must be ashamed of you.

* * * * *

EPISTLE TO MR JERVAS,

WITH MR DRYDEN'S TRANSLATION OF FRESNOY'S 'ART OF PAINTING.'

This verse be thine, my friend, nor thou refuse
This from no venal or ungrateful Muse.
Whether thy hand strike out some free design,
Where life awakes, and dawns at every line;
Or blend in beauteous tints the colour'd mass,
And from the canvas call the mimic face:
Read these instructive leaves, in which conspire
Fresnoy's close art, and Dryden's native fire:
And, reading, wish like theirs our fate and fame,
So mix'd our studies, and so join'd our name;   10
Like them to shine through long succeeding age,
So just thy skill, so regular my rage.

Smit with the love of sister-arts we came,
And met congenial, mingling flame with flame;
Like friendly colours found them both unite,
And each from each contract new strength and light.
How oft in pleasing tasks we wear the day,
While summer suns roll unperceived away!
How oft our slowly-growing works impart,
While images reflect from art to art!   20
How oft review; each finding, like a friend,
Something to blame, and something to commend!

What flattering scenes our wandering fancy wrought,
Rome's pompous glories rising to our thought!
Together o'er the Alps methinks we fly,
Fired with ideas of fair Italy.
With thee on Raphael's monument I mourn.
Or wait inspiring dreams at Maro's urn:
With thee repose where Tully once was laid,
Or seek some ruin's formidable shade: 30
While fancy brings the vanish'd piles to view.
And builds imaginary Rome anew.
Here thy well-studied marbles fix our eye;
A fading fresco here demands a sigh:

Each heavenly piece unwearied we compare,
Match Raphael's grace with thy loved Guide's air,
Carracci's strength, Correggio's softer line,
Paulo's free stroke, and Titian's warmth divine.

How finish'd with illustrious toil appears
This small, well-polish'd gem, the work of years![70]   40
Yet still how faint by precept is express'd
The living image in the painter's breast!
Thence endless streams of fair ideas flow,
Strike in the sketch, or in the picture glow;
Thence Beauty, waking all her forms, supplies
An angel's sweetness, or Bridgewater's eyes.

Muse! at that name thy sacred sorrows shed,
Those tears eternal, that embalm the dead;
Call round her tomb each object of desire,
Each purer frame inform'd with purer fire: 50
Bid her be all that cheers or softens life,
The tender sister, daughter, friend, and wife:
Bid her be all that makes mankind adore;
Then view this marble, and be vain no more!

Yet still her charms in breathing paint engage;
Her modest cheek shall warm a future age.
Beauty, frail flower that every season fears,
Blooms in thy colours for a thousand years.
Thus Churchill's race shall other hearts surprise,
And other beauties envy Worsley's eyes;[71]   60
Each pleasing Blount shall endless smiles bestow,
And soft Belinda's blush for ever glow.

Oh, lasting as those colours may they shine,
Free as thy stroke, yet faultless as thy line;
New graces yearly like thy works display,
Soft without weakness, without glaring gay;
Led by some rule, that guides, but not constrains;
And finish'd more through happiness than pains.
The kindred arts shall in their praise conspire,
One dip the pencil, and one string the lyre.   70
Yet should the Graces all thy figures place,
And breathe an air divine on every face;
Yet should the Muses bid my numbers roll

Strong as their charms, and gentle as their soul;
With Zeuxis' Helen thy Bridgewater vie,
And these be sung till Granville's Myra die:
Alas! how little from the grave we claim!
Thou but preserv'st a face, and I a name.

* * * * *

EPISTLE TO MISS BLOUNT,

WITH THE WORKS OF VOITURE.[72]

In these gay thoughts the Loves and Graces shine,
And all the writer lives in every line;
His easy art may happy nature seem,
Trifles themselves are elegant in him.
Sure, to charm all was his peculiar fate,
Who without flattery pleased the fair and great;
Still with esteem no less conversed than read;
With wit well-natured, and with books well-bred:
His heart, his mistress, and his friend did share,
His time, the Muse, the witty, and the fair.   10
Thus wisely careless, innocently gay,
Cheerful he play'd the trifle, Life, away;
Till Fate scarce felt his gentle breath suppress'd,
As smiling infants sport themselves to rest.
Even rival wits did Voiture's death deplore,
And the gay mourn'd who never mourn'd before;
The truest hearts for Voiture heaved with sighs,
Voiture was wept by all the brightest eyes:
The Smiles and Loves had died in Voiture's death,
But that for ever in his lines they breathe.   20

Let the strict life of graver mortals be
A long, exact, and serious comedy;
In every scene some moral let it teach,
And if it can, at once both please and preach.
Let mine an innocent gay farce appear,
And more diverting still than regular,
Have humour, wit, a native ease and grace,
Though not too strictly bound to time and place:
Critics in wit, or life, are hard to please,
Few write to those, and none can live to these.   30

Too much your sex is by their forms confined,
Severe to all, but most to womankind;
Custom, grown blind with age, must be your guide;
Your pleasure is a vice, but not your pride;
By nature yielding, stubborn but for fame;

Made slaves by honour, and made fools by shame.
Marriage may all those petty tyrants chase,
But sets up one, a greater, in their place;
Well might you wish for change, by those accursed,
But the last tyrant ever proves the worst.   40
Still in constraint your suffering sex remains,
Or bound in formal, or in real chains:
Whole years neglected, for some months adored,
The fawning servant turns a haughty lord.
Ah, quit not the free innocence of life,
For the dull glory of a virtuous wife;
Nor let false shows, or empty titles please:
Aim not at joy, but rest content with ease!

The gods, to curse Pamela with her prayers,
Gave the gilt coach and dappled Flanders mares,   50
The shining robes, rich jewels, beds of state,
And, to complete her bliss, a fool for mate.
She glares in balls, front boxes, and the Ring,
A vain, unquiet, glittering, wretched thing!
Pride, pomp, and state but reach her outward part:
She sighs, and is no duchess at her heart.

But, madam, if the Fates withstand, and you
Are destined Hymen's willing victim too:
Trust not too much your now resistless charms,
Those, age or sickness, soon or late, disarms: 60
Good-humour only teaches charms to last,
Still makes new conquests, and maintains the past;
Love, raised on beauty, will like that decay,
Our hearts may bear its slender chain a day;
As flowery bands in wantonness are worn,
A morning's pleasure, and at evening torn;
This binds in ties more easy, yet more strong,
The willing heart, and only holds it long.

Thus Voiture's early care still shone the same,
And Monthansier[73] was only changed in name: 70
By this, even now they live, even now they charm,
Their wit still sparkling, and their flames still warm.

Now crown'd with myrtle, on the Elysian coast,
Amid those lovers, joys his gentle ghost:

Pleased, while with smiles his happy lines you view,
And finds a fairer Rambouillet in you.
The brightest eyes of France inspired his Muse;
The brightest eyes of Britain now peruse;
And dead, as living, 'tis our author's pride
Still to charm those who charm the world beside.

*   *   *   *   *

EPISTLE TO MRS TERESA BLOUNT.

ON HER LEAVING THE TOWN AFTER THE CORONATION.[74]

As some fond virgin, whom her mother's care
Drags from the town to wholesome country air,
Just when she learns to roll a melting eye,
And hear a spark, yet think no danger nigh;
From the dear man unwilling she must sever,
Yet takes one kiss before she parts for ever:
Thus from the world fair Zephalinda flew,
Saw others happy, and with sighs withdrew;
Not that their pleasures caused her discontent,
She sigh'd not that they staid, but that she went. 10

She went to plain-work, and to purling brooks,
Old-fashion'd halls, dull aunts, and croaking rooks:
She went from opera, park, assembly, play,
To morning-walks, and prayers three hours a-day:
To part her time 'twixt reading and bohea,
To muse, and spill her solitary tea;
Or o'er cold coffee trifle with the spoon,
Count the slow clock, and dine exact at noon;
Divert her eyes with pictures in the fire,
Hum half a tune, tell stories to the 'squire; 20
Up to her godly garret after seven,
There starve and pray, for that's the way to heaven.

Some 'squire, perhaps, you take delight to rack;
Whose game is whist, whose treat, a toast in sack;
Who visits with a gun, presents you birds,
Then gives a smacking buss, and cries—No words!
Or with his hound comes hallooing from the stable,
Makes love with nods, and knees beneath a table;
Whose laughs are hearty, though his jests are coarse,
And loves you best of all things—but his horse. 30

In some fair evening, on your elbow laid,
You dream of triumphs in the rural shade;
In pensive thought recall the fancied scene,
See coronations rise on every green;

Before you pass the imaginary sights
Of lords, and earls, and dukes, and garter'd knights,
While the spread fan o'ershades your closing eyes;
Then give one flirt, and all the vision flies.
Thus vanish sceptres, coronets, and balls,
And leave you in lone woods, or empty walls! 40

So when your slave, at some dear idle time,
(Not plagued with headaches, or the want of rhyme)
Stands in the streets, abstracted from the crew,
And while he seems to study, thinks of you;
Just when his fancy paints your sprightly eyes,
Or sees the blush of soft Parthenia rise,
Gay pats my shoulder, and you vanish quite,
Streets, chairs, and coxcombs rush upon my sight;
Vex'd to be still in town, I knit my brow,
Look sour, and hum a tune, as you do now. 50

* * * * *

TO MRS M. B.[75] ON HER BIRTHDAY.

Oh, be thou blest with all that Heaven can send,
Long health, long youth, long pleasure, and a friend:
Not with those toys the female world admire,
Riches that vex, and vanities that tire.
With added years, if life bring nothing new,
But, like a sieve, let every blessing through,
Some joy still lost, as each vain year runs o'er,
And all we gain, some sad reflection more;
Is that a birthday? 'tis alas! too clear
'Tis but the funeral of the former year.   10

Let joy or ease, let affluence or content,
And the gay conscience of a life well spent,
Calm every thought, inspirit every grace,
Glow in thy heart, and smile upon thy face
Let day improve on day, and year on year,
Without a pain, a trouble, or a fear;
Till death unfelt that tender frame destroy,
In some soft dream, or ecstasy of joy,
Peaceful sleep out the Sabbath of the tomb,
And wake to raptures in a life to come.   20

*   *   *   *   *

TO MR THOMAS SOUTHERN,[76] ON HIS BIRTHDAY, 1742.

Resign'd to live, prepared to die,
With not one sin, but poetry,
This day Tom's fair account has run
(Without a blot) to eighty-one.
Kind Boyle, before his poet lays
A table,[77] with a cloth of bays;
And Ireland, mother of sweet singers,
Presents her harp[78] still to his fingers.
The feast, his towering genius marks
In yonder wild goose and the larks;　　　　10
The mushrooms show his wit was sudden;
And for his judgment, lo, a pudden!
Roast beef, though old, proclaims him stout,
And grace, although a bard, devout.
May Tom, whom Heaven sent down to raise
The price of prologues[79] and of plays,
Be every birthday more a winner,
Digest his thirty-thousandth dinner;
Walk to his grave without reproach,
And scorn a rascal and a coach.　　　　20

* * * * *

VARIATION.

VER. 15. Originally thus in the MS.:—

And oh, since Death must that fair frame destroy,
Die, by some sudden ecstasy of joy;
In some soft dream may thy mild soul remove,
And be thy latest gasp a sigh of love.

TO MR JOHN MOORE,

AUTHOR OF THE CELEBRATED WORM-POWDER.

1 How much, egregious Moore, are we
   Deceived by shows and forms!
Whate'er we think, whate'er we see,
   All humankind are worms.

2 Man is a very worm by birth,
   Vile reptile, weak and vain!
A while he crawls upon the earth,
   Then shrinks to earth again.

3 That woman is a worm, we find
   E'er since our grandame's evil;
She first conversed with her own kind,
   That ancient worm, the Devil.

4 The learn'd themselves we book-worms name,
   The blockhead is a slow-worm;
The nymph whose tail is all on flame,
   Is aptly term'd a glow-worm:

5 The fops are painted butterflies,
   That flutter for a day;
First from a worm they take their rise,
   And in a worm decay.

6 The flatterer an earwig grows;
   Thus worms suit all conditions;
Misers are muck-worms, silk-worms beaux.
   And death-watches, physicians.

7 That statesmen have the worm, is seen
   By all their winding play;
Their conscience is a worm within,
   That gnaws them night and day.

8 Ah, Moore! thy skill were well employ'd,
   And greater gain would rise,

If thou couldst make the courtier void
　　　The worm that never dies!

9　O learned friend of Abchurch Lane,
　　　Who sett'st our entrails free!
　　Vain is thy art, thy powder vain,
　　　Since worms shall eat even thee.

10 Our fate thou only canst adjourn
　　　Some few short years—no more;
　　Even Button's Wits to worms shall turn,
　　　Who maggots were before.

TO MR C.,[80] ST JAMES'S PLACE.

1 Few words are best; I wish you well:
   Bethel, I'm told, will soon be here;
  Some morning walks along the Mall,
   And evening friends, will end the year.

2 If in this interval, between
   The falling leaf and coming frost,
  You please to see, on Twit'nam green,
   Your friend, your poet, and your host:

3 For three whole days you here may rest
   From office business, news, and strife;
  And (what most folks would think a jest)
   Want nothing else except your wife.

    *   *   *   *   *

EPITAPHS.

I. ON CHARLES EARL OF DORSET, IN THE CHURCH OF WITHYAM, IN SUSSEX.

'His saltem accumulem donis, et fungar inani Munere!'

VIRG.

Dorset, the grace of courts, the Muses' pride,
Patron of arts, and judge of nature, died.
The scourge of pride, though sanctified or great,
Of fops in learning, and of knaves in state:
Yet soft his nature, though severe his lay,
His anger moral, and his wisdom gay.
Bless'd satirist! who touch'd the mean so true,
As show'd vice had his hate and pity too.
Blest courtier! who could king and country please,
Yet sacred keep his friendships, and his ease.
Blest peer! his great forefathers' every grace
Reflecting, and reflected in his race;
Where other Buckhursts, other Dorsets shine,
And patriots still, or poets, deck the line.

II. ON SIR WILLIAM TRUMBULL.[81]

A pleasing form; a firm, yet cautious mind;
Sincere, though prudent; constant, yet resign'd:
Honour unchanged, a principle profess'd,
Fix'd to one side, but moderate to the rest:
An honest courtier, yet a patriot too;
Just to his prince, and to his country true:
Fill'd with the sense of age, the fire of youth,
A scorn of wrangling, yet a zeal for truth;
A generous faith, from superstition free:
A love to peace, and hate of tyranny;
Such this man was; who now, from earth removed,
At length enjoys that liberty he loved.

III. ON THE HON. SIMON HARCOURT, ONLY SON OF THE LORD CHANCELLOR HARCOURT, AT THE CHURCH OF STANTON HARCOURT, IN OXFORDSHIRE, 1720.

To this sad shrine, whoe'er thou art, draw near;
Here lies the friend most loved, the son most dear:
Who ne'er knew joy, but friendship might divide,
Or gave his father grief but when he died.

How vain is reason, eloquence how weak!
If Pope must tell what Harcourt cannot speak.
Oh, let thy once-loved friend inscribe thy stone,
And, with a father's sorrows, mix his own!

IV. ON JAMES CRAGGS, ESQ. IN WESTMINSTER ABBEY.

JACOBUS CRAGGS REGI MAGNAE BRITANNIA A SECRETIS ET CONSILIIS SANCTIORIBUS, PRINCIPIS PARITER AC POPULI AMOR ET DELICIAE: VIXIT TITULIS ET INVIDIA MAJOR ANNOS, HEU PAUCOS, XXXV. OB. FEB. XVI. MDCCXX.

Statesman, yet friend to Truth! of soul sincere,
In action faithful, and in honour clear!
Who broke no promise, served no private end,
Who gain'd no title, and who lost no friend;
Ennobled by himself, by all approved,
Praised, wept, and honour'd by the Muse he loved.

V. INTENDED FOR MR ROWE, IN WESTMINSTER ABBEY.

Thy relics, Rowe, to this fair urn we trust,
And sacred place by Dryden's awful dust:
Beneath a rude and nameless stone he lies,
To which thy tomb shall guide inquiring eyes.
Peace to thy gentle shade, and endless rest!
Blest in thy genius, in thy love, too, blest!
One grateful woman to thy fame supplies
What a whole thankless land to his denies.

VI. ON MRS CORBET, WHO DIED OF A CANCER IN HER BREAST.

Here rests a woman, good without pretence,
Blest with plain reason, and with sober sense:
No conquests she, but o'er herself, desired,
No arts essay'd, but not to be admired.
Passion and pride were to her soul unknown,
Convinced that virtue only is our own.
So unaffected, so composed a mind;
So firm, yet soft; so strong, yet so refined;
Heaven, as its purest gold, by tortures tried;
The saint sustain'd it, but the woman died.

VII. ON THE MONUMENT OF THE HONOURABLE EGBERT DIGBY, AND HIS SISTER MARY.

ERECTED BY THEIR FATHER THE LORD DIGBY, IN THE CHURCH OF SHERBORNE, IN DORSETSHIRE, 1727.

Go! fair example of untainted youth,
Of modest wisdom, and pacific truth:
Composed in sufferings, and in joy sedate,
Good without noise, without pretension great.
Just of thy word, in every thought sincere,
Who knew no wish but what the world might hear:
Of softest manners, unaffected mind,
Lover of peace, and friend of human kind:
Go live! for Heaven's eternal year is thine,[82]
Go, and exalt thy moral to divine.

And thou, bless'd maid! attendant on his doom,
Pensive hast follow'd to the silent tomb,
Steer'd the same course to the same quiet shore,
Not parted long, and now to part no more!
Go then, where only bliss sincere is known!
Go, where to love and to enjoy are one!

Yet take these tears, Mortality's relief,
And till we share your joys, forgive our grief:
These little rites, a stone, a verse receive;
'Tis all a father, all a friend can give!

VIII. ON SIR GODFREY KNELLER, IN WESTMINSTER ABBEY, 1723.

Kneller, by Heaven, and not a master, taught,
Whose art was Nature, and whose pictures Thought;
Now for two ages having snatch'd from Fate
Whate'er was beauteous, or whate'er was great,
Lies crown'd with princes' honours, poets' lays,
Due to his merit, and brave thirst of praise.

Living, great Nature fear'd he might outvie
Her works; and, dying, fears herself may die.

IX. ON GENERAL HENRY WITHERS, IN WESTMINSTER ABBEY, 1729.

Here, Withers, rest! thou bravest, gentlest mind,
Thy country's friend, but more of human kind.
Oh, born to arms! oh, worth in youth approved!
Oh, soft humanity, in age beloved!
For thee the hardy veteran drops a tear,
And the gay courtier feels the sigh sincere.
Withers, adieu! yet not with thee remove
Thy martial spirit, or thy social love!
Amidst corruption, luxury, and rage,
Still leave some ancient virtues to our age:
Nor let us say (those English glories gone)
The last true Briton lies beneath this stone.

X. ON MR ELIJAH FENTON,[83] AT EASTHAMSTEAD, IN BERKS, 1730.

This modest stone, what few vain marbles can,
May truly say, Here lies an honest man:
A poet, blest beyond the poet's fate,
Whom Heaven kept sacred from the proud and great:
Foe to loud praise, and friend to learned ease,
Content with science in the vale of peace.
Calmly he look'd on either life, and here
Saw nothing to regret, or there to fear;
From Nature's temperate feast rose satisfied,

Thank'd Heaven that he had lived, and that he died.

XI. ON MR GAY, IN WESTMINSTER ABBEY, 1732.

Of manners gentle, of affections mild;
In wit, a man; simplicity, a child:
With native humour tempering virtuous rage,
Form'd to delight at once and lash the age:
Above temptation in a low estate,
And uncorrupted, even among the great:
A safe companion, and an easy friend,
Unblamed through life, lamented in thy end.
These are thy honours! not that here thy bust
Is mix'd with heroes, or with kings thy dust;
But that the worthy and the good shall say,
Striking their pensive bosoms—Here lies Gay.

XII. INTENDED FOR SIR ISAAC NEWTON, IN WESTMINSTER ABBEY.

ISAACUS NEWTONUS:
QUEM IMMORTALEM
TESTANTUR TEMPUS, NATURA, COELUM:
  MORTALEM
  HOC MARMOR FATETUR.

Nature and Nature's laws lay hid in night
God said, Let Newton be! and all was light.

XIII. ON DR FRANCIS ATTERBURY,[84] BISHOP OF ROCHESTER, WHO DIED IN EXILE AT PARIS, 1732.

SHE.

Yes, we have lived—one pang, and then we part!
May Heaven, dear father! now have all thy heart.
Yet ah! how once we loved, remember still,
Till you are dust like me.

HE.
                Dear shade! I will:
Then mix this dust with thine—O spotless ghost!
O more than fortune, friends, or country lost!
Is there on earth one care, one wish beside?
Yes—Save my country, Heaven!
               —He said, and died.

XIV. ON EDMUND DUKE OF BUCKINGHAM, WHO DIED IN THE NINETEENTH YEAR OF HIS AGE, 1735.

If modest youth, with cool reflection crown'd,
And every opening virtue blooming round,
Could save a parent's justest pride from fate,
Or add one patriot to a sinking state;
This weeping marble had not ask'd thy tear,
Or sadly told how many hopes lie here!
The living virtue now had shone approved,
The senate heard him, and his country loved.
Yet softer honours, and less noisy fame
Attend the shade of gentle Buckingham:
In whom a race, for courage famed and art,
Ends in the milder merit of the heart;
And chiefs or sages long to Britain given,
Pays the last tribute of a saint to Heaven.

XV. FOR ONE WHO WOULD NOT BE BURIED IN WESTMINSTER ABBEY.

Heroes and kings! your distance keep:
In peace let one poor poet sleep,
Who never flatter'd folks like you:
Let Horace blush, and Virgil too.

XVI. ANOTHER, ON THE SAME.

Under this marble, or under this sill,
Or under this turf, or e'en what they will;
Whatever an heir, or a friend in his stead,

Or any good creature shall lay o'er my head,
Lies one who ne'er cared, and still cares not a pin
What they said, or may say, of the mortal within:
But who, living and dying, serene still and free,
Trusts in God, that as well as he was, he shall be.

XVII. ON TWO LOVERS STRUCK DEAD BY LIGHTNING.[85]

When Eastern lovers feed the funeral fire,
On the same pile the faithful pair expire.
Here pitying Heaven that virtue mutual found,
And blasted both, that it might neither wound.
Hearts so sincere, the Almighty saw well pleased,
Sent his own lightning, and the victims seized.

[Lord Harcourt, on whose property the unfortunate pair lived, was apprehensive that the country people would not understand the above, and Pope wrote the subjoined]:—

NEAR THIS PLACE LIE THE BODIES OF
JOHN HEWET AND SARAH DREW,
AN INDUSTRIOUS YOUNG MAN,
AND VIRTUOUS MAIDEN OF THIS PARISH;
WHO, BEING AT HARVEST-WORK
(WITH SEVERAL OTHERS),
WERE IN ONE INSTANT KILLED BY LIGHTNING,
THE LAST DAY OF JULY 1718.

Think not, by rigorous judgment seized,
  A pair so faithful could expire;
Victims so pure Heaven saw well pleased,
  And snatch'd them in celestial fire.

Live well, and fear no sudden fate;
  When God calls virtue to the grave,
Alike 'tis justice soon or late,
  Mercy alike to kill or save.

Virtue unmoved can hear the call,
  And face the flash that melts the ball.

AN ESSAY ON MAN:

IN FOUR EPISTLES TO HENRY ST JOHN, LORD BOLINGBROKE.

THE DESIGN.

Having proposed to write some pieces on human life and manners, such as (to use my Lord Bacon's expression) come home to men's business and bosoms, I thought it more satisfactory to begin with considering man in the abstract, his nature and his state; since, to prove any moral duty, to enforce any moral precept, or to examine the perfection or imperfection of any creature whatsoever, it is necessary first to know what condition and relation it is placed in, and what is the proper end and purpose of its being.

The science of human nature is, like all other sciences, reduced to a few clear points: there are not many certain truths in this world. It is therefore in the anatomy of the mind as in that of the body; more good will accrue to mankind by attending to the large, open, and perceptible parts, than by studying too much such finer nerves and vessels, the conformations and uses of which will for ever escape our observation. The disputes are all upon these last, and, I will venture to say, they have less sharpened the wits than the hearts of men against each other, and have diminished the practice, more than advanced the theory, of morality. If I could flatter myself that this essay has any merit, it is in steering betwixt the extremes of doctrines seemingly opposite, in passing over terms utterly unintelligible, and in forming a *temperate* yet not *inconsistent*, and a *short* yet not *imperfect* system of ethics.

This I might have done in prose; but I chose verse, and even rhyme, for two reasons. The one will appear obvious; that principles, maxims, or precepts so written, both strike the reader more strongly at first, and are more easily retained by him afterwards: the other may seem odd, but is true; I found I could express them more shortly this way than in prose itself; and nothing is more certain, than that much of the force as well as grace of arguments or instructions, depends on their conciseness. I was unable to treat this part of my subject more in detail, without becoming dry and tedious; or more poetically, without sacrificing perspicuity to ornament, without wandering from the precision, or breaking the chain of reasoning: If any man can unite all these without diminution of any of them, I freely confess he will compass a thing above my capacity.

What is now published, is only to be considered as a general map of Man, marking out no more than the greater parts, their extent, their limits, and their connexion, but leaving the particular to be more fully delineated in the charts which are to follow. Consequently, these epistles in their progress (if I have health and leisure to make any progress) will be less dry, and more susceptible of poetical ornament. I am here only opening the *fountains*, and clearing the passage. To deduce the *rivers*, to follow them in their course, and to observe their effects, may be a task more agreeable.

EPISTLE I.

ARGUMENT

OF THE NATURE AND STATE OF MAN WITH RESPECT TO THE UNIVERSE.

Of man in the abstract.—

I. That we can judge only with regard to our own system, being ignorant of the relations of systems and things, ver. 17, &c. II. That Man is not to be deemed imperfect, but a being suited to his place and rank in the creation, agreeable to the general order of things, and conformable to ends and relations to him unknown, ver. 35, &c. III. That it is partly upon his ignorance of future events, and partly upon the hope of a future state, that all his happiness in the present depends, ver. 77, &c. IV. The pride of aiming at more knowledge, and pretending to more perfection, the cause of Man's error and misery. The impiety of putting himself in the place of God, and judging of the fitness or unfitness, perfection or imperfection, justice or injustice of his dispensations, ver. 109, &c. V. The absurdity of conceiting himself the final cause of the creation, or expecting that perfection in the moral world, which is not in the natural, ver. 131, &c. VI. The unreasonableness of his complaints against Providence, while on the one hand he demands the perfections of the angels, and on the other the bodily qualifications of the brutes; though to possess any of the sensitive faculties in a higher degree, would render him miserable, ver. 173, &c. VII. That throughout the whole visible world, an universal order and gradation in the sensual and mental faculties is observed, which causes a subordination of creature to creature, and of all creatures to Man. The gradations of sense, instinct, thought, reflection, reason; that reason alone countervails all the other faculties, ver. 207. VIII. How much further this order and subordination of living creatures may extend, above and below us; were any part of which broken, not that part only, but the whole connected creation must be destroyed, ver. 233. IX. The extravagance, madness, and pride of such a desire, ver. 259. X. The consequence of all, the absolute submission due to Providence, both as to our present and future state, ver. 281, &c. to the end.

AWAKE, my St John! leave all meaner things
To low ambition, and the pride of kings.
Let us (since life can little more supply

Than just to look about us and to die)
Expatiate free o'er all this scene of Man;
A mighty maze! but not without a plan;
A wild, where weeds and flowers promiscuous shoot;
Or garden, tempting with forbidden fruit.
Together let us beat this ample field,
Try what the open, what the covert yield;   10
The latent tracts, the giddy heights, explore
Of all who blindly creep, or sightless soar;
Eye Nature's walks, shoot folly as it flies,
And catch the manners living as they rise;
Laugh where we must, be candid where we can;
But vindicate the ways of God to Man.[86]

I. Say first, of God above, or Man below,
What can we reason, but from what we know?
Of Man, what see we but his station here,
From which to reason, or to which refer?   20
Through worlds unnumber'd, though the God be known,
'Tis ours to trace him only in our own.
He who through vast immensity can pierce,
See worlds on worlds compose one universe,
Observe how system into system runs,
What other planets circle other suns,
What varied being peoples every star,
May tell why Heaven has made us as we are.
But of this frame the bearings, and the ties,
The strong connexions, nice dependencies,   30
Gradations just, has thy pervading soul
Look'd through? or can a part contain the whole?

Is the great chain, that draws all to agree,
And drawn, supports, upheld by God, or thee?

II. Presumptuous Man! the reason wouldst thou find,
Why form'd so weak, so little, and so blind?
First, if thou canst, the harder reason guess,
Why form'd no weaker, blinder, and no less?
Ask of thy mother earth, why oaks are made
Taller or stronger than the weeds they shade?   40
Or ask of yonder argent fields above,
Why Jove's satellites are less than Jove?

Of systems possible, if 'tis confess'd
That Wisdom infinite must form the best,
Where all must full or not coherent be,
And all that rises, rise in due degree;
Then, in the scale of reasoning life, 'tis plain,
There must be, somewhere, such a rank as Man:
And all the question (wrangle e'er so long)
Is only this, if God has placed him wrong?   50

Respecting Man, whatever wrong we call,
May, must be right, as relative to all.
In human works, though labour'd on with pain,
A thousand movements scarce one purpose gain;
In God's, one single can its end produce;
Yet serves to second, too, some other use.
So Man, who here seems principal alone,
Perhaps acts second to some sphere unknown,
Touches some wheel, or verges to some goal;
'Tis but a part we see, and not a whole.   60

When the proud steed shall know why Man restrains
His fiery course, or drives him o'er the plains;
When the dull ox, why now he breaks the clod,
Is now a victim, and now Egypt's god:[87]
Then shall man's pride and dulness comprehend
His actions', passions', being's use and end;
Why doing, suffering, check'd, impell'd; and why
This hour a slave, the next a deity.

Then say not Man's imperfect, Heaven in fault;
Say rather, Man's as perfect as he ought: 70
His knowledge measured to his state and place;
His time a moment, and a point his space.
If to be perfect in a certain sphere,
What matter, soon or late, or here or there?
The blest to-day is as completely so,
As who began a thousand years ago.

III. Heaven from all creatures hides the book of Fate,
All but the page prescribed, their present state:
From brutes what men, from men what spirits know:
Or who could suffer being here below?   80
The lamb thy riot dooms to bleed to-day,

Had he thy reason, would he skip and play?
Pleased to the last, he crops the flowery food,
And licks the hand just raised to shed his blood.
Oh blindness to the future! kindly given,
That each may fill the circle mark'd by Heaven:
Who sees with equal eye, as God of all,
A hero perish, or a sparrow fall,
Atoms or systems into ruin hurl'd,
And now a bubble burst, and now a world.   90

Hope humbly then; with trembling pinions soar;
Wait the great teacher, Death; and God adore.
What future bliss, He gives not thee to know,
But gives that hope to be thy blessing now.
Hope springs eternal in the human breast:
Man never Is, but always To be blest:
The soul, uneasy and confined from home,
Rests and expatiates in a life to come.

Lo, the poor Indian! whose untutor'd mind
Sees God in clouds, or hears him in the wind;   100
His soul, proud science never taught to stray
Far as the solar walk, or milky-way;
Yet simple nature to his hope has given,
Behind the cloud-topp'd hill, an humbler heaven;
Some safer world in depth of woods embraced,
Some happier island in the watery waste,
Where slaves once more their native land behold,
No fiends torment, no Christians thirst for gold.
To be, contents his natural desire,
He asks no angel's wing, no seraph's fire;   110
But thinks, admitted to that equal sky,
His faithful dog shall bear him company.

IV. Go, wiser thou! and in thy scale of sense,
Weigh thy opinion against Providence;
Call imperfection what thou fanciest such,
Say, here he gives too little, there too much:
Destroy all creatures for thy sport or gust,
Yet cry, If Man's unhappy, God's unjust:
If Man alone engross not Heaven's high care,
Alone made perfect here, immortal there: 120
Snatch from his hand the balance and the rod,

Re-judge his justice, be the God of God.
In pride, in reasoning pride, our error lies;
All quit their sphere, and rush into the skies.
Pride still is aiming at the blest abodes,
Men would be angels, angels would be gods.
Aspiring to be gods, if angels fell,
Aspiring to be angels, men rebel:
And who but wishes to invert the laws
Of ORDER, sins against the Eternal Cause.   130

V. Ask for what end the heavenly bodies shine,
Earth for whose use? Pride answers, "Tis for mine:
For me kind Nature wakes her genial power,
Suckles each herb, and spreads out every flower;
Annual for me the grape, the rose renew,
The juice nectareous, and the balmy dew;
For me, the mine a thousand treasures brings;
For me, health gushes from a thousand springs;
Seas roll to waft me, suns to light me rise;
My footstool earth, my canopy the skies.'   140

But errs not Nature from this gracious end,
From burning suns when livid deaths descend,
When earthquakes swallow, or when tempests sweep
Towns to one grave, whole nations to the deep?
'No' 'tis replied, 'the first Almighty Cause
Acts not by partial, but by general laws;
Th' exceptions few; some change, since all began:
And what created perfect?'—Why then Man?
If the great end be human happiness,
Then Nature deviates; and can Man do less?   150
As much that end a constant course requires
Of showers and sunshine, as of Man's desires;
As much eternal springs and cloudless skies,
As men for ever temperate, calm, and wise.
If plagues or earthquakes break not Heaven's design,
Why then a Borgia, or a Catiline?
Who knows but He, whose hand the lightning forms,
Who heaves old Ocean, and who wings the storms,
Pours fierce ambition in a Caesar's mind,
Or turns young Ammon loose to scourge mankind?   150
From pride, from pride, our very reasoning springs;
Account for moral, as for natural things:

Why charge we Heaven in those, in these acquit?
In both, to reason right, is to submit.

Better for us, perhaps, it might appear,
Were there all harmony, all virtue here;
That never air or ocean felt the wind,
That never passion discomposed the mind.
But all subsists by elemental strife;
And passions are the elements of life.　　　170
The general order, since the whole began,
Is kept in Nature, and is kept in Man.

VI. What would this Man? Now upward will he soar,
And, little less than angel, would be more;
Now looking downwards, just as grieved appears
To want the strength of bulls, the fur of bears.
Made for his use all creatures if he call,
Say, what their use, had he the powers of all?
Nature to these, without profusion, kind,
The proper organs, proper powers assign'd;　　　180
Each seeming want compensated, of course,
Here with degrees of swiftness, there of force;
All in exact proportion to the state;
Nothing to add, and nothing to abate.
Each beast, each insect, happy in its own:
Is Heaven unkind to Man, and Man alone?
Shall he alone, whom rational we call,
Be pleased with nothing, if not bless'd with all?

The bliss of Man (could pride that blessing find)
Is not to act or think beyond mankind;　　　190
No powers of body or of soul to share,
But what his nature and his state can bear.
Why has not Man a microscopic eye?
For this plain reason, Man is not a fly.
Say, what the use, were finer optics given,
T'inspect a mite, not comprehend the heaven?
Or touch, if tremblingly alive all o'er,
To smart and agonise at every pore?
Or, quick effluvia darting through the brain,
Die of a rose in aromatic pain?　　　200
If nature thunder'd in his opening ears,
And stunn'd him with the music of the spheres,

How would he wish that Heaven had left him still
The whispering zephyr, and the purling rill?
Who finds not Providence all good and wise,
Alike in what it gives, and what denies?

VII. Far as Creation's ample range extends,
The scale of sensual, mental powers ascends:
Mark how it mounts, to Man's imperial race,
From the green myriads in the peopled grass: 210
What modes of sight betwixt each wide extreme,
The mole's dim curtain, and the lynx's beam!
Of smell, the headlong lioness between,
And hound sagacious on the tainted green:
Of hearing, from the life that fills the flood,
To that which warbles through the vernal wood:
The spider's touch, how exquisitely fine!
Feels at each thread, and lives along the line:
In the nice bee, what sense so subtly true
From poisonous herbs extracts the healing dew!   220
How instinct varies in the grovelling swine,
Compared, half-reasoning elephant, with thine!
'Twixt that and reason, what a nice barrier:
For ever separate, yet for ever near!
Remembrance and reflection how allied;
What thin partitions[88] sense from thought divide:
And middle natures, how they long to join,
Yet never pass th' insuperable line!
Without this just gradation, could they be
Subjected, these to those, or all to thee?   230
The powers of all subdued by thee alone,
Is not thy reason all these powers in one?

VIII. See, through this air, this ocean, and this earth,
All matter quick, and bursting into birth:
Above, how high progressive life may go!
Around, how wide! how deep extend below!
Vast chain of being! which from God began,
Natures ethereal, human, angel, man,
Beast, bird, fish, insect, what no eye can see,
No glass can reach; from Infinite to Thee,   240
From Thee to Nothing.—On superior powers
Were we to press, inferior might on ours:
Or in the full creation leave a void,

Where, one step broken, the great scale's destroy'd:
From Nature's chain whatever link you strike,
Tenth, or ten thousandth, breaks the chain alike.

And, if each system in gradation roll
Alike essential to th' amazing whole,
The least confusion but in one, not all
That system only, but the whole must fall.   250
Let earth, unbalanced, from her orbit fly,
Planets and suns run lawless through the sky;
Let ruling angels from their spheres be hurl'd,
Being on being wreck'd, and world on world;
Heaven's whole foundations to their centre nod,
And Nature trembles to the throne of God.
All this dread order break—for whom? for thee?
Vile worm!—oh madness! pride! impiety!

IX. What if the foot, ordain'd the dust to tread,
Or hand, to toil, aspired to be the head   260
What if the head, the eye, or ear repined
To serve mere engines to the ruling mind?
Just as absurd for any part to claim
To be another, in this general frame;
Just as absurd, to mourn the tasks or pains,
The great directing Mind of All ordains.

All are but parts of one stupendous whole,
Whose body Nature is, and God the soul;
That, changed through all, and yet in all the same;
Great in the earth, as in th' ethereal frame: 270
Warms in the sun, refreshes in the breeze,
Glows in the stars, and blossoms in the trees,
Lives through all life, extends through all extent.
Spreads undivided, operates unspent;
Breathes in our soul, informs our mortal part,
As full, as perfect, in a hair as heart;
As full, as perfect, in vile Man that mourns,
As the rapt Seraph that adores and burns:
To Him no high, no low, no great, no small;
He fills, He bounds, connects, and equals all.   280

X. Cease then, nor Order imperfection name:
Our proper bliss depends on what we blame.

Know thy own point: this kind, this due degree
Of blindness, weakness, Heaven bestows on thee.
Submit—in this, or any other sphere,
Secure to be as bless'd as thou canst bear:
Safe in the hand of one disposing Power,
Or in the natal, or the mortal hour.
All Nature is but Art, unknown to thee;
All chance, direction, which thou canst not see;   290
All discord, harmony not understood;
All partial evil, universal good:
And, spite of pride, in erring reason's spite,
One truth is clear, WHATEVER IS, IS RIGHT.

* * * * *

VARIATIONS.

In former editions, VER 64—

Now wears a garland, an Egyptian god.

Altered as above for the reason given in the note.

After VER. 68 the following lines in first edit.—

If to be perfect in a certain sphere,
What matters, soon or late, or here or there?
The blest to-day is as completely so
As who began ten thousand years ago.

After VER. 88 in the MS.—

No great, no little; 'tis as much decreed
That Virgil's gnat should die as Caesar bleed.

In the first folio and quarto:—

What bliss above He gives not thee to know,
But gives that hope to be thy bliss below.

After VER. 108 in the first edition:—

But does he say the Maker is not good,

Till he's exalted to what state he would:
Himself alone high Heaven's peculiar care,
Alone made happy when he will, and where?

VER. 238, first edition —

Ethereal essence, spirit, substance, man.

After VER. 282 in the MS. —

Reason, to think of God when she pretends,
Begins a censor, an adorer ends.

EPISTLE II.

ARGUMENT.

OF THE NATURE AND STATE OF MAN WITH RESPECT TO HIMSELF AS AN INDIVIDUAL.

I. The business of Man not to pry into God, but to study himself. His middle nature; his powers and frailties, ver. 1 to 19. The limits of his capacity, ver. 19, &c. II. The two principles of Man, self-love and reason, both necessary, ver. 53, &c. Self-love the stronger, and why, ver. 67, &c. Their end the same, ver. 81, &c. III. The passions, and their use, ver. 93-130. The predominant passion, and its force, ver. 132-160. Its necessity, in directing men to different purposes, ver. 165, &c. Its providential use, in fixing our principle, and ascertaining our virtue, ver. 177. IV. Virtue and vice joined in our mixed nature; the limits near, yet the things separate and evident: What is the office of reason, ver. 202-216. V. How odious vice in itself, and how we deceive ourselves into it, ver. 217. VI. That, however, the ends of Providence and general good are answered in our passions and imperfections, ver. 238, &c. How usefully these are distributed to all orders of men, ver. 241. How useful they are to society, ver. 251. And to the individuals, ver. 263. In every state, and every age of life, ver. 273, &c.

I. KNOW then thyself, presume not God to scan;
The proper study of mankind is Man.
Placed on this isthmus of a middle state,
A being darkly wise, and rudely great:
With too much knowledge for the sceptic side,
With too much weakness for the stoic's pride,
He hangs between; in doubt to act, or rest;
In doubt to deem himself a god, or beast;
In doubt his mind or body to prefer;
Born but to die, and reasoning but to err; 10
Alike in ignorance, his reason such,
Whether he thinks too little, or too much:
Chaos of thought and passion, all confused;
Still by himself abused, or disabused;
Created half to rise, and half to fall;
Great lord of all things, yet a prey to all;
Sole judge of truth, in endless error hurl'd:

The glory, jest, and riddle of the world![89]

Go, wondrous creature! mount where science guides,
Go, measure earth, weigh air, and state the tides;   20
Instruct the planets in what orbs to run,
Correct old Time, and regulate the sun;
Go, soar with Plato to the empyreal sphere,
To the first Good, first Perfect, and first Fair;
Or tread the mazy round his followers trod,
And quitting sense call imitating God;
As eastern priests in giddy circles run,
And turn their heads to imitate the sun.
Go, teach Eternal Wisdom how to rule—
Then drop into thyself, and be a fool!   30

Superior beings, when of late they saw
A mortal man unfold all Nature's law,
Admired such wisdom in an earthly shape,
And show'd a Newton as we show an ape.

Could he, whose rules the rapid comet bind,
Describe or fix one movement of his mind?
Who saw its fires here rise, and there descend,
Explain his own beginning, or his end?
Alas, what wonder! Man's superior part
Uncheck'd may rise, and climb from art to art;   40
But when his own great work is but begun,
What reason weaves, by passion is undone.

Trace Science, then, with modesty thy guide;
First strip off all her equipage of pride;
Deduct what is but vanity, or dress,
Or learning's luxury, or idleness;
Or tricks to show the stretch of human brain.
Mere curious pleasure, or ingenious pain;
Expunge the whole, or lop th' excrescent parts
Of all our vices have created arts;   50
Then see how little the remaining sum,
Which served the past, and must the times to come!

II. Two principles in human nature reign—
Self-love, to urge, and reason, to restrain;
Nor this a good, nor that a bad we call,

Each works its end, to move or govern all:
And to their proper operation still,
Ascribe all good; to their improper, ill.

Self-love, the spring of motion, acts the soul;
Reason's comparing balance rules the whole.　　60
Man, but for that, no action could attend,
And, but for this, were active to no end:
Fix'd like a plant on his peculiar spot,
To draw nutrition, propagate, and rot;
Or, meteor-like, flame lawless through the void,
Destroying others, by himself destroy'd.

Most strength the moving principle requires;
Active its task, it prompts, impels, inspires.
Sedate and quiet the comparing lies,
Form'd but to check, deliberate, and advise.　　70
Self-love, still stronger, as its objects nigh;
Reason's at distance, and in prospect lie:
That sees immediate good by present sense;
Reason, the future and the consequence.
Thicker than arguments, temptations throng,
At best more watchful this, but that more strong.
The action of the stronger to suspend
Reason still use, to reason still attend.
Attention, habit and experience gains;
Each strengthens reason, and self-love restrains.　　80

Let subtle schoolmen teach these friends to fight,
More studious to divide than to unite;
And grace and virtue, sense and reason split,
With all the rash dexterity of wit.
Wits, just like fools, at war about a name,
Have full as oft no meaning, or the same.
Self-love and reason to one end aspire,
Pain their aversion, pleasure their desire;
But greedy that its object would devour,
This taste the honey, and not wound the flower:　　90
Pleasure, or wrong or rightly understood,
Our greatest evil, or our greatest good.

III. Modes of self-love the passions we may call:
'Tis real good, or seeming, moves them all:

But since not every good we can divide,
And reason bids us for our own provide;
Passions, though selfish, if their means be fair,
List under reason, and deserve her care;
Those, that imparted, court a nobler aim,
Exalt their kind, and take some virtue's name. 100

In lazy apathy let Stoics boast
Their virtue fix'd; 'tis fix'd as in a frost;
Contracted all, retiring to the breast;
But strength of mind is exercise, not rest:
The rising tempest puts in act the soul,
Parts it may ravage, but preserves the whole.
On life's vast ocean diversely we sail,
Reason the card, but passion is the gale;
Nor God alone in the still calm we find,
He mounts the storm, and walks upon the wind. 110

Passions, like elements, though born to fight,
Yet, mix'd and soften'd, in his work unite:
These 'tis enough to temper and employ;
But what composes Man, can Man destroy?
Suffice that reason keep to Nature's road;
Subject, compound them, follow her and God.
Love, Hope, and Joy, fair Pleasure's smiling train,
Hate, Fear, and Grief, the family of Pain,
These mix'd with art, and to due bounds confined,
Make and maintain the balance of the mind: 120
The lights and shades, whose well-accorded strife
Gives all the strength and colour of our life.

Pleasures are ever in our hands or eyes;
And when, in act, they cease, in prospect, rise:
Present to grasp, and future still to find,
The whole employ of body and of mind.
All spread their charms, but charm not all alike;
On different senses different objects strike;
Hence different passions more or less inflame,
As strong or weak, the organs of the frame; 130
And hence one master passion in the breast,
Like Aaron's serpent, swallows up the rest.
As Man, perhaps, the moment of his breath,
Receives the lurking principle of death;

The young disease, that must subdue at length,
Grows with his growth, and strengthens with his strength:
So, cast and mingled with his very frame,
The mind's disease, its ruling passion came;
Each vital humour which should feed the whole,
Soon flows to this, in body and in soul: 140
Whatever warms the heart, or fills the head,
As the mind opens, and its functions spread,
Imagination plies her dangerous art,
And pours it all upon the peccant part.

Nature its mother, habit is its nurse;
Wit, spirit, faculties, but make it worse;
Reason itself but gives it edge and power;
As Heaven's blest beam turns vinegar more sour.

We, wretched subjects, though to lawful sway,
In this weak queen, some favourite still obey: 150
Ah! if she lend not arms, as well as rules,
What can she more than tell us we are fools?
Teach us to mourn our nature, not to mend,
A sharp accuser, but a helpless friend!
Or from a judge turn pleader, to persuade
The choice we make, or justify it made;
Proud of an easy conquest all along,
She but removes weak passions for the strong:
So, when small humours gather to a gout,
The doctor fancies he has driven them out.   160

Yes, Nature's road must ever be preferr'd;
Reason is here no guide, but still a guard:
'Tis hers to rectify, not overthrow,
And treat this passion more as friend than foe:
A mightier power the strong direction sends,
And several men impels to several ends:
Like varying winds, by other passions tost,
This drives them constant to a certain coast.
Let power or knowledge, gold or glory, please,
Or (oft more strong than all) the love of ease; 170
Through life 'tis follow'd, even at life's expense;
The merchant's toil, the sage's indolence,
The monk's humility, the hero's pride,
All, all alike, find reason on their side.

Th' eternal Art educing good from ill,
Grafts on this passion our best principle:
'Tis thus the mercury of Man is fix'd,
Strong grows the virtue with his nature mix'd;
The dross cements what else were too refined
And in one interest body acts with mind.   180

As fruits, ungrateful to the planter's care,
On savage stocks inserted, learn to bear;
The surest virtues thus from passions shoot,
Wild nature's vigour working at the root.
What crops of wit and honesty appear
From spleen, from obstinacy, hate, or fear!
See anger, zeal and fortitude supply;
Even avarice, prudence; sloth, philosophy;
Lust, through some certain strainers well refined,
Is gentle love, and charms all womankind;   190
Envy, to which th' ignoble mind's a slave,
Is emulation in the learn'd or brave;
Nor virtue, male or female, can we name,

But what will grow on pride, or grow on shame.
Thus Nature gives us (let it check our pride)
The virtue nearest to our vice allied:
Reason the bias turns to good from ill,
And Nero reigns a Titus, if he will.
The fiery soul abhorr'd in Catiline,
In Decius charms, in Curtius is divine: 200
The same ambition can destroy or save,
And makes a patriot, as it makes a knave.

IV. This light and darkness in our chaos join'd
What shall divide? the God within the mind.

Extremes in Nature equal ends produce,
In man they join to some mysterious use;
Though each by turns the other's bound invade,
As, in some well-wrought picture, light and shade,
And oft so mix, the difference is too nice
Where ends the virtue, or begins the vice.   210

Fools! who from hence into the notion fall,
That vice or virtue there is none at all.

If white and black blend, soften, and unite
A thousand ways, is there no black or white?
Ask your own heart, and nothing is so plain;
'Tis to mistake them, costs the time and pain.

V. Vice is a monster of so frightful mien,
As, to be hated, needs but to be seen;
Yet seen too oft, familiar with her face,
We first endure, then pity, then embrace.　　　220
But where th' extreme of vice, was ne'er agreed:
Ask where's the north? at York, 'tis on the Tweed;
In Scotland, at the Orcades; and there,
At Greenland, Zembla, or the Lord knows where.
No creature owns it in the first degree,
But thinks his neighbour further gone than he;
Even those who dwell beneath its very zone,
Or never feel the rage, or never own;
What happier natures shrink at with affright,
The hard inhabitant contends is right.　　　230

Virtuous and vicious every man must be,
Few in th' extreme, but all in the degree;
The rogue and fool by fits is fair and wise;
And even the best, by fits, what they despise.
'Tis but by parts we follow good or ill;
For, vice or virtue, self directs it still;
Each individual seeks a several goal;
But Heaven's great view is one, and that the whole.
That counterworks each folly and caprice;
That disappoints th' effect of every vice;　　　240
That, happy frailties to all ranks applied;
Shame to the virgin, to the matron pride,
Fear to the statesman, rashness to the chief,
To kings presumption, and to crowds belief:
That, virtue's ends from vanity can raise,
Which seeks no interest, no reward but praise;
And build on wants, and on defects of mind,
The joy, the peace, the glory of mankind.

Heaven forming each on other to depend,
A master, or a servant, or a friend,　　　250
Bids each on other for assistance call,
Till one man's weakness grows the strength of all.

Wants, frailties, passions, closer still ally
The common interest, or endear the tie.
To these we owe true friendship, love sincere,
Each home-felt joy that life inherits here;
Yet from the same we learn, in its decline,
Those joys, those loves, those interests to resign;
Taught half by reason, half by mere decay,
To welcome death, and calmly pass away.   260
Whate'er the passion, knowledge, fame, or pelf,
Not one will change his neighbour with himself.
The learn'd is happy Nature to explore;
The fool is happy that he knows no more;
The rich is happy in the plenty given,
The poor contents him with the care of Heaven.
See the blind beggar dance, the cripple sing,
The sot a hero, lunatic a king;
The starving chemist in his golden views
Supremely bless'd, the poet in his Muse.   270
See some strange comfort every state attend,
And pride bestow'd on all, a common friend;
See some fit passion every age supply,
Hope travels through, nor quits us when we die.

Behold the child, by Nature's kindly law,
Pleased with a rattle, tickled with a straw:
Some livelier plaything gives his youth delight,
A little louder, but as empty quite:
Scarfs, garters, gold, amuse his riper stage,
And beads and prayer-books are the toys of age: 280
Pleased with this bauble still, as that before;
Till, tired, he sleeps, and life's poor play is o'er.

Meanwhile opinion gilds with varying rays
Those painted clouds that beautify our days;
Each want of happiness by hope supplied,
And each vacuity of sense by pride:
These build as fast as knowledge can destroy;
In Folly's cup still laughs the bubble, joy;
One prospect lost, another still we gain;
And not a vanity is given in vain;   290
Even mean self-love becomes, by force divine,
The scale to measure others' wants by thine.
See! and confess, one comfort still must rise,

'Tis this, Though Man's a fool, yet God is wise.

* * * * *

VARIATIONS.

VER. 2, first edition —

The only science of mankind is Man.

After VER. 18, in the MS. —

For more perfection than this state can bear,
In vain we sigh, 'Heaven made us as we are.'
As wisely, sure, a modest ape might aim
To be like Man, whose faculties and frame
He sees, he feels, as you or I to be
An angel thing we neither know nor see.
Observe how near he edges on our race;
What human tricks! how risible of face!
'It must be so — why else have I the sense
Of more than monkey charms and excellence?
Why else to walk on two so oft essay'd?
And why this ardent longing for a maid?'
So pug might plead, and call his gods unkind,
Till set on end and married to his mind.
Go, reasoning thing! assume the doctor's chair,
As Plato deep, as Seneca severe:
Fix moral fitness, and to God give rule,
Then drop into thyself, &c.

VER. 21, edition fourth and fifth —

Show by what rules the wandering planets stray,
Correct old Time, and teach the sun his way.

VER. 35, first edition —

Could He, who taught each planet where to roll,
Describe or fix one movement of the soul?
Who mark'd their points to rise or to descend,
Explain his own beginning or his end?

After VER. 86, in the MS.—

Of good and evil gods what frighted fools,
Of good and evil reason puzzled schools,
Deceived, deceiving, taught, &c.

After VER. 108, in the MS.—

A tedious voyage! where how useless lies
The compass, if no powerful gusts arise?

After VER. 112, in the MS.—

The soft reward the virtuous, or invite;
The fierce, the vicious punish or affright.

After VER. 194, in the MS.—

How oft, with passion, Virtue points her charms!
Then shines the hero, then the patriot warms.
Peleus' great son, or Brutus, who had known,
Had Lucrece been a whore, or Helen none!
But virtues opposite to make agree,
That, Reason! is thy task; and worthy thee.
Hard task, cries Bibulus, and reason weak:
Make it a point, dear Marquess! or a pique.
Once, for a whim, persuade yourself to pay
A debt to reason, like a debt at play.
For right or wrong have mortals suffer'd more?
B—— for his prince, or —— for his whore?
Whose self-denials nature most control?
His, who would save a sixpence, or his soul?
Web for his health, a Chartreux for his sin,
Contend they not which soonest shall grow thin?
What we resolve, we can: but here's the fault,
We ne'er resolve to do the thing we ought.

After VER. 220, in the first edition, followed these—

A cheat! a whore! who starts not at the name,
In all the Inns of Court or Drury Lane?

After VER. 226, in the MS.—

The colonel swears the agent is a dog,
The scrivener vows th' attorney is a rogue.
Against the thief th' attorney loud inveighs,
For whose ten pound the county twenty pays.
The thief damns judges, and the knaves of state;
And dying, mourns small villains hang'd by great.

EPISTLE III.

ARGUMENT.

OF THE NATURE AND STATE OF MAN WITH RESPECT TO SOCIETY.

I. The whole universe one system of society, ver. 7, &c. Nothing made wholly for itself, nor yet wholly for another, ver. 27. The happiness of animals mutual, ver. 49. II. Reason or instinct operate alike to the good of each individual, ver. 79. Reason or instinct operate also to society, in all animals, ver. 109. III. How far society carried by instinct, ver. 115. How much farther by reason, ver. 128. IV. Of that which is called the state of nature, 144. Reason instructed by instinct in the invention of arts, ver. 166, and in the forms of society, ver. 176. V. Origin of political societies, ver. 196. Origin of monarchy, ver. 207. Patriarchal government, ver. 212. VI. Origin of true religion and government, from the same principle—of love, ver. 231, &c. Origin of superstition and tyranny, from the same principle—of fear, ver. 237, &c. The influence of self-love operating to the social and public good, ver. 266. Restoration of true religion and government on their first principle, ver. 285. Mixed government, ver. 288. Various forms of each, and the true end of all, ver. 300, &c.

Here then we rest: 'The Universal Cause
Acts to one end, but acts by various laws.'
In all the madness of superfluous health,
The trim of pride, the impudence of wealth,
Let this great truth be present night and day;
But most be present, if we preach or pray.

I. Look round our world; behold the chain of love
Combining all below and all above.
See plastic Nature working to this end,
The single atoms each to other tend,   10
Attract, attracted to, the next in place
Form'd and impell'd its neighbour to embrace.
See matter next, with various life endued,
Press to one centre still, the general Good.
See dying vegetables life sustain,
See life dissolving vegetate again:
All forms that perish other forms supply,

(By turns we catch the vital breath, and die)
Like bubbles on the sea of Matter born,
They rise, they break, and to that sea return.   20
Nothing is foreign: parts relate to whole;
One all-extending, all-preserving Soul
Connects each being, greatest with the least;
Made beast in aid of man, and man of beast;
All served, all serving: nothing stands alone;
The chain holds on, and where it ends, unknown.

Has God, thou fool! work'd solely for thy good,
Thy joy, thy pastime, thy attire, thy food?
Who for thy table feeds the wanton fawn,
For him as kindly spread the flowery lawn: 30
Is it for thee the lark ascends and sings?
Joy tunes his voice, joy elevates his wings.
Is it for thee the linnet pours his throat?
Loves of his own, and raptures swell the note.
The bounding steed you pompously bestride,
Shares with his lord the pleasure and the pride.
Is thine alone the seed that strews the plain?
The birds of heaven shall vindicate their grain.
Thine the full harvest of the golden year?
Part pays, and justly, the deserving steer: 40
The hog, that ploughs not, nor obeys thy call,
Lives on the labours of this lord of all.

Know, Nature's children all divide her care;
The fur that warms a monarch, warm'd a bear.
While Man exclaims, 'See all things for my use!'
'See man for mine!' replies a famper'd goose:
And just as short of reason he must fall,
Who thinks all made for one, not one for all.

Grant that the powerful still the weak control;
Be Man the wit and tyrant of the whole: 50
Nature that tyrant checks; he only knows,
And helps, another creature's wants and woes.
Say, will the falcon, stooping from above,
Smit with her varying plumage, spare the dove?
Admires the jay the insect's gilded wings?
Or hears the hawk when Philomela sings?
Man cares for all: to birds he gives his woods,

To beasts his pastures, and to fish his floods;
For some his interest prompts him to provide,
For more his pleasure, yet for more his pride: 60
All feed on one vain patron, and enjoy
Th' extensive blessing of his luxury.
That very life his learned hunger craves,
He saves from famine, from the savage saves;
Nay, feasts the animal he dooms his feast.
And, till he ends the being, makes it blest;
Which sees no more the stroke, or feels the pain,
Than favour'd Man by touch ethereal slain.
The creature had his feast of life before;
Thou too must perish, when thy feast is o'er!   70

To each unthinking being, Heaven, a friend,
Gives not the useless knowledge of its end:
To Man imparts it; but with such a view
As, while he dreads it, makes him hope it too:
The hour conceal'd, and so remote the fear,
Death still draws nearer, never seeming near.
Great standing miracle! that Heaven assign'd
Its only thinking thing this turn of mind.

II. Whether with reason or with instinct blest,
Know, all enjoy that power which suits them best;   80
To bliss alike by that direction tend,
And find the means proportion'd to their end.
Say, where full instinct is th' unerring guide,
What pope or council can they need beside?
Reason, however able, cool at best,
Cares not for service, or but serves when press'd,
Stays till we call, and then not often near;
But honest instinct comes a volunteer,
Sure never to o'ershoot, but just to hit;
While still too wide or short is human wit;   90
Sure by quick nature happiness to gain,
Which heavier reason labours at in vain.
This, too serves always, reason never long;
One must go right, the other may go wrong.
See then the acting and comparing powers
One in their nature, which are two in ours;
And reason raise o'er instinct as you can,
In this 'tis God directs, in that 'tis Man.

Who taught the nations of the field and wood
To shun their poison, and to choose their food? 100
Prescient, the tides or tempests to withstand,
Build on the wave, or arch beneath the sand?
Who made the spider parallels design,
Sure as De Moivre, without rule or line?
Who bid the stork, Columbus-like, explore
Heavens not his own, and worlds unknown before?
Who calls the council, states the certain day,
Who forms the phalanx, and who points the way?

III. God, in the nature of each being, founds
Its proper bliss, and sets its proper bounds: 110
But as he framed a whole, the whole to bless,
On mutual wants built mutual happiness:
So from the first, eternal Order ran,
And creature link'd to creature, man to man.
Whate'er of life all-quickening ether keeps,
Or breathes through air, or shoots beneath the deeps,
Or pours profuse on earth, one nature feeds
The vital flame, and swells the genial seeds.
Not Man alone, but all that roam the wood,
Or wing the sky, or roll along the flood, 120
Each loves itself, but not itself alone,
Each sex desires alike, till two are one.
Nor ends the pleasure with the fierce embrace;
They love themselves, a third time, in their race.
Thus beast and bird their common charge attend,
The mothers nurse it, and the sires defend;
The young dismiss'd to wander earth or air,
There stops the instinct, and there ends the care;
The link dissolves, each seeks a fresh embrace,
Another love succeeds, another race. 130
A longer care Man's helpless kind demands;
That longer care contracts more lasting bands:
Reflection, reason, still the ties improve,
At once extend the interest, and the love;
With choice we fix, with sympathy we burn;
Each virtue in each passion takes its turn;
And still new needs, new helps, new habits rise,
That graft benevolence on charities.
Still as one brood, and as another rose,
These natural love maintain'd, habitual those: 140

The last, scarce ripen'd into perfect man,
Saw helpless him from whom their life began:
Memory and forecast just returns engage,
That pointed back to youth, this on to age;
While pleasure, gratitude, and hope, combined,
Still spread the interest, and preserved the kind.

IV. Nor think, in Nature's state they blindly trod;
The state of Nature was the reign of God:
Self-love and social at her birth began,
Union the bond of all things, and of Man.   150
Pride then was not; nor arts, that pride to aid;
Man walk'd with beast, joint tenant of the shade;
The same his table, and the same his bed;
No murder clothed him, and no murder fed.
In the same temple, the resounding wood,
All vocal beings hymn'd their equal God:
The shrine with gore unstain'd, with gold undress'd,
Unbribed, unbloody, stood the blameless priest:
Heaven's attribute was universal care,
And Man's prerogative to rule, but spare.   160
Ah! how unlike the Man of times to come!
Of half that live the butcher and the tomb;
Who, foe to Nature, hears the general groan,
Murders their species, and betrays his own.
But just disease to luxury succeeds,
And every death its own avenger breeds;
The fury-passions from that blood began,
And turn'd on Man, a fiercer savage, Man.

See him from Nature rising slow to Art!
To copy instinct then was reason's part;   170
Thus then to Man the voice of Nature spake—
'Go, from the creatures thy instructions take:
Learn from the birds what food the thickets yield;
Learn from the beasts the physic of the field;
Thy arts of building from the bee receive;
Learn of the mole to plough, the worm to weave;
Learn of the little nautilus to sail,
Spread the thin oar, and catch the driving gale.
Here, too, all forms of social union find,
And hence let reason, late, instruct mankind: 180
Here subterranean works and cities see;

There towns aerial on the waving tree.
Learn each small people's genius, policies,
The ants' republic, and the realm of bees;
How those in common all their wealth bestow,
And anarchy without confusion know;
And these for ever, though a monarch reign,
Their separate cells and properties maintain.
Mark what unvaried laws preserve each state,
Laws wise as Nature, and as fix'd as Fate.   190
In vain thy reason finer webs shall draw,
Entangle Justice in her net of lay,
And right, too rigid, harden into wrong;
Still for the strong too weak, the weak too strong.
Yet go! and thus o'er all the creatures sway,
Thus let the wiser make the rest obey;
And for those arts mere instinct could afford,
Be crown'd as monarchs, or as gods adored.'

V. Great Nature spoke; observant men obey'd;
Cities were built, societies were made: 200
Here rose one little state; another near
Grew by like means, and join'd, through love or fear.
Did here the trees with ruddier burdens bend,
And there the streams in purer rills descend?
What war could ravish, commerce could bestow;
And he return'd a friend, who came a foe.
Converse and love mankind might strongly draw,
When love was liberty, and Nature law.
Thus states were form'd, the name of king unknown,
Till common interest placed the sway in one.   210
'Twas virtue only (or in arts or arms,
Diffusing blessings or averting harms),
The same which in a sire the sons obey'd,
A prince the father of a people made.

VI. Till then, by Nature crown'd, each patriarch sat,
King, priest, and parent of his growing state;
On him, their second Providence, they hung,
Their law his eye, their oracle his tongue.
He from the wondering furrow call'd the food,
Taught to command the fire, control the flood,   220
Draw forth the monsters of the abyss profound,
Or fetch the aerial eagle to the ground.

Till drooping, sickening, dying they began
Whom they revered as god to mourn as man:
Then, looking up from sire to sire, explored
One great first Father, and that first adored.
Or plain tradition that this All begun,
Convey'd unbroken faith from sire to son;
The worker from the work distinct was known,
And simple reason never sought but one: 230
Ere wit oblique had broke that steady light,
Man, like his Maker, saw that all was right;
To virtue, in the paths of pleasure, trod,
And own'd a Father when he own'd a God.
Love all the faith, and all the allegiance then;
For nature knew no right divine in men,
No ill could fear in God; and understood
A sovereign Being, but a sovereign good.
True faith, true policy, united ran,
That was but love of God, and this of Man. 240

Who first taught souls enslaved, and realms undone,
The enormous faith of many made for one;
That proud exception to all Nature's laws,
To invert the world, and counterwork its cause?
Force first made conquest, and that conquest, law;
'Till Superstition taught the tyrant awe,
Then shared the tyranny, then lent it aid,
And gods of conquerors, slaves of subjects made:
She, midst the lightning's blaze, and thunder's sound,
When rock'd the mountains, and when groan'd the ground, 250
She taught the weak to bend, the proud to pray,
To Power unseen, and mightier far than they:
She, from the rending earth and bursting skies,
Saw gods descend, and fiends infernal rise:
Here fix'd the dreadful, there the blest abodes;
Fear made her devils, and weak hope her gods;
Gods partial, changeful, passionate, unjust,
Whose attributes were rage, revenge, or lust;
Such as the souls of cowards might conceive,
And, form'd like tyrants, tyrants would believe. 260
Zeal then, not charity, became the guide;
And hell was built on spite, and heaven on pride.
Then sacred seem'd the ethereal vault no more;
Altars grew marble then, and reek'd with gore:

Then first the Flamen tasted living food;
Next his grim idol smear'd with human blood;
With Heaven's own thunders shook the world below,
And play'd the god an engine on his foe.

So drives self-love, through just and through unjust,
To one man's power, ambition, lucre, lust: 270
The same self-love, in all, becomes the cause
Of what restrains him, government and laws.
For, what one likes, if others like as well,
What serves one will, when many wills rebel?
How shall he keep what, sleeping or awake,
A weaker may surprise, a stronger take?
His safety must his liberty restrain:
All join to guard what each desires to gain.
Forced into virtue thus by self-defence,
Even kings learn'd justice and benevolence; 280
Self-love forsook the path it first pursued,
And found the private in the public good.

'Twas then the studious head or generous mind,
Follower of God, or friend of human kind,
Poet or patriot, rose but to restore
The faith and moral Nature gave before;
Relumed her ancient light, not kindled new;
If not God's image, yet his shadow drew;
Taught power's due use to people and to kings,
Taught not to slack, nor strain its tender strings, 290
The less, or greater, set so justly true,
That touching one must strike the other too;
Till jarring interests of themselves create
The according music of a well-mix'd state.
Such is the world's great harmony, that springs
From order, union, full consent of things:
Where small and great, where weak and mighty, made
To serve, not suffer; strengthen, not invade;
More powerful each as needful to the rest,
And in proportion as it blesses, bless'd; 300
Draw to one point, and to one centre bring
Beast, man, or angel, servant, lord, or king.

For forms of government let fools contest;
Whate'er is best administer'd is best:

For modes of faith let graceless zealots fight;
His can't be wrong whose life is in the right:
In faith and hope the world will disagree,
But all mankind's concern is charity:
All must be false that thwart this one great end;
And all of God that bless mankind, or mend.   310

Man, like the generous vine, supported lives;
The strength he gains is from the embrace he gives.
On their own axis as the planets run,
Yet make at once their circle round the sun;
So two consistent motions act the soul,
And one regards itself, and one the whole.

Thus God and Nature link'd the general frame,
And bade self-love and social be the same.

VARIATIONS.

VER. 1, in several quarto editions—

Learn, Dulness, learn! 'the Universal Cause,' &c.

After VER. 46, in the former editions—

What care to tend, to lodge, to cram, to treat him!
All this he knew; but not that 'twas to eat him.
As far as goose could judge, he reason'd right;
But as to Man, mistook the matter quite.

After VER. 84, in the MS.—

While Man, with opening views of various ways
Confounded, by the aid of knowledge strays:
Too weak to choose, yet choosing still in haste,
One moment gives the pleasure and distaste.

VER. 197, in the first edition—

Who for those arts they learn'd of brutes before,
As kings shall crown them, or as gods adore.

VER. 201, in the MSS. thus—

The neighbours leagued to guard their common spot:
And love was Nature's dictate, murder, not.
For want alone each animal contends,
Tigers with tigers, that removed, are friends.
Plain Nature's wants the common mother crown'd,
She pour'd her acorns, herbs, and streams around.
No treasure then for rapine to invade,
What need to fight for sunshine or for shade!
And half the cause of content was removed,
When beauty could be kind to all who loved.

EPISTLE IV.

ARGUMENT.

OF THE NATURE AND STATE OF MAN WITH RESPECT TO HAPPINESS.

I. False notions of happiness, philosophical and popular, answered from ver. 19 to ver. 27. II. It is the end of all men, and attainable by all, ver. 29. God intends happiness to be equal; and to be so, it must be social, since all particular happiness depends on general, and since he governs by general, not particular laws, ver. 35. As it is necessary for order, and the peace and welfare of society, that external goods should be unequal, happiness is not made to consist in these, ver. 51. But, notwithstanding that inequality, the balance of happiness among mankind is kept even by Providence, by the two passions of hope and fear, ver. 70. III. What the happiness of individuals is, as far as is consistent with the constitution of this world; and that the good man has here the advantage, ver. 77. The error of imputing to virtue what are only the calamities of nature, or of fortune, ver. 94. IV. The folly of expecting that God should alter his general laws in favour of particulars, ver. 121. V. That we are not judges who are good; but that, whoever they are, they must be happiest, ver. 131, &c. VI. That external goods are not the proper rewards, but often inconsistent with, or destructive of virtue, ver. 167. That even these can make no man happy without virtue: instanced in riches ver. 185; honours, ver. 193; nobility, ver. 205; greatness, ver. 217; fame, ver. 237; superior talents, ver. 259, &c. With pictures of human infelicity in men possessed of them all, ver. 269, &c. VII. That virtue only constitutes a happiness, whose object is universal, and whose prospect eternal, ver. 309, &c. That the perfection of virtue and happiness consists in a conformity to the order of Providence here, and a resignation to it here and hereafter, ver. 326, &c.

O Happiness! our being's end and aim!
Good, Pleasure, Ease, Content! whate'er thy name:
That something still which prompts th' eternal sigh,
For which we bear to live, or dare to die,
Which still so near us, yet beyond us lies,
O'erlook'd, seen double, by the fool, and wise.
Plant of celestial seed! if dropp'd below,

Say, in what mortal soil thou deign'st to grow?
Fair opening to some court's propitious shine,
Or deep with diamonds in the flaming mine? 10
Twined with the wreaths Parnassian laurels yield,
Or reap'd in iron harvests of the field?
Where grows?—where grows it not? If vain our toil,
We ought to blame the culture, not the soil:
Fix'd to no spot is happiness sincere,
Tis nowhere to be found, or everywhere;
'Tis never to be bought, but always free,
And, fled from monarchs, St John! dwells with thee.

I. Ask of the learn'd the way? the learn'd are blind;
This bids to serve, and that to shun mankind; 20
Some place the bliss in action, some in ease,
Those call it Pleasure, and Contentment these;
Some, sunk to beasts, find pleasure end in pain;
Some, swell'd to gods, confess even virtue vain;
Or, indolent, to each extreme they fall,
To trust in every thing, or doubt of all.

Who thus define it, say they more or less
Than this, that happiness is happiness?

II. Take Nature's path, and mad Opinion's leave;
All states can reach it, and all heads conceive; 30
Obvious her goods, in no extreme they dwell;
There needs but thinking right, and meaning well;
And, mourn our various portions as we please,
Equal is common sense, and common ease.

Remember, Man, 'The Universal Cause
Acts not by partial, but by general laws;'
And makes what happiness we justly call
Subsist, not in the good of one, but all.
There's not a blessing individuals find,
But some way leans and hearkens to the kind: 40
No bandit fierce, no tyrant mad with pride,
No cavern'd hermit, rests self-satisfied:
Who most to shun or hate mankind pretend,
Seek an admirer, or would fix a friend:
Abstract what others feel, what others think,
All pleasures sicken, and all glories sink:

Each has his share; and who would more obtain,
Shall find, the pleasure pays not half the pain.

Order is Heaven's first law; and, this confess'd,
Some are, and must be, greater than the rest, 50
More rich, more wise; but who infers from hence
That such are happier, shocks all common sense.
Heaven to mankind impartial we confess,
If all are equal in their happiness:
But mutual wants this happiness increase;
All Nature's difference keeps all Nature's peace.
Condition, circumstance, is not the thing;
Bliss is the same in subject or in king,
In who obtain defence, or who defend,
In him who is, or him who finds a friend: 60
Heaven breathes through every member of the whole
One common blessing, as one common soul.
But Fortune's gifts if each alike possess'd,
And each were equal, must not all contest?
If then to all Men happiness was meant,
God in externals could not place content.

Fortune her gifts may variously dispose,
And these be happy call'd, unhappy those;
But Heaven's just balance equal will appear,
While those are placed in hope, and these in fear: 70
Not present good or ill, the joy or curse,
But future views of better, or of worse.

O sons of earth! attempt ye still to rise,
By mountains piled on mountains, to the skies?
Heaven still with laughter the vain toil surveys,
And buries madmen in the heaps they raise.

III. Know, all the good that individuals find,
Or God and Nature meant to mere mankind,
Reason's whole pleasure, all the joys of sense,
Lie in three words—Health, Peace, and Competence, 80
But health consists with temperance alone;
And peace, O Virtue! peace is all thy own.
The good or bad the gifts of Fortune gain;
But these less taste them, as they worse obtain.
Say, in pursuit of profit or delight,

Who risk the most, that take wrong means, or right?
Of vice or virtue, whether bless'd or cursed,
Which meets contempt, or which compassion first?
Count all th' advantage prosperous vice attains,
'Tis but what virtue flies from and disdains: 90
And grant the bad what happiness they would,
One they must want, which is, to pass for good.

Oh, blind to truth, and God's whole scheme below,
Who fancy bliss to vice, to virtue woe!
Who sees and follows that great scheme the best,
Best knows the blessing, and will most be bless'd.
But fools, the good alone unhappy call,
For ills or accidents that chance to all.
See Falkland dies, the virtuous and the just!
See godlike Turenne prostrate on the dust! 100
See Sidney bleeds amid the martial strife!
Was this their virtue, or contempt of life?
Say, was it virtue, more though Heaven ne'er gave,
Lamented Digby! sunk thee to the grave?
Tell me, if virtue made the son expire,
Why, full of days and honour, lives the sire?
Why drew Marseilles' good bishop[90] purer breath,
When Nature sicken'd, and each gale was death?
Or why so long (in life if long can be)
Lent Heaven a parent to the poor and me? 110

What makes all physical or moral ill?
There deviates Nature, and here wanders Will.
God sends not ill, if rightly understood;
Or partial ill is universal good,
Or change admits, or Nature lets it fall;
Short, and but rare, till Man improved it all.
We just as wisely might of Heaven complain
That righteous Abel was destroy'd by Cain,
As that the virtuous son is ill at ease
When his lewd father gave the dire disease. 120

IV. Think we, like some weak prince, th' Eternal Cause,
Prone for his favourites to reverse his laws?
Shall burning AEtna, if a sage requires,
Forget to thunder, and recall her fires?
On air or sea new motions be impress'd,

O blameless Bethel![91] to relieve thy breast?
When the loose mountain trembles from on high,
Shall gravitation cease, if you go by?
Or some old temple, nodding to its fall,
For Chartres'[92] head reserve the hanging wall? 130

V. But still this world (so fitted for the knave)
Contents us not. A better shall we have?
A kingdom of the just then let it be:
But first consider how those just agree.
The good must merit God's peculiar care;
But who but God can tell us who they are?
One thinks on Calvin Heaven's own spirit fell;
Another deems him instrument of hell;
If Calvin feel Heaven's blessing, or its rod,
This cries there is, and that, there is no God. 140
What shocks one part will edify the rest,
Nor with one system can they all be bless'd.
The very best will variously incline,
And what rewards your virtue, punish mine.
Whatever is, is right.—This world, 'tis true,
Was made for Caesar—but for Titus too:
And which more bless'd? who chain'd his country, say,
Or he whose virtue sigh'd to lose a day?

'But sometimes virtue starves, while vice is fed.'
What then? Is the reward of virtue bread? 150
That, vice may merit, 'tis the price of toil;
The knave deserves it, when he tills the soil,
The knave deserves it, when he tempts the main,
Where Folly fights for kings, or dives for gain.
The good man may be weak, be indolent;
Nor is his claim to plenty, but content.
But grant him riches, your demand is o'er?
'No—shall the good want health, the good want power?'
Add health, and power, and every earthly thing,
'Why bounded power? why private? why no king?' 160
Nay, why external for internal given?
Why is not man a god, and earth a heaven?
Who ask and reason thus, will scarce conceive
God gives enough, while he has more to give:
Immense the power, immense were the demand;
Say, at what part of nature will they stand?

VI. What nothing earthly gives, or can destroy,
The soul's calm sunshine, and the heartfelt joy,
Is virtue's prize: a better would you fix?
Then give humility a coach and six,   170
Justice a conqueror's sword, or truth a gown,
Or public spirit its great cure, a crown.
Weak, foolish man! will Heaven reward us there
With the same trash mad mortals wish for here?
The boy and man an individual makes,
Yet sigh'st thou now for apples and for cakes?
Go, like the Indian, in another life
Expect thy dog, thy bottle, and thy wife;
As well as dream such trifles are assign'd,
As toys and empires, for a godlike mind.   180
Rewards, that either would to virtue bring
No joy, or be destructive of the thing;
How oft by these at sixty are undone
The virtues of a saint at twenty-one!
To whom can riches give repute, or trust,
Content, or pleasure, but the good and just?
Judges and senates have been bought for gold,
Esteem and love were never to be sold.
O fool! to think God hates the worthy mind,
The lover and the love of human kind,   190
Whose life is healthful, and whose conscience clear,
Because he wants a thousand pounds a year.

Honour and shame from no condition rise;
Act well your part; there all the honour lies.
Fortune in men has some small difference made—
One flaunts in rags, one flutters in brocade;
The cobbler apron'd, and the parson gown'd,
The friar hooded, and the monarch crown'd.
'What differ more' (you cry) 'than crown and cowl?'
I'll tell you, friend!—a wise man and a fool.   200
You'll find, if once the monarch acts the monk,
Or, cobbler-like, the parson will be drunk,
Worth makes the man, and want of it the fellow;
The rest is all but leather or prunella.

Stuck o'er with titles, and hung round with strings,
That thou may'st be by kings, or whores of kings,
Boast the pure blood of an illustrious race,

In quiet flow from Lucrece to Lucrece:
But by your fathers' worth if yours you rate,
Count me those only who were good and great. 210
Go! if your ancient but ignoble blood
Has crept through scoundrels ever since the flood,
Go! and pretend your family is young;
Nor own, your fathers have been fools so long.
What can ennoble sots, or slaves, or cowards?
Alas! not all the blood of all the Howards.

Look next on greatness; say where greatness lies?
'Where, but among the heroes and the wise?'
Heroes are much the same, the point's agreed,
From Macedonia's madman to the Swede; 220
The whole strange purpose of their lives, to find
Or make an enemy of all mankind!
Not one looks backward, onward still he goes,
Yet ne'er looks forward further than his nose.
No less alike the politic and wise;
All sly slow things, with circumspective eyes:
Men in their loose unguarded hours they take,
Not that themselves are wise, but others weak.
But grant that those can conquer, these can cheat;
'Tis phrase absurd to call a villain great: 230
Who wickedly is wise, or madly brave,
Is but the more a fool, the more a knave.
Who noble ends by noble means obtains,
Or failing, smiles in exile or in chains,
Like good Aurelius let him reign, or bleed
Like Socrates, that man is great indeed.

What's fame? A fancied life in others' breath,
A thing beyond us, even before our death.
Just what you hear, you have; and what's unknown
The same (my Lord) if Tully's, or your own. 240
All that we feel of it begins and ends
In the small circle of our foes or friends;
To all beside as much an empty shade
An Eugene living, as a Caesar dead;
Alike or when, or where, they shone, or shine,
Or on the Rubicon, or on the Rhine.
A wit's a feather, and a chief a rod;
An honest man's the noblest work of God.

Fame but from death a villain's name can save,
As justice tears his body from the grave,   250
When what t' oblivion better were resign'd,
Is hung on high, to poison half mankind.
All fame is foreign, but of true desert;
Plays round the head, but comes not to the heart:
One self-approving hour whole years out-weighs
Of stupid starers, and of loud huzzas;
And more true joy Marcellus exiled feels,
Than Caesar with a senate at his heels.

In parts superior what advantage lies?
Tell (for you can) what is it to be wise?   260
'Tis but to know how little can be known;
To see all others' faults, and feel our own:
Condemn'd in business or in arts to drudge,
Without a second, or without a judge.
Truths would you teach, or save a sinking land?
All fear, none aid you, and few understand.
Painful pre-eminence! yourself to view
Above life's weakness, and its comforts too.

Bring then these blessings to a strict account;
Make fair deductions; see to what they mount: 270
How much of other each is sure to cost;
How each for other oft is wholly lost;
How inconsistent greater goods with these;
How sometimes life is risk'd, and always ease:
Think, and if still the things thy envy call,
Say, wouldst thou be the man to whom they fall?
To sigh for ribands if thou art so silly,
Mark how they grace Lord Umbra, or Sir Billy:
Is yellow dirt the passion of thy life?
Look but on Gripus, or on Gripus' wife: 280
If parts allure thee, think how Bacon shined,
The wisest, brightest, meanest of mankind:
Or, ravish'd with the whistling of a name,
See Cromwell,[93] damn'd to everlasting fame!
If all, united, thy ambition call,
From ancient story learn to scorn them all.
There, in the rich, the honour'd, famed, and great,
See the false scale of happiness complete!
In hearts of kings, or arms of queens who lay,

How happy! those to ruin, these betray.   290
Mark by what wretched steps their glory grows,
From dirt and sea-weed as proud Venice rose;
In each how guilt and greatness equal ran,
And all that raised the hero, sunk the man:
Now Europe's laurels on their brows behold,
But stain'd with blood, or ill exchanged for gold:
Then see them broke with toils, or sunk in ease,
Or infamous for plunder'd provinces.
Oh wealth ill-fated! which no act of fame
E'er taught to shine, or sanctified from shame!   300
What greater bliss attends their close of life?
Some greedy minion, or imperious wife.
The trophied arches, storied halls invade,
And haunt their slumbers in the pompous shade.
Alas! not dazzled with their noontide ray,
Compute the morn and evening to the day;
The whole amount of that enormous fame,
A tale that blends their glory with their shame!

VII. Know then this truth (enough for man to know)
'Virtue alone is happiness below.'   310
The only point where human bliss stands still,
And tastes the good without the fall to ill;
Where only merit constant pay receives,
Is bless'd in what it takes, and what it gives;
The joy unequall'd, if its end it gain,
And if it lose, attended with no pain:
Without satiety, though e'er so bless'd,
And but more relish'd as the more distress'd:
The broadest mirth unfeeling Folly wears,
Less pleasing far than Virtue's very tears: 320
Good, from each object, from each place acquired,
For ever exercised, yet never tired;
Never elated, while one man's oppress'd;
Never dejected, while another's bless'd;
And where no wants, no wishes can remain,
Since but to wish more virtue, is to gain.

See the sole bliss Heaven could on all bestow!
Which who but feels can taste, but thinks can know:
Yet poor with fortune, and with learning blind,
The bad must miss; the good, untaught, will find;   330

Slave to no sect, who takes no private road,
But looks through Nature up to Nature's God;
Pursues that chain which links th' immense design,
Joins Heaven and Earth, and mortal and divine;
Sees, that no being any bliss can know,
But touches some above, and some below;
Learns, from this union of the rising whole,
The first, last purpose of the human soul;
And knows where faith, law, morals, all began,
All end, in love of God, and love of Man.   340

For him alone Hope leads from goal to goal,
And opens still, and opens on his soul;
Till lengthen'd on to Faith, and unconfined,
It pours the bliss that fills up all the mind.
He sees why Nature plants in Man alone
Hope of known bliss, and faith in bliss unknown:
(Nature, whose dictates to no other kind
Are given in vain, but what they seek they find)
Wise is her present; she connects in this
His greatest virtue with his greatest bliss;   350
At once his own bright prospect to be bless'd,
And strongest motive to assist the rest.

Self-love thus push'd to social, to divine,
Gives thee to make thy neighbour's blessing thine.
Is this too little for the boundless heart?
Extend it, let thy enemies have part;
Grasp the whole worlds of Reason, Life, and Sense,
In one close system of Benevolence:
Happier as kinder, in whate'er degree,
And height of bliss but height of charity.   360

God loves from whole to parts: but human soul
Must rise from individual to the whole.
Self-love but serves the virtuous mind to wake,
As the small pebble stirs the peaceful lake;
The centre moved, a circle straight succeeds,
Another still, and still another spreads;
Friend, parent, neighbour, first it will embrace;
His country next; and next all human race;
Wide and more wide, th' o'erflowings of the mind
Take every creature in, of every kind;   370

Earth smiles around, with boundless bounty bless'd,
And Heaven beholds its image in his breast.

Come then, my friend, my genius! come along;
O master of the poet, and the song!
And while the Muse now stoops, or now ascends,
To Man's low passions, or their glorious ends,
Teach me, like thee, in various Nature wise,
To fall with dignity, with temper rise;
Form'd by thy converse, happily to steer
From grave to gay, from lively to severe;   380
Correct with spirit, eloquent with ease,
Intent to reason, or polite to please.
Oh! while along the stream of Time thy name
Expanded flies, and gathers all its fame,
Say, shall my little bark attendant sail,
Pursue the triumph, and partake the gale?
When statesmen, heroes, kings, in dust repose,
Whose sons shall blush their fathers were thy foes,
Shall then this verse to future age pretend
Thou wert my guide, philosopher, and friend?   390
That, urged by thee, I turn'd the tuneful art.
From sounds to things, from fancy to the heart;
For Wit's false mirror held up Nature's light;
Show'd erring pride, Whatever is, is right;
That Reason, Passion, answer one great aim;
That true Self-love and Social are the same;
That Virtue only makes our bliss below;
And all our knowledge is, Ourselves to know.

* * * * *

VARIATIONS.

VER. 1, in the MS. thus—

O Happiness! to which we all aspire,
Wing'd with strong hope, and borne by full desire;
That ease, for which in want, in wealth we sigh;
That ease, for which we labour and we die

After VER. 52, in the MS. —

Say not, 'Heaven's here profuse, there poorly saves,
And for one monarch makes a thousand slaves,'
You'll find, when causes and their ends are known,
'Twas for the thousand Heaven has made that one.

After VER. 66. in the MS.—

'Tis peace of mind alone is at a stay;
The rest mad Fortune gives or takes away.
All other bliss by accident's debarr'd;
But virtue's in the instant a reward:
In hardest trials operates the best,
And more is relish'd as the more distress'd.

After VER. 92, in the MS.—

Let sober moralists correct their speech,
No bad man's happy: he is great or rich.

After VER. 116, in the MS.—

Of every evil, since the world began,
The real source is not in God, but man.

After VER. 142, in some editions—

Give each a system, all must be at strife;
What different systems for a man and wife?

After VER. 172, in the MS.—

Say, what rewards this idle world imparts,
Or fit for searching heads or honest hearts.

VER. 207, in the MS. thus—

The richest blood, right-honourably old,
Down from Lucretia to Lucretia roll'd,
May swell thy heart, and gallop in thy breast,
Without one dash of usher or of priest:
Thy pride as much despise all other pride
As Christ-church once all colleges beside.

After VER. 316, in the MS.—

Even while it seems unequal to dispose,
And chequers all the good man's joys with woes,
'Tis but to teach him to support each state,
With patience this, with moderation that;
And raise his base on that one solid joy,
Which conscience gives, and nothing can destroy.

VER. 373, in the MS. thus—

And now transported o'er so vast a plain,
While the wing'd courser flies with all her rein,
While heavenward now her mounting wing she feels,
Now scatter'd fools fly trembling from her heels,
Wilt thou, my St John! keep her course in sight,
Confine her fury, and assist her flight?

VER. 397, in the MS. thus—

That just to find a God is all we can,
And all the study of mankind is Man.

EPISTLE TO DR ARBUTHNOT;

OR, PROLOGUE TO THE SATIRES.

ADVERTISEMENT.

This paper is a sort of bill of complaint, begun many years since, and drawn up by snatches, as the several occasions offered. I had no thoughts of publishing it, till it pleased some persons of rank and fortune (the authors of 'Verses to the Imitator of Horace, ' and of an 'Epistle to a Doctor of Divinity from a Nobleman at Hampton Court') to attack, in a very extraordinary manner, not only my writings (of which, being public, the public is judge) but my person, morals, and family, whereof, to those who know me not, a truer information may be requisite. Being divided between the necessity to say something of myself, and my own laziness to undertake so awkward a task, I thought it the shortest way to put the last hand to this epistle. If it have anything pleasing, it will be that by which I am most desirous to please, the truth and the sentiment; and if anything offensive, it will be only to those I am least sorry to offend, the vicious or the ungenerous.

Many will know their own pictures in it, there being not a circumstance but what is true; but I have, for the most part, spared their names, and they may escape being laughed at, if they please.

I would have some of them know, it was owing to the request of the learned and candid friend to whom it is inscribed, that I make not as free use of theirs as they have done of mine. However, I shall have this advantage and honour on my side, that whereas, by their proceeding, any abuse may be directed at any man, no injury can possibly be done by mine, since a nameless character can never be found out, but by its truth and likeness.

P. Shut, shut the door, good John![94] fatigued, I said,
Tie up the knocker, say I'm sick, I'm dead.
The Dog-star rages! nay, 'tis past a doubt,
All Bedlam, or Parnassus, is let out:
Fire in each eye, and papers in each hand,
They rave, recite, and madden round the land.

What walls can guard me, or what shades can hide?
They pierce my thickets, through my grot they glide,
By land, by water, they renew the charge,
They stop the chariot, and they board the barge.   10
No place is sacred, not the church is free,
Even Sunday shines no Sabbath-day to me:
Then from the Mint[95] walks forth the man of rhyme,
Happy! to catch me, just at dinner-time.

Is there a parson, much bemused in beer,
A maudlin poetess, a rhyming peer,
A clerk, foredoom'd his father's soul to cross,
Who pens a stanza, when he should engross?
Is there, who, lock'd from ink and paper, scrawls
With desperate charcoal round his darken'd walls?   20
All fly to Twit'nam, and in humble strain
Apply to me, to keep them mad or vain.
Arthur, whose giddy son neglects the laws,
Imputes to me and my damn'd works the cause:
Poor Cornus sees his frantic wife elope,
And curses wit, and poetry, and Pope.

Friend to my life! (which did not you prolong,
The world had wanted many an idle song)
What drop or nostrum can this plague remove?
Or which must end me, a fool's wrath or love?   30
A dire dilemma! either way I'm sped,
If foes, they write, if friends, they read me dead.
Seized and tied down to judge, how wretched I!
Who can't be silent, and who will not lie:
To laugh, were want of goodness and of grace,
And to be grave, exceeds all power of face.
I sit with sad civility, I read
With honest anguish, and an aching head;
And drop at last, but in unwilling ears,
This saving counsel, 'Keep your piece nine years.'   40

'Nine years!' cries he, who high in Drury-lane,
Lull'd by soft zephyrs through the broken pane,
Rhymes ere he wakes, and prints before Term ends,
Obliged by hunger, and request of friends:
'The piece, you think, is incorrect? why take it,
I'm all submission, what you'd have it, make it.'

Three things another's modest wishes bound,
My friendship, and a prologue, and ten pound.

Pitholeon[96] sends to me: 'You know his Grace,
I want a patron; ask him for a place.'   50
Pitholeon libell'd me—'But here's a letter
Informs you, sir, 'twas when he knew no better.
Dare you refuse him? Curll invites to dine,
He'll write a journal, or he'll turn divine.'

Bless me! a packet.—"Tis a stranger sues,
A virgin tragedy, an orphan Muse.'
If I dislike it, 'Furies, death, and rage!'
If I approve, 'Commend it to the stage.'
There (thank my stars) my whole commission ends,
The players and I are, luckily, no friends.   60
Fired that the house reject him, "Sdeath! I'll print it,
And shame the fools—Your interest, sir, with Lintot.'
Lintot, dull rogue! will think your price too much:
'Not, sir, if you revise it, and retouch.'
All my demurs but double his attacks;
At last he whispers, 'Do; and we go snacks.'
Glad of a quarrel, straight I clap the door:
Sir, let me see your works and you no more.

'Tis sung, when Midas' ears began to spring
(Midas, a sacred person and a king),   70
His very minister who spied them first,
(Some say his queen) was forced to speak, or burst.
And is not mine, my friend, a sorer case,
When every coxcomb perks them in my face?

A. Good friend, forbear! you deal in dangerous things.
I'd never name queens, ministers, or kings;
Keep close to ears, and those let asses prick,
'Tis nothing——

P.   Nothing? if they bite and kick?
Out with it, Dunciad! let the secret pass,
That secret to each fool, that he's an ass: 80
The truth once told (and wherefore should we lie?)
The queen of Midas slept, and so may I.

You think this cruel? Take it for a rule,
No creature smarts so little as a fool.
Let peals of laughter, Codrus! round thee break,
Thou unconcern'd canst hear the mighty crack:
Pit, box, and gallery in convulsions hurl'd,
Thou stand'st unshook amidst a bursting world.
Who shames a scribbler? break one cobweb through,
He spins the slight, self-pleasing thread anew: 90
Destroy his fib or sophistry, in vain,
The creature's at his dirty work again,
Throned in the centre of his thin designs,
Proud of a vast extent of flimsy lines!
Whom have I hurt? has poet yet, or peer,
Lost the arch'd eyebrow, or Parnassian sneer?
And has not Colly still his lord, and whore?
His butchers, Henley,[97] his freemasons, Moore?[98]
Does not one table Bavius still admit?
Still to one bishop,[99] Philips seem a wit   100
Still Sappho— —

A.   Hold! for God-sake—you'll offend,
No names—be calm—learn prudence of a friend:
I too could write, and I am twice as tall;
But foes like these— —

P.   One flatterer's worse than all.
Of all mad creatures, if the learn'd are right,
It is the slaver kills, and not the bite.
A fool quite angry is quite innocent:
Alas! 'tis ten times worse when they repent.

One dedicates in high heroic prose,
And ridicules beyond a hundred foes: 110
One from all Grub-street will my fame defend,
And, more abusive, calls himself my friend.
This prints my letters, that expects a bribe,
And others roar aloud, 'Subscribe, subscribe!'

There are, who to my person pay their court:
I cough like Horace, and, though lean, am short,
Ammon's great son one shoulder had too high,
Such Ovid's nose, and, 'Sir! you have an eye'—
Go on, obliging creatures! make me see

All that disgraced my betters, met in me. 120
Say for my comfort, languishing in bed,
'Just so immortal Maro held his head:'
And, when I die, be sure you let me know
Great Homer died three thousand years ago.

Why did I write? what sin to me unknown
Dipp'd me in ink, my parents', or my own?
As yet a child, nor yet a fool to fame,
I lisp'd in numbers, for the numbers came.
I left no calling for this idle trade,
No duty broke, no father disobey'd. 130
The Muse but served to ease some friend, not wife,
To help me through this long disease, my life,
To second, Arbuthnot! thy art and care,
And teach the being you preserved to bear.

But why then publish? Granville the polite,
And knowing Walsh, would tell me I could write;
Well-natured Garth inflamed with early praise,
And Congreve loved, and Swift endured my lays;
The courtly Talbot, Somers, Sheffield read,
Even mitred Rochester would nod the head, 140
And St John's self (great Dryden's friends before)
With open arms received one poet more.
Happy my studies, when by these approved!
Happier their author, when by these beloved!
From these the world will judge of men and books,
Not from the Burnets,[100] Oldmixons, and Cookes.

Soft were my numbers; who could take offence
While pure description held the place of sense?
Like gentle Fanny's was my flowery theme,
'A painted mistress, or a purling stream.' 150
Yet then did Gildon[101] draw his venal quill;
I wish'd the man a dinner, and sat still.
Yet then did Dennis rave in furious fret;
I never answer'd—I was not in debt.
If want provoked, or madness made them print,
I waged no war with Bedlam or the Mint.

Did some more sober critic come abroad—
If wrong, I smiled; if right, I kiss'd the rod.

Pains, reading, study, are their just pretence,
And all they want is spirit, taste, and sense.   160
Commas and points they set exactly right,
And 'twere a sin to rob them of their mite.
Yet ne'er one sprig of laurel graced these ribalds,
From slashing Bentley down to piddling Tibbalds:
Each wight, who reads not, and but scans and spells,
Each word-catcher, that lives on syllables,
Even such small critics some regard may claim,
Preserved in Milton's or in Shakspeare's name.
Pretty! in amber to observe the forms
Of hairs, or straws, or dirt, or grubs, or worms!   170
The things, we know, are neither rich nor rare,
But wonder how the devil they got there.

Were others angry—I excused them too;
Well might they rage, I gave them but their due.
A man's true merit 'tis not hard to find;
But each man's secret standard in his mind,
That casting-weight pride adds to emptiness,
This, who can gratify for who can guess?
The bard whom pilfer'd Pastorals renown,
Who turns a Persian tale[102] for half-a-crown,   180
Just writes to make his barrenness appear,
And strains from hard-bound brains eight lines a year;
He who, still wanting, though he lives on theft,
Steals much, spends little, yet has nothing left:
And he who, now to sense, now nonsense leaning,
Means not, but blunders round about a meaning:
And he, whose fustian's so sublimely bad,
It is not poetry, but prose run mad:
All these, my modest satire bade translate,
And own'd that nine such poets made a Tate.   190
How did they fume, and stamp, and roar, and chafe!
And swear, not Addison himself was safe.

Peace to all such! but were there one whose fires
True genius kindles, and fair fame inspires;
Blest with each talent and each art to please,
And born to write, converse, and live with ease:
Should such a man, too fond to rule alone,
Bear, like the Turk, no brother near the throne,
View him with scornful, yet with jealous eyes,

And hate for arts that caused himself to rise;   200
Damn with faint praise, assent with civil leer,
And, without sneering, teach the rest to sneer;
Willing to wound, and yet afraid to strike,
Just hint a fault, and hesitate dislike;
Alike reserved to blame, or to commend,
A timorous foe, and a suspicious friend;
Dreading e'en fools, by flatterers besieged,
And so obliging, that he ne'er obliged;
Like Cato, give his little senate laws,
And sit attentive to his own applause;   210
While wits and Templars every sentence raise,
And wonder with a foolish face of praise—
Who but must laugh, if such a man there be?
Who would not weep, if Atticus were he?

What though my name stood rubric on the walls,
Or plaster'd posts, with claps, in capitals?
Or smoking forth, a hundred hawkers' load,
On wings of winds came flying all abroad?
I sought no homage from the race that write;
I kept, like Asian monarchs, from their sight: 220
Poems I heeded (now be-rhymed so long)
No more than thou, great George! a birthday song.
I ne'er with wits or witlings pass'd my days,
To spread about the itch of verse and praise;
Nor like a puppy, daggled through the town,
To fetch and carry sing-song up and down;
Nor at rehearsals sweat, and mouth'd, and cried,
With handkerchief and orange at my side;
But sick of fops, and poetry, and prate,
To Bufo left the whole Castalian state.   230

Proud as Apollo on his forked hill,
Sat full-blown Bufo,[103] puff'd by every quill;
Fed with soft dedication all day long,
Horace and he went hand in hand in song.
His library (where busts of poets dead
And a true Pindar stood without a head)
Received of wits an undistinguish'd race,
Who first his judgment ask'd, and then a place:
Much they extoll'd his pictures, much his seat,
And flatter'd every day, and some days eat: 240

Till, grown more frugal in his riper days,
He paid some bards with port, and some with praise,
To some a dry rehearsal was assign'd,
And others (harder still) he paid in kind.
Dryden alone (what wonder?) came not nigh,
Dryden alone escaped this judging eye:
But still the great have kindness in reserve,
He help'd to bury whom he help'd to starve.

May some choice patron bless each gray-goose quill!
May every Bavius have his Bufo still!   250
So when a statesman wants a day's defence,
Or envy holds a whole week's war with sense,
Or simple pride for flattery makes demands,
May dunce by dunce be whistled off my hands!
Bless'd be the great! for those they take away,
And those they left me; for they left me Gay;
Left me to see neglected genius bloom,
Neglected die, and tell it on his tomb:
Of all thy blameless life, the sole return
My verse, and Queensberry weeping o'er thy urn!   260

Oh let me live my own, and die so too!
(To live and die is all I have to do:)
Maintain a poet's dignity and ease,
And see what friends, and read what books I please:
Above a patron, though I condescend
Sometimes to call a minister my friend.
I was not born for courts or great affairs;
I pay my debts, believe, and say my prayers;
Can sleep without a poem in my head,
Nor know if Dennis be alive or dead.   270

Why am I ask'd what next shall see the light?
Heavens! was I born for nothing but to write?
Has life no joys for me? or (to be grave)
Have I no friend to serve, no soul to save?
'I found him close with Swift—Indeed? no doubt
(Cries prating Balbus) something will come out.'
'Tis all in vain, deny it as I will.
'No, such a genius never can lie still;'
And then for mine obligingly mistakes
The first lampoon Sir Will[104] or Bubo[105] makes.   280

Poor guiltless I! and can I choose but smile,
When every coxcomb knows me by my style?

Cursed be the verse, how well soe'er it flow,
That tends to make one worthy man my foe,
Give virtue scandal, innocence a fear,
Or from the soft-eyed virgin steal a tear!
But he who hurts a harmless neighbour's peace,
Insults fallen worth, or beauty in distress,
Who loves a lie, lame slander helps about,
Who writes a libel, or who copies out: 290
That fop, whose pride affects a patron's name,
Yet, absent, wounds an author's honest fame:
Who can your merit selfishly approve,
And show the sense of it without the love;
Who has the vanity to call you friend,
Yet wants the honour, injured, to defend;
Who tells whate'er you think, whate'er you say,
And, if he lie not, must at least betray:
Who to the dean, and silver bell[106] can swear,
And sees at Canons what was never there; 300
Who reads, but—with a lust to misapply,
Make satire a lampoon, and fiction, lie;
A lash like mine no honest man shall dread,
But all such babbling blockheads in his stead.
Let Sporus[107] tremble—

A.   What? that thing of silk,
Sporus, that mere white curd of ass's milk?
Satire or sense, alas! can Sporus feel?
Who breaks a butterfly upon a wheel?

P. Yet let me flap this bug with gilded wings,
This painted child of dirt, that stinks and stings; 310
Whose buzz the witty and the fair annoys,
Yet wit ne'er tastes, and beauty ne'er enjoys;
So well-bred spaniels civilly delight
In mumbling of the game they dare not bite.
Eternal smiles his emptiness betray,
As shallow streams run dimpling all the way.
Whether in florid impotence he speaks,
And, as the prompter breathes, the puppet squeaks;
Or at the ear of Eve, familiar toad!

Half-froth, half-venom, spits himself abroad,   320
In puns or politics, or tales, or lies,
Or spite, or smut, or rhymes, or blasphemies.
His wit all see-saw, between that and this,
Now high, now low, now master up, now miss,
And he himself one vile antithesis.
Amphibious thing! that, acting either part,
The trifling head, or the corrupted heart,
Fop at the toilet, flatterer at the board,
Now trips a lady, and now struts a lord.
Eve's tempter thus the Rabbins have express'd,   330
A cherub's face, a reptile all the rest,
Beauty that shocks you, parts that none will trust,
Wit that can creep, and pride that licks the dust.

Not Fortune's worshipper, nor Fashion's fool,
Not Lucre's madman, nor Ambition's tool,
Not proud, nor servile; be one poet's praise,
That, if he pleased, he pleased by manly ways:
That flattery, even to kings, he held a shame,
And thought a lie in verse or prose the same.
That not in Fancy's maze he wander'd long,   340
But stoop'd to Truth, and moralised his song:
That not for Fame, but Virtue's better end,
He stood the furious foe, the timid friend,
The damning critic, half-approving wit,
The coxcomb hit, or fearing to be hit;
Laugh'd at the loss of friends he never had,
The dull, the proud, the wicked, and the mad;
The distant threats of vengeance on his head,
The blow unfelt, the tear he never shed;
The tale revived, the lie so oft o'erthrown,[108]   350
Th' imputed trash,[109] and dulness not his own;
The morals blacken'd when the writings 'scape,
The libell'd person, and the pictured shape;
Abuse,[110] on all he loved, or loved him, spread,
A friend in exile, or a father dead;
The whisper that, to greatness still too near,
Perhaps yet vibrates on his sovereign's ear—
Welcome for thee, fair Virtue! all the past:
For thee, fair Virtue! welcome even the last!

A. But why insult the poor, affront the great?   360

P. A knave's a knave, to me, in every state:
Alike my scorn, if he succeed or fail,
Sporus at court, or Japhet in a jail,
A hireling scribbler, or a hireling peer,
Knight of the post corrupt, or of the shire;
If on a pillory, or near a throne,
He gain his prince's ear, or lose his own.

Yet soft by nature, more a dupe than wit,
Sappho[111] can tell you how this man was bit:
This dreaded satirist Dennis will confess   370
Foe to his pride, but friend to his distress:
So humble, he has knock'd at Tibbald's door,
Has drunk with Cibber, nay, has rhymed for Moore.
Full ten years slander'd, did he once reply?
Three thousand suns went down on Welsted's[112] lie.
To please a mistress one aspersed his life;
He lash'd him not, but let her be his wife:
Let Budgell[113] charge low Grub-street on his quill,
And write whate'er he pleased, except his will;[114]
Let the two Curlls of town and court[115] abuse   380
His father, mother, body, soul, and Muse.
Yet why that father held it for a rule,
It was a sin to call our neighbour fool:
That harmless mother thought no wife a whore:
Hear this, and spare his family, James Moore!
Unspotted names, and memorable long!
If there be force in virtue, or in song.

Of gentle blood (part shed in honour's cause,
While yet in Britain honour had applause)
Each parent sprung— —

A.   What fortune, pray?— —

P.   Their own,   390
And better got, than Bestia's from the throne.
Born to no pride, inheriting no strife,
Nor marrying discord in a noble wife,[116]
Stranger to civil and religious rage,
The good man walk'd innoxious through his age.
No courts he saw, no suits would ever try,
Nor dared an oath,[117] nor hazarded a lie.

Unlearn'd, he knew no schoolman's subtle art,
No language but the language of the heart.
By nature honest, by experience wise,   400
Healthy by temperance, and by exercise;
His life, though long, to sickness pass'd unknown,
His death was instant, and without a groan.
O grant me thus to live, and thus to die!
Who sprung from kings shall know less joy than I.

O friend! may each domestic bliss be thine!
Be no unpleasing melancholy mine:
Me, let the tender office long engage,
To rock the cradle of reposing age,
With lenient arts extend a mother's breath,   410
Make languor smile, and smooth the bed of death,
Explore the thought, explain the asking eye,
And keep a while one parent from the sky!
On cares like these if length of days attend,
May Heaven, to bless those days, preserve my friend,
Preserve him social, cheerful, and serene,
And just as rich as when he served a Queen.

A. Whether that blessing be denied or given,
Thus far was right, the rest belongs to Heaven.

*　　*　　*　　*　　*

VARIATIONS.

After VER. 20 in the MS.—

Is there a bard in durance? turn them free,
With all their brandish'd reams they run to me:
Is there a 'prentice, having seen two plays,
Who would do something in his semptress' praise?

VER. 29 in the first edition—

Dear Doctor, tell me, is not this a curse?
Say, is their anger or their friendship worse?

VER. 53 in the MS.—

If you refuse, he goes, as fates incline,
To plague Sir Robert, or to turn divine.

VER. 60 in the former edition—

Cibber and I are luckily no friends.

VER. 111 in the MS.—

For song, for silence, some expect a bribe;
And others roar aloud, 'Subscribe, subscribe!'
Time, praise, or money, is the least they crave;
Yet each declares the other fool or knave.

After VER. 124 in the MS.—

But, friend, this shape, which you and Curll[118] admire
Came not from Ammon's son, but from my sire:[119]
And for my head, if you'll the truth excuse,
I had it from my mother,[120] not the Muse.
Happy, if he, in whom these frailties join'd,
Had heir'd as well the virtues of the mind.

After VER. 208 in the MS.—

Who, if two wits on rival themes contest,
Approves of each, but likes the worst the best.

After VER. 234 in the MS.—

To bards reciting he vouchsafed a nod,
And snuff'd their incense like a gracious god.
Our ministers like gladiators live,
'Tis half their bus'ness blows to ward, or give;
The good their virtue would effect, or sense,
Dies between exigents and self-defence.

After VER. 270 in the MS.—

Friendships from youth I sought, and seek them still;
Fame, like the wind, may breathe where'er it will.
The world I knew, but made it not my school,
And in a course of flattery lived no fool.

After VER. 282 in the MS.—

P. What if I sing Augustus, great and good?
A. You did so lately, was it understood?
P. Be nice no more, but, with a mouth profound,
    As rumbling D——s or a Norfolk hound;
    With George and Fred'ric roughen every verse,
    Then smooth up all and Caroline rehearse.
A. No—the high task to lift up kings to god
    Leave to court-sermons, and to birthday odes.
    On themes like these, superior far to thine,
    Let laurell'd Cibber and great Arnal shine.
P. Why write at all?
A.   Yes, silence if you keep,
    The town, the court, the wits, the dunces weep.

VER. 368 in the MS.—

Once, and but once, his heedless youth was bit,
And liked that dangerous thing, a female wit:
Safe as he thought, though all the prudent chid.
He writ no libels, but my lady did:
Great odds in amorous or poetic game,
Where woman's is the sin, and man's the shame.

After VER. 405 in the MS.—

And of myself, too, something must I say?
Take then this verse, the trifle of a day.
And if it live, it lives but to commend
The man whose heart has ne'er forgot a friend,
Or head, an author: critic, yet polite,
And friend to learning, yet too wise to write.

    *   *   *   *   *

SATIRES AND EPISTLES OF HORACE IMITATED.

ADVERTISEMENT.

The occasion of publishing these 'Imitations' was the clamour raised on some of my 'Epistles. ' An answer from Horace was both more full, and of more dignity, than any I could have made in my own person; and the example of much greater freedom in so eminent a divine as Dr Donne, seemed a proof with what indignation and contempt a Christian may treat vice or folly, in ever so low or ever so high a station. Both these authors were acceptable to the princes and ministers under whom they lived. The satires of Dr Donne I versified, at the desire of the Earl of Oxford while he was Lord Treasurer, and of the Duke of Shrewsbury who had been Secretary of State; neither of whom looked upon a satire on vicious courts as any reflection on those they served in. And, indeed, there is not in the world a greater error than that which fools are so apt to fall into, and knaves with good reason to encourage, the mistaking a satirist for a libeller; whereas to a true satirist nothing is so odious as a libeller, for the same reason as to a man truly virtuous nothing is so hateful as a hypocrite.

'Uni aequus virtati atque ejus amicis.'

SATIRE I. TO MR FORTESCUE.[121]

P. There are (I scarce can think it, but am told)
There are, to whom my satire seems too bold:
Scarce to wise Peter complaisant enough,
And something said of Chartres much too rough.
The lines are weak, another's pleased to say,
Lord Fanny[122] spins a thousand such a day.
Timorous by nature, of the rich in awe,
I come to counsel learned in the law:
'You'll give me, like a friend both sage and free,
Advice; and (as you use) without a fee.'   10

F. I'd write no more.

P.   Not write? but then I think,

And for my soul I cannot sleep a wink.
I nod in company, I wake at night,
Fools rush into my head, and so I write.

F. You could not do a worse thing for your life.
Why, if the nights seem tedious—take a wife:
Or rather truly, if your point be rest,
Lettuce and cowslip-wine; *probatum est.*
But talk with Celsus, Celsus will advise
Hartshorn, or something that shall close your eyes.   20
Or, if you needs must write, write Caesar's praise,
You'll gain at least a knighthood, or the bays.

P. What! like Sir Richard, rumbling, rough, and fierce,
With arms, and George, and Brunswick crowd the verse,
Rend with tremendous sound your ears asunder,
With gun, drum, trumpet, blunderbuss, and thunder?
Or, nobly wild, with Budgell's fire and force,
Paint angels trembling round his falling horse?[123]

F. Then all your Muse's softer art display,
Let Carolina smooth the tuneful lay,   30
Lull with Amelia's liquid name the Nine,
And sweetly flow through all the royal line.

P. Alas! few verses touch their nicer ear;
They scarce can bear their Laureate twice a-year;
And justly Caesar scorns the poet's lays,
It is to history he trusts for praise.

F. Better be Cibber, I'll maintain it still,
Than ridicule all taste, blaspheme quadrille,
Abuse the city's best good men in metre,
And laugh at peers that put their trust in Peter.   40
Even those you touch not, hate you.

P.   What should ail them?

F. A hundred smart in Timon and in Balaam:
The fewer still you name, you wound the more;
Bond is but one, but Harpax is a score.

P. Each mortal has his pleasure: none deny

Scarsdale his bottle, Darty his ham-pie;
Ridotta sips and dances, till she see
The doubling lustres dance as fast as she;
F— — loves the Senate, Hockley-hole his brother,
Like in all else, as one egg to another.   50
I love to pour out all myself, as plain
As downright Shippen,[124] or as old Montaigne:
In them, as certain to be loved as seen,
The soul stood forth, nor kept a thought within;
In me what spots (for spots I have) appear,
Will prove at least the medium must be clear.
In this impartial glass, my Muse intends
Fair to expose myself, my foes, my friends;
Publish the present age; but, where my text
Is vice too high, reserve it for the next: 60
My foes shall wish my life a longer date,
And every friend the less lament my fate,
My head and heart thus flowing through my quill,
Verse-man or prose-man, term me which you will,
Papist or Protestant, or both between,
Like good Erasmus, in an honest mean,
In moderation placing all my glory,
While Tories call me Whig, and Whigs a Tory.

Satire's my weapon, but I'm too discreet
To run a-muck, and tilt at all I meet;   70
I only wear it in a land of hectors,
Thieves, supercargoes, sharpers, and directors.
Save but our army! and let Jove incrust
Swords, pikes, and guns, with everlasting rust!
Peace is my dear delight—not Fleury's more:
But touch me, and no minister so sore.
Whoe'er offends, at some unlucky time
Slides into verse, and hitches in a rhyme,
Sacred to ridicule his whole life long,
And the sad burthen of some merry song.   80

Slander or poison dread from Delia's rage,
Hard words or hanging, if your judge be Page.
From furious Sappho scarce a milder fate,
Pox'd by her love, or libell'd by her hate.
Its proper power to hurt, each creature feels;
Bulls aim their horns, and asses lift their heels;

'Tis a bear's talent not to kick, but hug;
And no man wonders he's not stung by pug.
So drink with Walters, or with Chartres eat,
They'll never poison you, they'll only cheat.   90

Then, learned sir! (to cut the matter short)
Whate'er my fate, or well or ill at court,
Whether old age, with faint but cheerful ray,
Attends to gild the evening of my day,
Or death's black wing already be display'd,
To wrap me in the universal shade;
Whether the darken'd room to muse invite,
Or whiten'd wall provoke the skewer to write:
In durance, exile, Bedlam, or the Mint,
Like Lee[125] or Budgell,[126] I will rhyme and print.   100

F. Alas, young man! your days can ne'er be long,
In flower of age you perish for a song!
Plums and directors, Shylock and his wife,
Will club their testers, now, to take your life!

P. What? arm'd for Virtue, when I point the pen,
Brand the bold front of shameless guilty men;
Dash the proud gamester in his gilded car;
Bare the mean heart that lurks beneath a star;
Can there be wanting to defend her cause,
Lights of the Church, or guardians of the laws?   110
Could pension'd Boileau lash, in honest strain,
Flatterers and bigots even in Louis' reign?
Could Laureate Dryden pimp and friar engage,
Yet neither Charles nor James be in a rage?
And I not strip the gilding off a knave,
Unplaced, unpension'd, no man's heir, or slave?
I will, or perish in the generous cause:
Hear this, and tremble! you who 'scape the laws.
Yes, while I live, no rich or noble knave
Shall walk the world, in credit, to his grave.   120
TO VIRTUE ONLY, AND HER FRIENDS, A FRIEND,
The world beside may murmur, or commend.
Know, all the distant din that world can keep,
Rolls o'er my grotto, and but soothes my sleep.
There, my retreat the best companions grace,
Chiefs out of war, and statesmen out of place.

There St John mingles with my friendly bowl
The feast of reason and the flow of soul:
And he, whose lightning[127] pierced th' Iberian lines,
Now forms my quincunx, and now ranks my vines,   130
Or tames the genius of the stubborn plain,
Almost as quickly as he conquer'd Spain.

Envy must own, I live among the great,
No pimp of pleasure, and no spy of state,
With eyes that pry not, tongue that ne'er repeats,
Fond to spread friendships, but to cover heats;
To help who want, to forward who excel;—
This, all who know me, know; who love me, tell;
And who unknown defame me, let them be
Scribblers or peers, alike are mob to me.   140
This is my plea, on this I rest my cause—
What saith my counsel, learned in the laws?

F. Your plea is good; but still, I say, beware!
Laws are explain'd by men—so have a care!
It stands on record, that in Richard's times
A man was hang'd for very honest rhymes.
Consult the statute: *quart.* I think, it is,
Edwardi Sext. or *prim, et quint. Eliz.*
See 'Libels, Satires'—here you have it—read.

P. Libels and satires! lawless things indeed!   150
But grave epistles, bringing vice to light,
Such as a king might read, a bishop write,
Such as Sir Robert would approve—

F.   Indeed?
The case is alter'd—you may then proceed;
In such a cause the plaintiff will be hiss'd,
My lords the judges laugh, and you're dismiss'd.

*   *   *   *   *

SATIRE II. TO MR BETHEL.

What, and how great, the virtue and the art
To live on little with a cheerful heart;
(A doctrine sage, but truly none of mine)
Let's talk, my friends, but talk before we dine;
Not when a gilt buffet's reflected pride
Turns you from sound philosophy aside;
Not when from plate to plate your eyeballs roll,
And the brain dances to the mantling bowl.

Hear Bethel's sermon, one not versed in schools,
But strong in sense, and wise without the rules.   10

Go, work, hunt, exercise! (he thus began)
Then scorn a homely dinner, if you can.
Your wine lock'd up, your butler stroll'd abroad,
Or fish denied (the river yet unthaw'd),
If then plain bread and milk will do the feat,
The pleasure lies in you, and not the meat.

Preach as I please, I doubt our curious men
Will choose a pheasant still before a hen;
Yet hens of Guinea full as good I hold,
Except you eat the feathers green and gold.   20
Of carps and mullets why prefer the great,
(Though cut in pieces ere my lord can eat)
Yet for small turbots such esteem profess?
Because God made these large, the other less.

Oldfield,[128] with more than harpy throat endued,
Cries, 'Send me, gods! a whole hog barbecued!'
Oh, blast it, south-winds! till a stench exhale
Rank as the ripeness of a rabbit's tail.
By what criterion do ye eat, d' ye think,
If this is prized for sweetness, that for stink?   30
When the tired glutton labours through a treat,
He finds no relish in the sweetest meat,
He calls for something bitter, something sour,
And the rich feast concludes extremely poor:
Cheap eggs, and herbs, and olives still we see;
Thus much is left of old simplicity!

The robin redbreast till of late had rest,
And children sacred held a martin's nest,
Till beccaficos sold so devilish dear
To one that was, or would have been, a peer. 40
Let me extol a cat, on oysters fed,
I'll have a party at the Bedford-head;[129]
Or even to crack live crawfish recommend;
I'd never doubt at court to make a friend.

'Tis yet in vain, I own, to keep a pother
About one vice, and fall into the other:
Between excess and famine lies a mean;
Plain, but not sordid; though not splendid, clean.

Avidien, or his wife (no matter which,
For him you'll call a dog, and her a bitch) 50
Sell their presented partridges, and fruits,
And humbly live on rabbits and on roots:
One half-pint bottle serves them both to dine,
And is at once their vinegar and wine.
But on some lucky day (as when they found
A lost bank-bill, or heard their son was drown'd)
At such a feast, old vinegar to spare,
Is what two souls so generous cannot bear:
Oil, though it stink, they drop by drop impart, 60
But souse the cabbage with a bounteous heart.

He knows to live, who keeps the middle state,
And neither leans on this side, nor on that;
Nor stops, for one bad cork, his butler's pay;
Swears, like Albutius, a good cook away;
Nor lets, like Naevius, every error pass,
The musty wine, foul cloth, or greasy glass.
Now hear what blessings temperance can bring:
(Thus said our friend, and what he said I sing)
First health: the stomach (cramm'd from every dish, 70
A tomb of boil'd and roast, and flesh and fish,
Where bile, and wind, and phlegm, and acid jar,
And all the man is one intestine war)
Remembers oft the school-boy's simple fare,
The temperate sleeps, and spirits light as air.

How pale each worshipful and reverend guest

Rise from a clergy or a city feast!
What life in all that ample body, say?
What heavenly particle inspires the clay?
The soul subsides, and wickedly inclines   80
To seem but mortal, even in sound divines.

On morning wings how active springs the mind
That leaves the load of yesterday behind!
How easy every labour it pursues!
How coming to the poet every Muse!
Not but we may exceed some holy time,
Or tired in search of truth, or search of rhyme;
Ill health some just indulgence may engage,
And more the sickness of long life, old age;
For fainting age what cordial drop remains,   90
If our intemperate youth the vessel drains?

Our fathers praised rank ven'son. You suppose,
Perhaps, young men! our fathers had no nose.
Not so: a buck was then a week's repast,
And 'twas their point, I ween, to make it last;
More pleased to keep it till their friends could come,
Than eat the sweetest by themselves at home.
Why had not I in those good times my birth,
Ere coxcomb-pies or coxcombs were on earth?

Unworthy he, the voice of fame to hear—   100
That sweetest music to an honest ear—
(For, faith! Lord Fanny, you are in the wrong,
The world's good word is better than a song,)
Who has not learn'd, fresh sturgeon and ham-pie
Are no rewards for want, and infamy!
When luxury has lick'd up all thy pelf,
Cursed by thy neighbours, thy trustees, thyself,
To friends, to fortune, to mankind a shame,
Think how posterity will treat thy name;
And buy a rope, that future times may tell   110
Thou hast at least bestow'd one penny well.

'Right,' cries his lordship, 'for a rogue in need
To have a taste is insolence indeed:
In me 'tis noble, suits my birth and state,
My wealth unwieldy, and my heap too great.'

Then, like the sun, let bounty spread her ray,
And shine that superfluity away.
Oh, impudence of wealth! with all thy store,
How dar'st thou let one worthy man be poor?
Shall half the new-built churches round thee fall? 120
Make quays, build bridges, or repair Whitehall:
Or to thy country let that heap be lent,
As Marlbro's was, but not at five per cent.

Who thinks that Fortune cannot change her mind,
Prepares a dreadful jest for all mankind.
And who stands safest? tell me, is it he
That spreads and swells in puff'd prosperity,
Or, blest with little, whose preventing care
In peace provides fit arms against a war?

Thus Bethel spoke, who always speaks his thought, 130
And always thinks the very thing he ought:
His equal mind I copy what I can,
And as I love, would imitate the man.
In South-sea days not happier, when surmised
The lord of thousands, than if now excised;
In forest planted by a father's hand,
Than in five acres now of rented land.
Content with little, I can piddle here
On broccoli and mutton, round the year;
But ancient friends (though poor, or out of play) 140
That touch my bell, I cannot turn away.
'Tis true, no turbots dignify my boards,
But gudgeons, flounders, what my Thames affords:
To Hounslow Heath I point, and Bansted Down,
Thence comes your mutton, and these chicks my own:
From yon old walnut-tree a shower shall fall;
And grapes, long lingering on my only wall,
And figs from standard and espalier join;
The devil is in you if you cannot dine:
Then cheerful healths (your mistress shall have place) 150
And, what's more rare, a poet shall say grace.

Fortune not much of humbling me can boast;
Though double tax'd, how little have I lost?
My life's amusements have been just the same,
Before and after standing armies came.

My lands are sold, my father's house is gone;
I'll hire another's; is not that my own,
And yours, my friends? through whose free-opening gate
None comes too early, none departs too late;
(For I, who hold sage Homer's rule the best,   160
Welcome the coming, speed the going guest).
'Pray Heaven it last!' (cries Swift) 'as you go on;
I wish to God this house had been your own:
Pity to build, without a son or wife:
Why, you'll enjoy it only all your life.'
Well, if the use be mine, can it concern one,
Whether the name belong to Pope or Vernon?
What's property, dear Swift? You see it alter
From you to me, from me to Peter Walter;
Or, in a mortgage, prove a lawyer's share;   170
Or, in a jointure, vanish from the heir;
Or in pure equity (the case not clear)
The Chancery takes your rents for twenty year:
At best, it falls to some ungracious son,
Who cries, 'My father's damn'd, and all's my own.'
Shades, that to Bacon could retreat afford,
Become the portion of a booby lord;
And Helmsley, once proud Buckingham's[130] delight,
Slides to a scrivener or a city knight.
Let lands and houses have what lords they will,   180
Let us be fix'd, and our own masters still.

*   *   *   *   *

THE FIRST EPISTLE OF THE FIRST BOOK OF HORACE.

TO LORD BOLINGBROKE.

St John, whose love indulged my labours past,
Matures my present, and shall bound my last!
Why will you break the Sabbath of my days?
Now sick alike of envy and of praise.
Public too long, ah, let me hide my age!
See, modest Cibber now has left the stage:
Our generals now, retired to their estates,
Hang their old trophies o'er the garden gates,
In life's cool evening satiate of applause,
Nor fond of bleeding, even in Brunswick's cause.   10

A voice there is, that whispers in my ear,
('Tis reason's voice, which sometimes one can hear)
'Friend Pope! be prudent, let your Muse take breath,
And never gallop Pegasus to death;
Lest, still and stately, void of fire or force,
You limp, like Blackmore on a Lord Mayor's horse.'

Farewell, then, verse, and love, and every toy,
The rhymes and rattles of the man or boy;
What right, what true, what fit we justly call,
Let this be all my care—for this is all: 20
To lay this harvest up, and hoard with haste
What every day will want, and most, the last.

But ask not, to what doctors I apply;
Sworn to no master, of no sect am I:
As drives the storm, at any door I knock:
And house with Montaigne now, or now with Locke.
Sometimes a patriot, active in debate,
Mix with the world, and battle for the state,
Free as young Lyttelton, her cause pursue,
Still true to virtue, and as warm as true: 30
Sometimes with Aristippus,[131] or St Paul,
Indulge my candour, and grow all to all;
Back to my native moderation slide,
And win my way by yielding to the tide.

Long, as to him who works for debt, the day,
Long as the night to her whose love's away,
Long as the year's dull circle seems to run,
When the brisk minor pants for twenty-one:
So slow the unprofitable moments roll,
That lock up all the functions of my soul;   40
That keep me from myself; and still delay
Life's instant business to a future day:
That task, which, as we follow, or despise,
The eldest is a fool, the youngest wise.
Which done, the poorest can no wants endure;
And which, not done, the richest must be poor.

Late as it is, I put myself to school,
And feel some comfort not to be a fool.
Weak though I am of limb, and short of sight,
Far from a lynx, and not a giant quite;   50
I'll do what Mead and Cheselden advise,
To keep these limbs, and to preserve these eyes.
Not to go back, is somewhat to advance,
And men must walk at least before they dance.

Say, does thy blood rebel, thy bosom move
With wretched avarice, or as wretched love?
Know, there are words and spells which can control
Between the fits this fever of the soul:
Know, there are rhymes, which, fresh and fresh applied,
Will cure the arrant'st puppy of his pride.   60
Be furious, envious, slothful, mad, or drunk,
Slave to a wife, or vassal to a punk,
A Switz, a High-Dutch, or a Low-Dutch bear;
All that we ask is but a patient ear.

'Tis the first virtue, vices to abhor:
And the first wisdom, to be fool no more.
But to the world no bugbear is so great,
As want of figure, and a small estate.
To either India see the merchant fly,
Scared at the spectre of pale poverty!   70
See him, with pains of body, pangs of soul,
Burn through the tropic, freeze beneath the pole!
Wilt thou do nothing for a nobler end,
Nothing, to make philosophy thy friend?

To stop thy foolish views, thy long desires,
And ease thy heart of all that it admires?

Here, Wisdom calls: 'Seek Virtue first, be bold!
As gold to silver, Virtue is to gold.'
There, London's voice: 'Get money, money still!
And then let virtue follow, if she will.'   80
This, this the saving doctrine, preach'd to all,
From low St James's up to high St Paul;
From him whose quill stands quiver'd at his ear,
To him who notches sticks[132] at Westminster.

Barnard[133] in spirit, sense, and truth abounds;
'Pray then, what wants he?' Fourscore thousand pounds;
A pension, or such harness for a slave
As Bug now has, and Dorimant would have.
Barnard, thou art a cit, with all thy worth;
But Bug and D— —l, their Honours, and so forth.   90

Yet every child another song will sing,
'Virtue, brave boys! 'tis virtue makes a king.'
True, conscious honour is to feel no sin,
He's arm'd without that's innocent within;
Be this thy screen, and this thy wall of brass;
Compared to this, a minister's an ass.

And say, to which shall our applause belong,
This new court-jargon, or the good old song?
The modern language of corrupted peers,
Or what was spoke at Cressy and Poictiers?   100
Who counsels best? who whispers, 'Be but great,
With praise or infamy leave that to fate;
Get place and wealth, if possible, with grace;
If not, by any means get wealth and place.'
For what? to have a box where eunuchs sing,
And foremost in the circle eye a king.
Or he, who bids thee face with steady view
Proud fortune, and look shallow greatness through:
And, while he bids thee, sets th' example too?
If such a doctrine, in St James's air,   110
Should chance to make the well-dress'd rabble stare;
If honest S— —z take scandal at a spark,
That less admires the palace than the park:

Faith, I shall give the answer Reynard gave:
'I cannot like, dread sir, your royal cave:
Because I see, by all the tracks about,
Full many a beast goes in, but none comes out.'
Adieu to virtue, if you're once a slave:
Send her to court, you send her to her grave.

Well, if a king's a lion, at the least   120
The people are a many-headed beast:
Can they direct what measures to pursue,
Who know themselves so little what to do?
Alike in nothing but one lust of gold,
Just half the land would buy, and half be sold:
Their country's wealth our mightier misers drain,
Or cross, to plunder provinces, the main;
The rest, some farm the poor-box, some the pews;
Some keep assemblies, and would keep the stews;
Some with fat bucks on childless dotards fawn;   130
Some win rich widows by their chine and brawn;
While with the silent growth of ten per cent,
In dirt and darkness, hundreds stink content.

Of all these ways, if each pursues his own,
Satire, be kind, and let the wretch alone:
But show me one who has it in his power
To act consistent with himself an hour.
Sir Job sail'd forth, the evening bright and still,
'No place on earth' (he cried) 'like Greenwich hill!'
Up starts a palace, lo, the obedient base   140
Slopes at its foot, the woods its sides embrace,
The silver Thames reflects its marble face.
Now let some whimsy, or that devil within,
Which guides all those who know not what they mean,
But give the knight (or give his lady) spleen;
'Away, away! take all your scaffolds down,
For, snug's the word: my dear! we'll live in town.'

At amorous Flavio is the stocking thrown?
That very night he longs to lie alone.
The fool, whose wife elopes some thrice a quarter,   150
For matrimonial solace dies a martyr.
Did ever Proteus, Merlin, any witch,
Transform themselves so strangely as the rich?

Well, but the poor—the poor have the same itch;
They change their weekly barber, weekly news,
Prefer a new japanner to their shoes,
Discharge their garrets, move their beds, and run
(They know not whither) in a chaise and one;
They hire their sculler, and when once aboard,
Grow sick, and damn the climate—like a lord.   160

You laugh, half-beau, half-sloven if I stand;
My wig all powder, and all snuff my band;
You laugh, if coat and breeches strangely vary,
White gloves, and linen worthy Lady Mary![134]
But, when no prelate's lawn with hair-shirt lined
Is half so incoherent as my mind,
When (each opinion with the next at strife,
One ebb and flow of follies all my life)
I plant, root up; I build, and then confound;
Turn round to square, and square again to round;   170
You never change one muscle of your face,
You think this madness but a common case,
Nor once to Chancery, nor to Hale apply;
Yet hang your lip, to see a seam awry!
Careless how ill I with myself agree,
Kind to my dress, my figure, not to me.
Is this my guide, philosopher, and friend?
This, he who loves me, and who ought to mend?
Who ought to make me (what he can, or none),
That man divine whom Wisdom calls her own;   180
Great without title, without fortune bless'd;
Rich even when plunder'd, honour'd while oppress'd;
Loved without youth, and follow'd without power;
At home, though exiled; free, though in the Tower;
In short, that reasoning, high, immortal thing,
Just less than Jove, and much above a king,
Nay, half in heaven—except (what's mighty odd)
A fit of vapours clouds this demi-god.

*   *   *   *   *

THE SIXTH EPISTLE OF THE FIRST BOOK OF HORACE.

TO MR MURRAY.[135]

'Not to admire, is all the art I know,
To make men happy, and to keep them so.'
(Plain truth, dear Murray, needs no flowers of speech,
So take it in the very words of Creech.)[136]

This vault of air, this congregated ball,
Self-centred sun, and stars that rise and fall,
There are, my friend! whose philosophic eyes
Look through and trust the Ruler with his skies,
To Him commit the hour, the day, the year,
And view this dreadful All without a fear.   10

Admire we then what earth's low entrails hold,
Arabian shores, or Indian seas infold;
All the mad trade of fools and slaves for gold?
Or popularity? or stars and strings?
The mob's applauses, or the gifts of kings?
Say with what eyes we ought at courts to gaze,
And pay the great our homage of amaze?

If weak the pleasure that from these can spring,
The fear to want them is as weak a thing:
Whether we dread, or whether we desire,   20
In either case, believe me, we admire;
Whether we joy or grieve, the same the curse,
Surprised at better, or surprised at worse.
Thus good or bad, to one extreme betray
The unbalanced mind, and snatch the man away:
For virtue's self may too much zeal be had;
The worst of madmen is a saint run mad.

Go then, and, if you can, admire the state
Of beaming diamonds, and reflected plate;
Procure a taste to double the surprise,   30
And gaze on Parian charms with learned eyes:
Be struck with bright brocade, or Tyrian dye,
Our birthday nobles' splendid livery.
If not so pleased, at council-board rejoice,

To see their judgments hang upon thy voice;
From morn to night, at Senate, Rolls, and Hall,
Plead much, read more, dine late, or not at all.
But wherefore all this labour, all this strife?
For fame, for riches, for a noble wife?
Shall one whom nature, learning, birth, conspired 40
To form, not to admire, but be admired,
Sigh, while his Chloe, blind to wit and worth,
Weds the rich dulness of some son of earth?
Yet time ennobles, or degrades each line;
It brighten'd Craggs's,[137] and may darken thine:
And what is fame? the meanest have their day,
The greatest can but blaze, and pass away.
Graced as thou art, with all the power of words,
So known, so honour'd, at the House of Lords:
Conspicuous scene! another yet is nigh 50
(More silent far) where kings and poets lie;
Where Murray (long enough his country's pride)
Shall be no more than Tully, or than Hyde!

Rack'd with sciatics, martyr'd with the stone,
Will any mortal let himself alone?
See Ward by batter'd beaux invited over,
And desperate misery lays hold on Dover.
The case is easier in the mind's disease;
There all men may be cured, whene'er they please.
Would ye be blest? despise low joys, low gains; 60
Disdain whatever Cornbury[138] disdains;
Be virtuous, and be happy for your pains.

But art thou one, whom new opinions sway,
One who believes as Tindal[139] leads the way,
Who virtue and a church alike disowns,
Thinks that but words, and this but brick and stones?
Fly then, on all the wings of wild desire,
Admire whate'er the maddest can admire:
Is wealth thy passion? Hence! from pole to pole,
Where winds can carry, or where waves can roll, 70
For Indian spices, for Peruvian gold,
Prevent the greedy, and outbid the bold:
Advance thy golden mountain to the skies;
On the broad base of fifty thousand rise,
Add one round hundred, and (if that's not fair)

Add fifty more, and bring it to a square.
For, mark the advantage; just so many score
Will gain a wife with half as many more,
Procure her beauty, make that beauty chaste,
And then such friends—as cannot fail to last.   80
A man of wealth is dubb'd a man of worth,
Venus shall give him form, and Anstis[140] birth.
(Believe me, many a German prince is worse,
Who, proud of pedigree, is poor of purse).
His wealth brave Timon gloriously confounds;
Ask'd for a groat, he gives a hundred pounds;
Or if three ladies like a luckless play,[141]
Takes the whole house upon the poet's day.
Now, in such exigencies not to need,
Upon my word, you must be rich indeed;   90
A noble superfluity it craves,
Not for yourself, but for your fools and knaves;
Something, which for your honour they may cheat,
And which it much becomes you to forget.
If wealth alone then make and keep us bless'd,
Still, still be getting, never, never rest.

But if to power and place your passion lie,
If in the pomp of life consist the joy;
Then hire a slave, or (if you will) a lord   100
To do the honours, and to give the word;
Tell at your levee, as the crowds approach,
To whom to nod, whom take into your coach,
Whom honour with your hand: to make remarks,
Who rules in Cornwall, or who rules in Berks:
'This may be troublesome, is near the chair:
That makes three members, this can choose a mayor.'
Instructed thus, you bow, embrace, protest,
Adopt him son, or cousin at the least,
Then turn about, and laugh at your own jest.   110

Or if your life be one continued treat,
If to live well means nothing but to eat;
Up, up! cries Gluttony, 'tis break of day,
Go drive the deer, and drag the finny prey;
With hounds and horns go hunt an appetite—
So Russel did, but could not eat at night,
Call'd, happy dog! the beggar at his door,

And envied thirst and hunger to the poor.

Or shall we every decency confound,
Through taverns, stews, and bagnios take our round,   120
Go dine with Chartres, in each vice outdo
K—l's lewd cargo, or Ty—y's crew;
From Latian syrens, French Circaean feasts,
Return well travell'd, and transform'd to beasts,
Or for a titled punk, or foreign flame,
Renounce our country, and degrade our name?

If, after all, we must with Wilmot own,
The cordial drop of life is love alone,
And Swift cry wisely, '*Vive la bagatelle!*'
The man that loves and laughs, must sure do well.   130

Adieu—if this advice appear the worst,
E'en take the counsel which I gave you first:
Or better precepts if you can impart,
Why do, I'll follow them with all my heart.

*   *   *   *   *

THE FIRST EPISTLE OF THE SECOND BOOK OF HORACE.

ADVERTISEMENT.

The reflections of Horace, and the judgments past in his Epistle to Augustus, seemed so seasonable to the present times, that I could not help applying them to the use of my own country. The author thought them considerable enough to address them to his prince; whom he paints with all the great and good qualities of a monarch, upon whom the Romans depended for the increase of an absolute empire. But to make the poem entirely English, I was willing to add one or two of those which contribute to the happiness of a free people, and are more consistent with the welfare of our neighbours.

This epistle will show the learned world to have fallen into two mistakes: One, that Augustus was a patron of poets in general; whereas he not only prohibited all but the best writers to name him, but recommended that care even to the civil magistrate: *Admonebat praetores, ne paterentur nomen suum obsolefieri*, &c. The other, that this piece was only a general discourse of poetry; whereas it was an apology for the poets, in order to render Augustus more their patron. Horace here pleads the cause of his contemporaries, first against the taste of the town, whose humour it was to magnify the authors of the preceding age; secondly against the court and nobility, who encouraged only the writers for the theatre; and lastly against the emperor himself, who had conceived them of little use to the government. He shows (by a view of the progress of learning, and the change of taste among the Romans) that the introduction of the polite arts of Greece had given the writers of his time great advantages over their predecessors; that their morals were much improved, and the license of those ancient poets restrained; that satire and comedy were become more just and useful; that whatever extravagances were left on the stage, were owing to the ill taste of the nobility; that poets, under due regulations, were in many respects useful to the state; and concludes, that it was upon them the emperor himself must depend for his fame with posterity.

We may further learn from this epistle, that Horace made his court to this great prince by writing with a decent freedom toward him, with a just contempt of his low flatterers, and with a manly regard to his own character.

TO AUGUSTUS.[142]

While you, great patron of mankind! sustain
The balanced world, and open all the main;
Your country, chief, in arms abroad defend,
At home, with morals, arts, and laws amend;
How shall the Muse, from such a monarch, steal
An hour, and not defraud the public weal?

Edward and Henry, now the boast of fame,
And virtuous Alfred, a more sacred name,
After a life of generous toils endured,
The Gaul subdued, or property secured,   10
Ambition humbled, mighty cities storm'd,
Or laws establish'd, and the world reform'd;
Closed their long glories with a sigh, to find
The unwilling gratitude of base mankind!
All human virtue, to its latest breath,
Finds envy never conquer'd, but by death.
The great Alcides, every labour past,
Had still this monster to subdue at last.
Sure fate of all, beneath whose rising ray
Each star of meaner merit fades away!   20
Oppress'd we feel the beam directly beat,
Those suns of glory please not till they set.

To thee, the world its present homage pays,
The harvest early, but mature the praise:
Great friend of liberty! in kings a name
Above all Greek, above all Roman fame:
Whose word is truth, as sacred and revered,
As Heaven's own oracles from altars heard.
Wonder of kings! like whom, to mortal eyes
None e'er has risen, and none e'er shall rise.   30

Just in one instance, be it yet confess'd,
Your people, sir, are partial in the rest:
Foes to all living worth except your own,
And advocates for folly dead and gone.
Authors, like coins, grow dear as they grow old;
It is the rust we value, not the gold.
Chaucer's worst ribaldry is learn'd by rote,

And beastly Skelton[143] heads of houses quote:
One likes no language but the 'Faery Queen';
A Scot will fight for 'Christ's Kirk o' the Green';[144]   40
And each true Briton is to Ben so civil,
He swears the Muses met him at The Devil.[145]

Though justly Greece her eldest sons admires,
Why should not we be wiser than our sires?
In every public virtue we excel;
We build, we paint, we sing, we dance as well,
And learned Athens to our art must stoop,
Could she behold us tumbling through a hoop.

If time improve our wit as well as wine,
Say at what age a poet grows divine?   50
Shall we, or shall we not, account him so,
Who died, perhaps, an hundred years ago?
End all dispute; and fix the year precise
When British bards begin t' immortalise?

'Who lasts a century can have no flaw,
I hold that wit a classic, good in law.'
Suppose he wants a year, will you compound?
And shall we deem him ancient, right and sound,
Or damn to all eternity at once,
At ninety-nine, a modern and a dunce?   60

'We shall not quarrel for a year or two;
By courtesy of England, he may do.'

Then, by the rule that made the horse-tail bare,[146]
I pluck out year by year, as hair by hair,
And melt down ancients like a heap of snow:
While you, to measure merits, look in Stowe,
And estimating authors by the year,
Bestow a garland only on a bier.

Shakspeare (whom you and every play-house bill
Style the divine, the matchless, what you will),   70
For gain, not glory, wing'd his roving flight,
And grew immortal in his own despite.
Ben, old and poor, as little seem'd to heed
The life to come, in every poet's creed.

Who now reads Cowley? if he pleases yet,
His moral pleases, not his pointed wit;
Forgot his epic, nay, Pindaric art,
But still I love the language of his heart.

'Yet surely, surely, these were famous men!
What boy but hears the sayings of old Ben?   80
In all debates where critics bear a part,
Not one but nods and talks of Johnson's art,
Of Shakspeare's nature, and of Cowley's wit;
How Beaumont's judgment check'd what Fletcher writ;
How Shadwell hasty, Wycherley was slow;
But, for the passions, Southern sure and Rowe.
These, only these, support the crowded stage,
From eldest Heywood down to Cibber's age.'

All this may be; the people's voice is odd,
It is, and it is not, the voice of God.   90
To Gammer Gurton[147] if it give the bays,
And yet deny the 'Careless Husband' praise,
Or say our fathers never broke a rule;
Why then, I say, the public is a fool.
But let them own, that greater faults than we
They had, and greater virtues, I'll agree.
Spenser himself affects the obsolete,
And Sydney's verse halts ill on Roman feet:
Milton's strong pinion now not Heaven can bound,
Now serpent-like, in prose he sweeps the ground,   100
In quibbles, angel and archangel join,
And God the Father turns a school-divine.
Not that I'd lop the beauties from his book,
Like slashing Bentley with his desperate hook,
Or damn all Shakspeare, like the affected fool
At court, who hates whate'er he read at school.

But for the wits of either Charles's days,
The mob of gentlemen who wrote with ease;
Sprat, Carew, Sedley, and a hundred more,
(Like twinkling stars the Miscellanies o'er)   110
One simile, that solitary shines
In the dry desert of a thousand lines,
Or lengthen'd thought that gleams through many a page,
Has sanctified whole poems for an age.

I lose my patience, and I own it too,
When works are censured, not as bad, but new;
While if our elders break all reason's laws,
These fools demand not pardon, but applause.

On Avon's bank, where flowers eternal blow,
If I but ask, if any weed can grow? 120
One tragic sentence if I dare deride
Which Betterton's grave action dignified,
Or well-mouth'd Booth with emphasis proclaims,
(Though but, perhaps, a muster-roll of names)
How will our fathers rise up in a rage,
And swear, all shame is lost in George's age!
You'd think no fools disgraced the former reign,
Did not some grave examples yet remain,
Who scorn a lad should teach his father skill,
And, having once been wrong, will be so still. 130
He who, to seem more deep than you or I,
Extols old bards, or Merlin's prophecy,
Mistake him not; he envies, not admires,
And to debase the sons, exalts the sires.
Had ancient times conspired to disallow
What then was new, what had been ancient now?
Or what remain'd so worthy to be read
By learned critics of the mighty dead?

In days of ease, when now the weary sword
Was sheathed, and luxury with Charles restored; 140
In every taste of foreign courts improved,
'All, by the king's example,[148] lived and loved.'
Then peers grew proud in horsemanship t' excel,
Newmarket's glory rose, as Britain's fell;
The soldier breathed the gallantries of France,
And every flowery courtier writ romance.
Then marble, soften'd into life, grew warm,
And yielding metal flow'd to human form:
Lely[149] on animated canvas stole
The sleepy eye, that spoke the melting soul. 150
No wonder then, when all was love and sport,
The willing Muses were debauch'd at court:
On each enervate string they taught the note
To pant, or tremble through an eunuch's throat.

But Britain, changeful as a child at play,
Now calls in princes, and now turns away.
Now Whig, now Tory, what we loved we hate;
Now all for pleasure, now for Church and State;
Now for prerogative, and now for laws;
Effects unhappy! from a noble cause. 160

Time was, a sober Englishman would knock
His servants up, and rise by five o'clock,
Instruct his family in every rule,
And send his wife to church, his son to school.
To worship like his fathers, was his care;
To teach their frugal virtues to his heir;
To prove, that luxury could never hold;
And place, on good security, his gold.
Now times are changed, and one poetic itch
Has seized the court and city, poor and rich: 170
Sons, sires, and grandsires, all will wear the bays,
Our wives read Milton, and our daughters plays,
To theatres, and to rehearsals throng,
And all our grace at table is a song.
I, who so oft renounce the Muses, lie,
Not — —'s self e'er tells more fibs than I;
When sick of muse, our follies we deplore,
And promise our best friends to rhyme no more;
We wake next morning in a raging fit,
And call for pen and ink to show our wit. 180

He served a 'prenticeship, who sets up shop;
Ward tried on puppies, and the poor, his drop;
E'en Radcliffe's doctors travel first to France,
Nor dare to practise till they've learn'd to dance.
Who builds a bridge that never drove a pile?
(Should Ripley[150] venture, all the world would smile)
But those who cannot write, and those who can,
All rhyme, and scrawl, and scribble, to a man.

Yet, sir, reflect, the mischief is not great;
These madmen never hurt the Church or State: 190
Sometimes the folly benefits mankind;
And rarely avarice taints the tuneful mind.
Allow him but his plaything of a pen,
He ne'er rebels, or plots, like other men:

Flight of cashiers, or mobs, he'll never mind;
And knows no losses while the Muse is kind.
To cheat a friend, or ward, he leaves to Peter;
The good man heaps up nothing but mere metre,
Enjoys his garden and his book in quiet;
And then—a perfect hermit in his diet.   200

Of little use the man you may suppose,
Who says in verse what others say in prose;
Yet let me show, a poet's of some weight,
And (though no soldier) useful to the State.
What will a child learn sooner than a song?
What better teach a foreigner the tongue?
What's long or short, each accent where to place,
And speak in public with some sort of grace?
I scarce can think him such a worthless thing,
Unless he praise some monster of a king;   210
Or virtue or religion turn to sport,
To please a lewd or unbelieving court
Unhappy Dryden!—in all Charles's days,
Roscommon only boasts unspotted bays;
And in our own (excuse some courtly stains)
No whiter page than Addison remains.
He from the taste obscene reclaims our youth,
And sets the passions on the side of truth,
Forms the soft bosom with the gentlest art,
And pours each human virtue in the heart,   220
Let Ireland tell, how wit upheld her cause,
Her trade supported, and supplied her laws;
And leave on Swift this grateful verse engraved,
'The rights a court attack'd, a poet saved.'
Behold the hand that wrought a nation's cure,
Stretch'd to relieve the idiot and the poor,
Proud vice to brand, or injured worth adorn,
And stretch the ray to ages yet unborn.
Not but there are, who merit other palms;
Hopkins and Sternhold glad the heart with psalms: 230
The boys and girls whom charity maintains,
Implore your help in these pathetic strains:
How could devotion touch the country pews,
Unless the gods bestow'd a proper muse?
Verse cheers their leisure, verse assists their work,
Verse prays for peace, or sings down Pope and Turk.

The silenced preacher yields to potent strain,
And feels that grace his prayer besought in vain;
The blessing thrills through all the labouring throng,
And Heaven is won by violence of song. 240

Our rural ancestors, with little blest,
Patient of labour when the end was rest,
Indulged the day that housed their annual grain,
With feasts, and offerings, and a thankful strain:
The joy their wives, their sons, and servants share,
Ease of their toil, and partners of their care:
The laugh, the jest, attendants on the bowl,
Smooth'd every brow, and open'd every soul:
With growing years the pleasing license grew,
And taunts alternate innocently flew. 250
But times corrupt, and nature, ill-inclined,
Produced the point that left a sting behind;
Till friend with friend, and families at strife,
Triumphant malice raged through private life.
Who felt the wrong, or fear'd it, took the alarm,
Appeal'd to law, and justice lent her arm.
At length, by wholesome dread of statutes bound,
The poets learn'd to please, and not to wound:
Most warp'd to flattery's side; but some, more nice,
Preserved the freedom, and forbore the vice. 260
Hence satire rose, that just the medium hit,
And heals with morals what it hurts with wit.

We conquer'd France, but felt our captive's charms;
Her arts victorious triumph'd o'er our arms;
Britain to soft refinements less a foe,
Wit grew polite, and numbers learn'd to flow.
Waller was smooth; but Dryden taught to join
The varying verse, the full-resounding line,
The long majestic march, and energy divine:
Though still some traces of our rustic vein 270
And splayfoot verse remain'd, and will remain.
Late, very late, correctness grew our care,
When the tired nation breathed from civil war.
Exact Racine, and Corneille's noble fire,
Show'd us that France had something to admire.
Not but the tragic spirit was our own,
And full in Shakspeare, fair in Otway shone:

But Otway fail'd to polish or refine,
And fluent Shakspeare scarce effaced a line.
Even copious Dryden wanted, or forgot,   280
The last and greatest art, the art to blot.
Some doubt, if equal pains, or equal fire
The humbler muse of Comedy require.
But in known images of life, I guess
The labour greater, as the indulgence less.
Observe how seldom even the best succeed:
Tell me if Congreve's fools are fools indeed?
What pert, low dialogue has Farquhar writ!
How Van[151] wants grace, who never wanted wit!
The stage how loosely does Astraea[152] tread,   290
Who fairly puts all characters to bed:
And idle Cibber, how he breaks the laws,
To make poor Pinky eat with vast applause!
But fill their purse, our poets' work is done,
Alike to them, by pathos or by pun.

O you! whom Vanity's light bark conveys
On Fame's mad voyage by the wind of praise,
With what a shifting gale your course you ply,
For ever sunk too low, or borne too high!
Who pants for glory finds but short repose,   300
A breath revives him, or a breath o'erthrows.
Farewell the stage! if just as thrives the play,
The silly bard grows fat, or falls away.

There still remains, to mortify a wit,
The many-headed monster of the pit:
A senseless, worthless, and unhonour'd crowd;
Who, to disturb their betters mighty proud,
Clattering their sticks before ten lines are spoke.
Call for the farce, the bear, or the black-joke.
What dear delight to Britons farce affords!   310
Ever the taste of mobs, but now of lords;
(Taste, that eternal wanderer, which flies
From heads to ears, and now from ears to eyes).
The play stands still; damn action and discourse,
Back fly the scenes, and enter foot and horse;
Pageants on pageants, in long order drawn,
Peers, heralds, bishops, ermine, gold, and lawn;
The champion too; and, to complete the jest,

Old Edward's armour beams on Cibber's breast[153]
With laughter, sure, Democritus had died,   320
Had he beheld an audience gape so wide.
Let bear or elephant be e'er so white,
The people, sure, the people are the sight!
Ah, luckless poet! stretch thy lungs and roar,
That bear or elephant shall heed thee more;
While all its throats the gallery extends,
And all the thunder of the pit ascends!
Loud as the wolves, on Orcas' stormy steep,
Howl to the roarings of the Northern deep.
Such is the shout, the long-applauding note,   330
At Quin's high plume, or Oldfield's petticoat;
Or when from court a birthday suit bestow'd,
Sinks the lost actor in the tawdry load.
Booth enters—hark! the universal peal!
'But has he spoken?' Not a syllable.
What shook the stage, and made the people stare?
Cato's long wig, flower'd gown, and lacquer'd chair.

Yet lest you think I rally more than teach,
Or praise malignly arts I cannot reach,
Let me for once presume to instruct the times,   340
To know the poet from the man of rhymes:
'Tis he, who gives my breast a thousand pains,
Can make me feel each passion that he feigns;
Enrage, compose, with more than magic art,
With pity, and with terror, tear my heart:
And snatch me, o'er the earth, or through the air,
To Thebes, to Athens, when he will, and where.

But not this part of the poetic state
Alone, deserves the favour of the great:
Think of those authors, sir, who would rely   350
More on a reader's sense, than gazer's eye.
Or who shall wander where the Muses sing?
Who climb their mountain, or who taste their spring?
How shall we fill a library with wit,
When Merlin's cave is half unfurnish'd yet?

My liege! why writers little claim your thought,
I guess; and, with their leave, will tell the fault:
We poets are (upon a poet's word)

Of all mankind, the creatures most absurd:
The season, when to come, and when to go, 360
To sing, or cease to sing, we never know;
And if we will recite nine hours in ten,
You lose your patience, just like other men.
Then, too, we hurt ourselves, when to defend
A single verse, we quarrel with a friend;
Repeat unask'd; lament, the wit's too fine
For vulgar eyes, and point out every line.
But most, when straining with too weak a wing,
We needs will write epistles to the king;
And from the moment we oblige the town, 370
Expect a place, or pension from the crown;
Or dubb'd historians by express command,
To enrol your triumphs o'er the seas and land,
Be call'd to court to plan some work divine,
As once for Louis, Boileau and Racine.

Yet think, great sir! (so many virtues shown)
Ah think, what poet best may make them known?
Or choose, at least, some minister of grace,
Fit to bestow the Laureate's weighty place.

Charles, to late times to be transmitted fair, 380
Assign'd his figure to Bernini's[154] care;
And great Nassau to Kneller's hand decreed
To fix him graceful on the bounding steed;
So well in paint and stone they judged of merit:
But kings in wit may want discerning spirit.
The hero William, and the martyr Charles,
One knighted Blackmore, and one pension'd Quarles;
Which made old Ben and surly Dennis swear,
'No Lord's anointed, but a Russian bear.'

Not with such majesty, such bold relief, 390
The forms august of king, or conquering chief.
E'er swell'd on marble, as in verse have shined
(In polish'd verse) the manners and the mind.
Oh! could I mount on the Maeonian wing,
Your arms, your actions, your repose to sing!
What seas you traversed, and what fields you fought!
Your country's peace, how oft, how dearly bought!
How barbarous rage subsided at your word,

And nations wonder'd while they dropp'd the sword!
How, when you nodded, o'er the land and deep,   400
Peace stole her wing, and wrapp'd the world in sleep;
Till earth's extremes your mediation own,
And Asia's tyrants tremble at your throne—
But verse, alas! your Majesty disdains;
And I'm not used to panegyric strains:
The zeal of fools offends at any time,
But most of all, the zeal of fools in rhyme.
Besides, a fate attends on all I write,
That when I aim at praise, they say I bite.
A vile encomium doubly ridicules: 410
There's nothing blackens like the ink of fools.
If true, a woful likeness; and if lies,
'Praise undeserved is scandal in disguise:'
Well may he blush who gives it, or receives;
And when I flatter, let my dirty leaves
(Like journals, odes, and such forgotten things
As Eusden, Philips, Settle, writ of kings)
Clothe spice, line trunks, or fluttering in a row,
Befringe the rails of Bedlam and Soho.

* * * * *

THE SECOND EPISTLE OF THE SECOND BOOK OF HORACE.

'Ludentis speciem dabit, et torquebitur.'

—HOR.

Dear Colonel,[155] Cobham's and your country's friend!
You love a verse, take such as I can send.
A Frenchman comes, presents you with his boy,
Bows and begins—'The lad, sir, is of Blois:[156]
Observe his shape how clean! his locks how curl'd!
My only son;—I'd have him see the world:
His French is pure: his voice, too, you shall hear.
Sir, he's your slave, for twenty pound a-year.
Mere wax as yet, you fashion him with ease,
Your barber, cook, upholsterer, what you please: 10
A perfect genius at an opera song—
To say too much, might do my honour wrong.
Take him with all his virtues, on my word;
His whole ambition was to serve a lord;
But, sir, to you, with what would I not part?
Though, faith! I fear, 'twill break his mother's heart.
Once (and but once) I caught him in a lie,
And then, unwhipp'd, he had the grace to cry;
The fault he has I fairly shall reveal,
(Could you o'erlook but that) it is to steal.'   20

If, after this, you took the graceless lad,
Could you complain, my friend, he proved so bad?
Faith, in such case, if you should prosecute,
I think Sir Godfrey[157] should decide the suit;
Who sent the thief that stole the cash away,
And punish'd him that put it in his way.

Consider then, and judge me in this light;
I told you when I went, I could not write;
You said the same; and are you discontent
With laws, to which you gave your own assent?   30
Nay worse, to ask for verse at such a time!
D' ye think me good for nothing but to rhyme?

In Anna's wars, a soldier, poor and old,
Had dearly earn'd a little purse of gold:
Tired with a tedious march, one luckless night,
He slept, poor dog! and lost it to a doit.
This put the man in such a desperate mind,
Between revenge, and grief, and hunger join'd,
Against the foe, himself, and all mankind,
He leap'd the trenches, scaled a castle-wall,   40
Tore down a standard, took the fort and all.
'Prodigious well!' his great commander cried,
Gave him much praise, and some reward beside.
Next, pleased his excellence a town to batter;
(Its name I know not, and it's no great matter)
'Go on, my friend,' (he cried) 'see yonder walls!
Advance and conquer! go where glory calls!
More honours, more rewards attend the brave.'
Don't you remember what reply he gave?
'D' ye think me, noble general, such a sot?   50
Let him take castles who has ne'er a groat.'

Bred up at home, full early I begun
To read in Greek the wrath of Peleus' son.
Besides, my father taught me from a lad,
The better art to know the good from bad:
(And little sure imported to remove,
To hunt for truth in Maudlin's learned grove.)
But knottier points we knew not half so well,
Deprived us soon of our paternal cell;
And certain laws, by sufferers thought unjust.   60
Denied all posts of profit or of trust:
Hopes after hopes of pious Papists fail'd,
While mighty William's thundering arm prevail'd.
For right hereditary tax'd and fined,
He stuck to poverty with peace of mind;
And me, the Muses help'd to undergo it:
Convict a Papist he, and I a poet.
But (thanks to Homer) since I live and thrive.
Indebted to no prince or peer alive,
Sure I should want the care of ten Monroes,[158]   70
If I would scribble, rather than repose.

Years following years, steal something every day,
At last they steal us from ourselves away;

In one our frolics, one amusements end,
In one a mistress drops, in one a friend:
This subtle thief of life, this paltry time,
What will it leave me, if it snatch my rhyme?
If every wheel of that unwearied mill
That turn'd ten thousand verses, now stands still?

But, after all, what would you have me do?   80
When out of twenty I can please not two;
When this heroics only deigns to praise,
Sharp satire that, and that Pindaric lays?
One likes the pheasant's wing, and one the leg;
The vulgar boil, the learned roast an egg;
Hard task! to hit the palate of such guests,
When Oldfield loves, what Dartineuf[159] detests.

But grant I may relapse, for want of grace,
Again to rhyme; can London be the place?
Who there his Muse, or self, or soul attends,   90
In crowds, and courts, law, business, feasts, and friends?
My counsel sends to execute a deed:
A poet begs me I will hear him read:
In Palace-yard at nine you'll find me there—
At ten for certain, sir, in Bloomsbury Square—
Before the Lords at twelve my cause comes on—
There's a rehearsal, sir, exact at one.—
'Oh, but a wit can study in the streets,
And raise his mind above the mob he meets.'
Not quite so well, however, as one ought;   100
A hackney-coach may chance to spoil a thought:
And then a nodding beam, or pig of lead,
God knows, may hurt the very ablest head.
Have you not seen, at Guildhall's narrow pass,
Two aldermen dispute it with an ass?
And peers give way, exalted as they are,
Even to their own s-r-v—nce in a car?

Go, lofty poet! and in such a crowd,
Sing thy sonorous verse—but not aloud.
Alas! to grottos and to groves we run,   110
To ease and silence, every Muse's son:
Blackmore himself, for any grand effort,
Would drink and doze at Tooting or Earl's Court.[160]

How shall I rhyme in this eternal roar?
How match the bards whom none e'er match'd before?

The man, who, stretch'd in Isis' calm retreat,
To books and study gives seven years complete,
See! strew'd with learned dust, his nightcap on,
He walks, an object new beneath the sun!
The boys flock round him, and the people stare: 120
So stiff, so mute! some statue, you would swear,
Stepp'd from its pedestal to take the air!
And here, while town, and court, and city roars,
With mobs, and duns, and soldiers, at their doors:
Shall I, in London, act this idle part?
Composing songs,[161] for fools to get by heart?

The Temple late two brother sergeants saw,
Who deem'd each other oracles of law;
With equal talents, these congenial souls,
One lull'd th' Exchequer, and one stunn'd the Rolls;   130
Each had a gravity would make you split,
And shook his head at Murray, as a wit.
"Twas, sir, your law'—and 'Sir, your eloquence,'
'Yours, Cowper's manner—and yours, Talbot's sense.'

Thus we dispose of all poetic merit,
Yours Milton's genius, and mine Homer's spirit.
Call Tibbald Shakspeare, and he'll swear the Nine,
Dear Cibber! never match'd one ode of thine.
Lord! how we strut through Merlin's cave, to see
No poets there, but, Stephen,[162] you, and me.   140
Walk with respect behind, while we at ease
Weave laurel crowns, and take what names we please.
'My dear Tibullus!' if that will not do,
'Let me be Horace, and be Ovid you:'
Or 'I'm content, allow me Dryden's strains,
And you shall rise up Otway for your pains.'
Much do I suffer, much, to keep in peace
This jealous, waspish, wrong-head, rhyming race;
And much must flatter, if the whim should bite
To court applause by printing what I write: 150
But let the fit pass o'er, I'm wise enough
To stop my ears to their confounded stuff.

In vain bad rhymers all mankind reject,
They treat themselves with most profound respect;
'Tis to small purpose that you hold your tongue,
Each, praised within, is happy all day long,
But how severely with themselves proceed
The men, who write such verse as we can read?
Their own strict judges, not a word they spare
That wants, or force, or light, or weight, or care,   160
Howe'er unwillingly it quits its place,
Nay though at court (perhaps) it may find grace:
Such they'll degrade; and sometimes, in its stead,
In downright charity revive the dead;
Mark where a bold expressive phrase appears,
Bright through the rubbish of some hundred years;
Command old words, that long have slept, to wake,
Words that wise Bacon or brave Raleigh spake;
Or bid the new be English, ages hence,
(For use will father what's begot by sense)   170
Pour the full tide of eloquence along,
Serenely pure, and yet divinely strong,
Rich with the treasures of each foreign tongue;
Prune the luxuriant, the uncouth refine,
But show no mercy to an empty line:
Then polish all, with so much life and ease,
You think 'tis nature, and a knack to please:
But ease in writing flows from art, not chance;
As those move easiest who have learn'd to dance.

If such the plague and pains to write by rule,   180
Better (say I) be pleased, and play the fool;
Call, if you will, bad rhyming a disease,
It gives men happiness, or leaves them ease.
There lived *in primo Georgii* (they record)
A worthy member, no small fool, a lord;
Who, though the House was up, delighted sat,
Heard, noted, answer'd, as in full debate:
In all but this, a man of sober life,
Fond of his friend, and civil to his wife;
Not quite a madman, though a pasty fell,   190
And much too wise to walk into a well.
Him, the damn'd doctors and his friends immured,
They bled, they cupp'd, they purged; in short, they cured:
Whereat the gentleman began to stare—

'My friends!' he cried, 'pox take you for your care!
That from a patriot of distinguish'd note,
Have bled and purged me to a simple vote.'

Well, on the whole, plain prose must be my fate:
Wisdom (curse on it!) will come soon or late.
There is a time when poets will grow dull: 200
I'll e'en leave verses to the boys at school:
To rules of poetry no more confined,
I learn to smooth and harmonise my mind,
Teach every thought within its bounds to roll,
And keep the equal measure of the soul.

Soon as I enter at my country door,
My mind resumes the thread it dropped before;
Thoughts, which at Hyde-park-corner I forgot,
Meet, and rejoin me, in the pensive grot,
There all alone, and compliments apart,   210
I ask these sober questions of my heart:

If, when the more you drink, the more you crave,
You tell the doctor; when the more you have,
The more you want, why not with equal ease
Confess as well your folly, as disease?
The heart resolves this matter in a trice,
'Men only feel the smart, but not the vice.'

When golden angels cease to cure the evil,
You give all royal witchcraft to the devil:
When servile chaplains[163] cry, that birth and place 220
Indue a peer with honour, truth, and grace,
Look in that breast, most dirty D— —! be fair,
Say, can you find out one such lodger there?
Yet still, not heeding what your heart can teach,
You go to church to hear these flatterers preach.
Indeed, could wealth bestow or wit or merit,
A grain of courage, or a spark of spirit,
The wisest man might blush, I must agree,
If D— — loved sixpence more than he.

If there be truth in law, and use can give   230
A property, that's yours on which you live.
Delightful Abbs Court,[164] if its fields afford

Their fruits to you, confesses you its lord:
All Worldly's hens, nay, partridge, sold to town,
His ven'son, too, a guinea makes your own:
He bought at thousands, what with better wit
You purchase as you want, and bit by bit;
Now, or long since, what difference will be found?
You pay a penny, and he paid a pound.

Heathcote himself, and such large-acred men,   240
Lords of fat Ev'sham, or of Lincoln fen,
Buy every stick of wood that lends them heat,
Buy every pullet they afford to eat.
Yet these are wights who fondly call their own
Half that the devil o'erlooks from Lincoln town.
The laws of God, as well as of the land,
Abhor a perpetuity should stand:
Estates have wings, and hang in fortune's power
Loose on the point of every wavering hour,
Ready, by force, or of your own accord,   250
By sale, at least by death, to change their lord.
Man? and for ever? wretch! what wouldst thou have?
Heir urges heir, like wave impelling wave.
All vast possessions (just the same the case
Whether you call them villa, park, or chase)
Alas, my Bathurst! what will they avail!
Join Cotswood hills to Saperton's fair dale,
Let rising granaries and temples here,
There mingled farms and pyramids appear,
Link towns to towns with avenues of oak,   260
Enclose whole downs in walls,—'tis all a joke!
Inexorable death shall level all,
And trees, and stones, and farms, and farmer fall.

Gold, silver, ivory, vases sculptured high,
Paint, marble, gems, and robes of Persian dye,
There are who have not—and, thank Heaven, there are,
Who, if they have not, think not worth their care.

Talk what you will of taste, my friend, you'll find,
Two of a face, as soon as of a mind.
Why, of two brothers, rich and restless one   270
Ploughs, burns, manures, and toils from sun to sun;
The other slights, for women, sports, and wines,

All Townshend's turnips,[165] and all Grosvenor's mines:
Why one like Bu— —,[166] with pay and scorn content,
Bows and votes on, in court and parliament;
One, driven by strong benevolence of soul,
Shall fly, like Oglethorpe,[167] from pole to pole:
Is known alone to that Directing Power,
Who forms the genius in the natal hour;
That God of Nature, who, within us still,   280
Inclines our action, not constrains our will;
Various of temper, as of face or frame,
Each individual: His great end the same.

Yes, sir, how small soever be my heap,
A part I will enjoy, as well as keep.
My heir may sigh, and think it want of grace
A man so poor would live without a place:
But sure no statute in his favour says,
How free, or frugal, I shall pass my days:
I, who at some times spend, at others spare,   290
Divided between carelessness and care.
'Tis one thing madly to disperse my store:
Another, not to heed to treasure more;
Glad, like a boy, to snatch the first good day,
And pleased, if sordid want be far away.

What is't to me (a passenger, God wot!)
Whether my vessel be first-rate or not?
The ship itself may make a better figure,
But I that sail am neither less nor bigger.
I neither strut with every favouring breath,   300
Nor strive with all the tempest in my teeth.
In power, wit, figure, virtue, fortune, placed
Behind the foremost, and before the last.

'But why all this of avarice? I have none.'
I wish you joy, sir, of a tyrant gone;
But does no other lord it at this hour,
As wild and mad—the avarice of power?
Does neither rage inflame, nor fear appal?
Not the black fear of death, that saddens all?
With terrors round, can reason hold her throne,   310
Despise the known, nor tremble at the unknown?
Survey both worlds, intrepid and entire,

In spite of witches, devils, dreams, and fire?
Pleased to look forward, pleased to look behind,
And count each birthday with a grateful mind?
Has life no sourness, drawn so near its end?
Canst thou endure a foe, forgive a friend?
Has age but melted the rough parts away,
As winter-fruits grow mild ere they decay?
Or will you think, my friend, your business done,   320
When, of a hundred thorns, you pull out one?

Learn to live well, or fairly make your will;
You've play'd, and loved, and eat, and drank your fill:
Walk sober off, before a sprightlier age
Comes tittering on, and shoves you from the stage:
Leave such to trifle with more grace and ease,
Whom folly pleases, and whose follies please.

*   *   *   *   *

BOOK I. EPISTLE VII.

IMITATED IN THE MANNER OF DR SWIFT.

'Tis true, my lord, I gave my word,
I would be with you, June the third;
Changed it to August, and (in short)
Have kept it—as you do at court.
You humour me when I am sick,
Why not when I am splenetic?
In town, what objects could I meet?
The shops shut up in every street,
And funerals blackening all the doors,
And yet more melancholy whores: 10
And what a dust in every place!
And a thin court that wants your face,
And fevers raging up and down,
And W—— and H—— both in town!

'The dog-days are no more the case.'
'Tis true, but winter comes apace:
Then southward let your bard retire,
Hold out some months 'twixt sun and fire,
And you shall see, the first warm weather,
Me and the butterflies together.   20

My lord, your favours well I know;
'Tis with distinction you bestow;
And not to every one that comes,
Just as a Scotchman does his plums.
'Pray, take them, sir,—enough's a feast:
Eat some, and pocket up the rest.'
What! rob your boys? those pretty rogues
'No, sir, you'll leave them to the hogs.'
Thus fools with compliments besiege ye,
Contriving never to oblige ye.   30
Scatter your favours on a fop,
Ingratitude's the certain crop;
And 'tis but just, I'll tell ye wherefore,
You give the things you never care for.
A wise man always is, or should,

Be mighty ready to do good;
But makes a difference in his thought
Betwixt a guinea and a groat.

Now this I'll say, you'll find in me
A safe companion, and a free;   40
But if you'd have me always near—
A word, pray, in your honour's ear.
I hope it is your resolution
To give me back my constitution!
The sprightly wit, the lively eye,
Th' engaging smile, the gaiety,
That laugh'd down many a summer sun,
And kept you up so oft till one:
And all that voluntary vein,
As when Belinda[168] raised my strain.   50

A weasel once made shift to slink
In at a corn-loft through a chink;
But having amply stuff'd his skin,
Could not get out as he got in:
Which one belonging to the house
('Twas not a man, it was a mouse)
Observing, cried, 'You 'scape not so;
Lean as you came, sir, you must go.'

Sir, you may spare your application,
I'm no such beast, nor his relation;   60
Nor one that temperance advance,
Cramm'd to the throat with ortolans:
Extremely ready to resign
All that may make me none of mine.
South-Sea subscriptions take who please,
Leave me but liberty and ease.
'Twas what I said to Craggs and Child,
Who praised my modesty, and smiled.
Give me, I cried, (enough for me)
My bread, and independency!   70
So bought an annual rent or two,
And lived—just as you see I do;
Near fifty, and without a wife,
I trust that sinking fund, my life.
Can I retrench? Yes, mighty well,

Shrink back to my paternal cell,
A little house, with trees a-row,
And, like its master, very low.
There died my father, no man's debtor,
And there I'll die, nor worse, nor better.   80

To set this matter full before ye,
Our old friend Swift will tell his story.

'Harley, the nation's great support'—
But you may read it,—I stop short.

*　　*　　*　　*　　*

BOOK II. SATIRE VI. THE FIRST PART IMITATED IN THE YEAR 1714, BY DR SWIFT; THE LATTER PART ADDED AFTERWARDS.

I've often wish'd that I had clear,
For life, six hundred pounds a-year,
A handsome house to lodge a friend,
A river at my garden's end,
A terrace-walk, and half a rood
Of land, set out to plant a wood.

Well, now I have all this and more,
I ask not to increase my store;
But here a grievance seems to lie,
All this is mine but till I die;   10
I can't but think 'twould sound more clever,
To me and to my heirs for ever.

If I ne'er got or lost a groat,
By any trick, or any fault;
And if I pray by reason's rules,
And not like forty other fools:
As thus, 'Vouchsafe, O gracious Maker!
To grant me this and t' other acre:
Or, if it be thy will and pleasure,
Direct my plough to find a treasure:'   20
But only what my station fits,
And to be kept in my right wits.
Preserve, Almighty Providence!
Just what you gave me, competence:
And let me in these shades compose
Something in verse as true as prose;
Removed from all the ambitious scene,
Nor puff'd by pride, nor sunk by spleen.

In short, I'm perfectly content,
Let me but live on this side Trent;   30
Nor cross the Channel twice a-year,
To spend six months with statesmen here.

I must by all means come to town,
'Tis for the service of the crown.

'Lewis, the Dean will be of use,
Send for him up, take no excuse.'
The toil, the danger of the seas;
Great ministers ne'er think of these;
Or let it cost five hundred pound,
No matter where the money's found,   40
It is but so much more in debt,
And that they ne'er consider'd yet.

'Good Mr Dean, go change your gown,
Let my lord know you're come to town.'
I hurry me in haste away,
Not thinking it is levee-day;
And find his honour in a pound,
Hemm'd by a triple circle round,
Checquer'd with ribbons blue and green:
How should I thrust myself between?   50
Same wag observes me thus perplex'd,
And smiling, whispers to the next,
'I thought the Dean had been too proud,
To jostle here among a crowd.'
Another in a surly fit,
Tells me I have more zeal than wit,
'So eager to express your love,
You ne'er consider whom you shove,
But rudely press before a duke.'
I own, I'm pleased with this rebuke,   60
And take it kindly meant to show
What I desire the world should know.

I get a whisper, and withdraw;
When twenty fools I never saw
Come with petitions fairly penn'd,
Desiring I would stand their friend.

This, humbly offers me his case—
That, begs my interest for a place—
A hundred other men's affairs,
Like bees, are humming in my ears.   70
'To-morrow my appeal comes on,
Without your help the cause is gone'—
The duke expects my lord and you,
About some great affair, at two—

'Put my Lord Bolingbroke in mind,
To get my warrant quickly sign'd:
Consider, 'tis my first request.' —
Be satisfied, I'll do my best:
Then presently he falls to tease,
'You may for certain, if you please; 80
I doubt not, if his lordship knew —
And, Mr Dean, one word from you' —

'Tis (let me see) three years and more,
(October next it will be four)
Since Harley bid me first attend,
And chose me for an humble friend;
Would take me in his coach to chat,
And question me of this and that;
As, 'What's o'clock?' and, 'How's the wind?'
'Who's chariot's that we left behind?' 90
Or gravely try to read the lines
Writ underneath the country signs;
Or, 'Have you nothing new to-day
From Pope, from Parnell, or from Gay?'
Such tattle often entertains
My lord and me as far as Staines,
As once a week we travel down
To Windsor, and again to town,
Where all that passes, *inter nos*,
Might be proclaim'd at Charing Cross. 100

Yet some I know with envy swell,
Because they see me used so well:
'How think you of our friend the dean?
I wonder what some people mean;
My lord and he are grown so great,
Always together, tete-a-tete:
What, they admire him for his jokes —
See but the fortune of some folks!'
There flies about a strange report
Of some express arrived at court; 110
I'm stopp'd by all the fools I meet,
And catechised in every street.
'You, Mr Dean, frequent the great;
Inform us, will the Emperor treat?
Or do the prints and papers lie?'

Faith, sir, you know as much as I.
'Ah, Doctor, how you love to jest!
Tis now no secret'—I protest
'Tis one to me—'Then tell us, pray,
When are the troops to have their pay?'   120
And, though I solemnly declare
I know no more than my Lord Mayor,
They stand amazed, and think me grown
The closest mortal ever known.

Thus in a sea of folly toss'd,
My choicest hours of life are lost;
Yet always wishing to retreat,
Oh, could I see my country-seat!
There, leaning near a gentle brook,
Sleep, or peruse some ancient book,   130
And there in sweet oblivion drown
Those cares that haunt the court and town.
O charming noons! and nights divine!
Or when I sup, or when I dine,
My friends above, my folks below,
Chatting and laughing all a-row;
The beans and bacon set before 'em,
The grace-cup served with all decorum:
Each willing to be pleased, and please,
And even the very dogs at ease!   140
Here no man prates of idle things,
How this or that Italian sings,
A neighbour's madness, or his spouse's,
Or what's in either of the Houses:
But something much more our concern,
And quite a scandal not to learn:
Which is the happier or the wiser,
A man of merit, or a miser?
Whether we ought to choose our friends,
For their own worth, or our own ends?   150
What good, or better, we may call,
And what, the very best of all?

Our friend Dan Prior told (you know)
A tale extremely *a propos*:
Name a town life, and in a trice,
He had a story of two mice.

Once on a time (so runs the fable)
A country mouse, right hospitable,
Received a town mouse at his board,
Just as a farmer might a lord.   160
A frugal mouse upon the whole.
Yet loved his friend, and had a soul,
Knew what was handsome, and would do 't,
On just occasion, coute qui coute,
He brought him bacon (nothing lean);
Pudding, that might have pleased a dean;
Cheese, such as men in Suffolk make,
But wish'd it Stilton, for his sake;
Yet, to his guest though no way sparing,
He eat himself the rind and paring,   170
Our courtier scarce could touch a bit,
But show'd his breeding and his wit;
He did his best to seem to eat,
And cried, 'I vow you're mighty neat.
But, lord! my friend, this savage scene!
For God's sake, come, and live with men:
Consider, mice, like men, must die,
Both small and great, both you and I:
Then spend your life in joy and sport,
(This doctrine, friend, I learn'd at court).'   180

The veriest hermit in the nation
May yield, God knows, to strong temptation.
Away they come, through thick and thin,
To a tall house near Lincoln's Inn;
('Twas on the night of a debate,
When all their lordships had sat late.)

Behold the place where, if a poet
Shined in description, he might show it;
Tell how the moonbeam trembling falls,
And tips with silver[169] all the walls;   190
Palladian walls, Venetian doors,
Grotesco roofs, and stucco floors:
But let it (in a word) be said,
The moon was up, and men a-bed,
The napkins white, the carpet red:
The guests withdrawn had left the treat,
And down the mice sat, *tete-a-tete*.

Our courtier walks from dish to dish,
Tastes for his friend of fowl and fish;
Tells all their names, lays down the law,   200
'*Que ca est bon! Ah goutez ca!*
That jelly's rich, this malmsey healing,
Pray, dip your whiskers and your tail in.'
Was ever such a happy swain?
He stuffs and swills, and stuffs again.
'I'm quite ashamed—'tis mighty rude
To eat so much—but all's so good.
I have a thousand thanks to give—
My lord alone knows how to live.'
No sooner said, but from the hall   210
Rush chaplain, butler, dogs, and all:
'A rat! a rat! clap to the door'—
The cat comes bouncing on the floor.
O for the heart of Homer's mice,
Or gods to save them in a trice!
(It was by Providence they think,
For your damn'd stucco has no chink.)
'An't please your honour, quoth the peasant,
This same dessert is not so pleasant:
Give me again my hollow tree,   220
A crust of bread, and liberty!'

*   *   *   *   *

BOOK IV. ODE I. TO VENUS.

Again? new tumults in my breast?
  Ah, spare me, Venus! let me, let me rest!
I am not now, alas! the man
  As in the gentle reign of my Queen Anne.
Ah, sound no more thy soft alarms,
  Nor circle sober fifty with thy charms.
Mother too fierce of dear desires!
  Turn, turn to willing hearts your wanton fires,
To Number Five direct your doves,
  There spread round Murray all your blooming loves   10
Noble and young, who strikes the heart
  With every sprightly, every decent part;
Equal, the injured to defend,
  To charm the mistress, or to fix the friend.
He, with a hundred arts refined,
  Shall stretch thy conquests over half the kind;
To him each rival shall submit,
  Make but his riches equal to his wit.
Then shall thy form the marble grace,
  (Thy Grecian form) and Chloe lend the face: 20
His house, embosom'd in the grove,
  Sacred to social life and social love,
Shall glitter o'er the pendant green,
  Where Thames reflects the visionary scene:
Thither, the silver-sounding lyres
  Shall call the smiling Loves, and young Desires;
There, every Grace and Muse shall throng,
  Exalt the dance, or animate the song;
There, youths and nymphs, in consort gay,
  Shall hail the rising, close the parting day.   30
With me, alas! those joys are o'er;
  For me, the vernal garlands bloom no more.
Adieu![170] fond hope of mutual fire,
  The still believing, still-renew'd desire;
Adieu! the heart-expanding bowl,
  And all the kind deceivers of the soul!
But why? ah, tell me, ah, too dear!
  Steals down my cheek th' involuntary tear?
Why words so flowing, thoughts so free,

Stop, or turn nonsense, at one glance of thee?   40
Thee, dress'd in fancy's airy beam,
  Absent I follow through th' extended dream;
Now, now I seize, I clasp thy charms,
  And now you burst (ah, cruel!) from my arms;
And swiftly shoot along the Mall,
  Or softly glide by the canal,
Now shown by Cynthia's silver ray,
  And now on rolling waters snatch'd away.

*   *   *   *   *

PART OF THE NINTH ODE OF THE FOURTH BOOK.

1 Lest you should think that verse shall die,
    Which sounds the silver Thames along,
  Taught, on the wings of truth to fly
    Above the reach of vulgar song;

2 Though daring Milton sits sublime,
    In Spenser, native Muses play;
  Nor yet shall Waller yield to time,
    Nor pensive Cowley's moral lay.

3 Sages and chiefs long since had birth
    Ere Caesar was, or Newton named;
  These raised new empires o'er the earth,
    And those, new heavens and systems framed.

4 Vain was the chief's, the sage's pride!
    They had no poet, and they died.
  In vain they schemed, in vain they bled!
    They had no poet, and are dead.

THE SATIRES OF DR JOHN DONNE, DEAN OF ST PAUL'S,[171] VERSIFIED.

'Quid vetat et nosmet Lucili scripta legentes Quaerere, num illius, num rerum dura negarit Versiculos natura magis factos, et euntes Mollius?'

HOR.

SATIRE II.

Yes; thank my stars! as early as I knew
This town, I had the sense to hate it too:
Yet here, as ev'n in Hell, there must be still
One giant-vice, so excellently ill,
That all beside, one pities, not abhors;
As who knows Sappho, smiles at other whores.

I grant that poetry's a crying sin;
It brought (no doubt) the Excise and Army in:
Catch'd like the plague, or love, the Lord knows how,
But that the cure is starving, all allow.   10
Yet like the papist's is the poet's state,
Poor and disarm'd, and hardly worth your hate!

Here a lean bard, whose wit could never give
Himself a dinner, makes an actor live;
The thief condemn'd, in law already dead,
So prompts, and saves a rogue who cannot read.
Thus as the pipes of some carved organ move,
The gilded puppets dance and mount above.
Heaved by the breath the inspiring bellows blow:
The inspiring bellows lie and pant below.   20

One sings the fair; but songs no longer move;
No rat is rhymed to death, nor maid to love:
In love's, in nature's spite, the siege they hold,
And scorn the flesh, the devil, and all—but gold.
These write to lords, some mean reward to get,
As needy beggars sing at doors for meat.
Those write because all write, and so have still
Excuse for writing, and for writing ill.

Wretched indeed! but far more wretched yet
Is he who makes his meal on others' wit: 30
'Tis changed, no doubt, from what it was before,
His rank digestion makes it wit no more:
Sense, pass'd through him, no longer is the same;
For food digested takes another name.

I pass o'er all those confessors and martyrs,
Who live like Sutton, or who die like Chartres,
Out-cant old Esdras, or out-drink his heir,
Out-usure Jews, or Irishmen out-swear;
Wicked as pages, who in early years
Act sins which Prisca's confessor scarce hears. 40
Ev'n those I pardon, for whose sinful sake
Schoolmen new tenements in hell must make;
Of whose strange crimes no canonist can tell
In what commandment's large contents they dwell.

One, one man only breeds my just offence;
Whom crimes gave wealth, and wealth gave impudence:
Time, that at last matures a clap to pox,
Whose gentle progress makes a calf an ox,
And brings all natural events to pass,
Hath made him an attorney of an ass. 50
No young divine, new-beneficed, can be
More pert, more proud, more positive than he.
What further could I wish the fop to do,
But turn a wit, and scribble verses too;
Pierce the soft labyrinth of a lady's ear
With rhymes of this per cent, and that per year?
Or court a wife, spread out his wily parts,
Like nets or lime-twigs, for rich widows' hearts:
Call himself barrister to every wench,
And woo in language of the Pleas and Bench? 60
Language, which Boreas might to Auster hold
More rough than forty Germans when they scold.

Cursed be the wretch, so venal and so vain:
Paltry and proud, as drabs in Drury-lane.
'Tis such a bounty as was never known,
If Peter deigns to help you to your own:
What thanks, what praise, if Peter but supplies,
And what a solemn face, if he denies!

Grave, as when prisoners shake the head and swear
'Twas only suretiship that brought 'em there.   70
His office keeps your parchment fates entire,
He starves with cold to save them from the fire;
For you he walks the streets through rain or dust,
For not in chariots Peter puts his trust;
For you he sweats and labours at the laws,
Takes God to witness he affects your cause,
And lies to every lord in every thing,
Like a king's favourite, or like a king.
These are the talents that adorn them all,
From wicked Waters ev'n to godly Paul.[172]
Not more of simony beneath black gowns,   80
Not more of bastardy in heirs to crowns.
In shillings and in pence at first they deal;
And steal so little, few perceive they steal;
Till, like the sea, they compass all the land,
From Scots to Wight, from Mount to Dover strand:
And when rank widows purchase luscious nights,
Or when a duke to Jansen punts at White's,
Or city-heir in mortgage melts away;
Satan himself feels far less joy than they.
Piecemeal they win this acre first, then that,   90
Glean on, and gather up the whole estate.
Then strongly fencing ill-got wealth by law,
Indentures, covenants, articles they draw,
Large as the fields themselves, and larger far
Than civil codes, with all their glosses, are;
So vast, our new divines, we must confess,
Are fathers of the Church for writing less.
But let them write for you, each rogue impairs
The deeds, and dext'rously omits, *ses heires*:
No commentator can more slily pass   100
O'er a learn'd, unintelligible place;
Or, in quotation, shrewd divines leave out
Those words, that would against them clear the doubt.

So Luther thought the Pater-noster long,
When doom'd to say his beads and even-song;
But having cast his cowl, and left those laws,
Adds to Christ's prayer, the Power and Glory clause.

The lands are bought; but where are to be found

Those ancient woods, that shaded all the ground?
We see no new-built palaces aspire,   110
No kitchens emulate the vestal fire.
Where are those troops of poor, that throng'd of yore
The good old landlord's hospitable door?
Well, I could wish, that still in lordly domes
Some beasts were kill'd, though not whole hecatombs;
That both extremes were banish'd from their walls,
Carthusian fasts, and fulsome Bacchanals;
And all mankind might that just mean observe,
In which none e'er could surfeit, none could starve.
These as good works, 'tis true, we all allow;   120
But oh! these works are not in fashion now:
Like rich old wardrobes, things extremely rare,
Extremely fine, but what no man will wear.

Thus much I've said, I trust, without offence;
Let no court sycophant pervert my sense,
Nor sly informer watch these words to draw
Within the reach of treason, or the law.

    *   *   *   *   *

SATIRE IV.

Well, if it be my time to quit the stage,
Adieu to all the follies of the age!
I die in charity with fool and knave,
Secure of peace at least beyond the grave.
I've had my purgatory here betimes,
And paid for all my satires, all my rhymes.
The poet's hell, its tortures, fiends, and flames.
To this were trifles, toys, and empty names.

With foolish pride my heart was never fired,
Nor the vain itch t' admire, or be admired;   10
I hoped for no commission from his Grace;
I bought no benefice, I begg'd no place;
Had no new verses, nor new suit to show;
Yet went to court!—the devil would have it so.
But, as the fool that, in reforming days,
Would go to mass in jest (as story says)
Could not but think, to pay his fine was odd,
Since 'twas no form'd design of serving God;
So was I punish'd, as if full as proud,
As prone to ill, as negligent of good.   20
As deep in debt, without a thought to pay,
As vain, as idle, and as false as they
Who live at court, for going once that way!
Scarce was I enter'd, when, behold! there came
A thing which Adam had been posed to name;
Noah had refused it lodging in his ark,
Where all the race of reptiles might embark:
A verier monster than on Afric's shore
The sun e'er got, or slimy Nilus bore,
Or Sloane or Woodward's wondrous shelves contain,   30
Nay, all that lying travellers can feign.
The watch would hardly let him pass at noon,
At night, would swear him dropp'd out of the moon.
One whom the mob, when next we find or make
A Popish plot, shall for a Jesuit take,
And the wise justice, starting from his chair,
Cry, By your priesthood, tell me what you are?

Such was the wight; the apparel on his back,
Though coarse, was reverend, and though bare, was black:
The suit, if by the fashion one might guess,   40
Was velvet in the youth of good Queen Bess,
But mere tuff-taffety what now remain'd;
So time, that changes all things, had ordain'd!
Our sons shall see it leisurely decay,
First turn plain rash, then vanish quite away.

This thing has travell'd, speaks each language too,
And knows what's fit for every State to do;
Of whose best phrase and courtly accent join'd,
He forms one tongue, exotic and refined
Talkers I've learn'd to bear; Motteux I knew,   50
Henley himself I've heard, and Budgell too.
The Doctor's wormwood style, the hash of tongues
A pedant makes, the storm of Gonson's lungs,
The whole artillery of the terms of war,
And (all those plagues in one) the bawling Bar:
These I could bear; but not a rogue so civil,
Whose tongue will compliment you to the devil;
A tongue, that can cheat widows, cancel scores,
Make Scots speak treason, cozen subtlest whores,
With royal favourites in flattery vie,   60
And Oldmixon and Burnet both outlie.

He spies me out; I whisper, Gracious God!
What sin of mine could merit such a rod?
That all the shot of dulness now must be
From this thy blunderbuss discharged on me!
Permit (he cries) no stranger to your fame
To crave your sentiment, if — —'s your name.
What speech esteem you most? 'The King's,' said I.
But the best words?—'Oh, sir, the Dictionary.'
You miss my aim; I mean the most acute   70
And perfect speaker?—'Onslow, past dispute.'
But, sir, of writers? 'Swift, for closer style;
But Hoadley,[173] for a period of a mile.'
Why, yes, 'tis granted, these indeed may pass:
Good common linguists, and so Panurge was;
Nay, troth, the Apostles (though perhaps too rough)
Had once a pretty gift of tongues enough:
Yet these were all poor gentlemen! I dare

Affirm, 'twas travel made them what they were.

Thus others' talents having nicely shown,   80
He came by sure transition to his own:
Till I cried out, You prove yourself so able,
Pity you was not druggerman at Babel;
For had they found a linguist half so good,
I make no question but the tower had stood.
'Obliging sir! for courts you sure were made:
Why then for ever buried in the shade?
Spirits like you should see, and should be seen,
The king would smile on you—at least the queen.'
Ah, gentle sir! you courtiers so cajole us—   90
But Tully has it, *Nunquam minus solus*:
And as for courts, forgive me, if I say
No lessons now are taught the Spartan way:
Though in his pictures lust be full display'd,
Few are the converts Aretine has made;
And though the court show vice exceeding clear,
None should, by my advice, learn virtue there.

At this, entranced, he lifts his hands and eyes,
Squeaks like a high-stretch'd lutestring, and replies:
'Oh, 'tis the sweetest of all earthly things   100
To gaze on princes, and to talk of kings!'
Then, happy man who shows the tombs! said I,
He dwells amidst the royal family;
He every day, from king to king can walk,
Of all our Harries, all our Edwards talk,
And get by speaking truth of monarchs dead,
What few can of the living-ease and bread.
'Lord, sir, a mere mechanic! strangely low,
And coarse of phrase,—your English all are so.
How elegant your Frenchmen!' Mine, d'ye mean?   110
I have but one, I hope the fellow's clean.
'Oh! sir, politely so! nay, let me die:
Your only wearing is your paduasoy.'
Not, sir, my only, I have better still,
And this, you see, is but my dishabille.
Wild to get loose, his patience I provoke,
Mistake, confound, object at all he spoke.
But as coarse iron, sharpen'd, mangles more,
And itch most hurts when anger'd to a sore;

So when you plague a fool, 'tis still the curse,   120
You only make the matter worse and worse.

He pass'd it o'er; affects an easy smile
At all my peevishness, and turns his style.
He asks, 'What news?' I tell him of new plays,
New eunuchs, harlequins, and operas.
He hears, and as a still with simples in it
Between each drop it gives, stays half a minute,
Loth to enrich me with too quick replies,
By little, and by little, drops his lies.
Mere household trash! of birthnights, balls, and shows,   130
More than ten Hollinsheds, or Halls, or Stowes.
When the queen frown'd, or smiled, he knows; and what
A subtle minister may make of that:
Who sins with whom: who got his pension rug,
Or quicken'd a reversion by a drug:
Whose place is quarter'd out, three parts in four,
And whether to a bishop, or a whore:
Who, having lost his credit, pawn'd his rent,
Is therefore fit to have a government:
Who, in the secret, deals in stocks secure,   140
And cheats the unknowing widow and the poor:
Who makes a trust or charity a job,
And gets an act of parliament to rob:
Why turnpikes rise, and now no cit nor clown
Can gratis see the country, or the town:
Shortly no lad shall chuck, or lady vole,
But some excising courtier will have toll.
He tells what strumpet places sells for life,
What 'squire his lands, what citizen his wife:
And last (which proves him wiser still than all)   150
What lady's face is not a whited wall.

As one of Woodward's patients, sick, and sore,
I puke, I nauseate,—yet he thrusts in more:
Trim's Europe's balance, tops the statesman's part.
And talks Gazettes and Postboys o'er by heart.
Like a big wife at sight of loathsome meat
Ready to cast, I yawn, I sigh, and sweat.
Then as a licensed spy, whom nothing can
Silence or hurt, he libels the great man;
Swears every place entail'd for years to come,   160

In sure succession to the day of doom:
He names the price for every office paid,
And says our wars thrive ill, because delay'd:
Nay, hints 'tis by connivance of the court
That Spain robs on, and Dunkirk's still a port.
Not more amazement seized on Circe's guests,
To see themselves fall endlong into beasts,
Than mine, to find a subject, staid and wise,
Already half turn'd traitor by surprise.
I felt the infection slide from him to me,   170
As in the pox, some give it to get free;
And quick to swallow me, methought I saw
One of our giant statues ope its jaw.

In that nice moment, as another lie
Stood just a-tilt, the minister came by.
To him he flies, and bows, and bows again,
Then, close as Umbra, joins the dirty train.
Not Fannius' self more impudently near,
When half his nose is in his prince's ear.
I quaked at heart; and still afraid, to see   180
All the court fill'd with stranger things than he,
Ran out as fast, as one that pays his bail,
And dreads more actions, hurries from a jail.

Bear me, some god! oh quickly bear me hence
To wholesome solitude, the nurse of sense,
Where Contemplation prunes her ruffled wings,
And the free soul looks down to pity kings!
There sober thought pursued the amusing theme,
Till fancy colour'd it, and form'd a dream.
A vision hermits can to Hell transport,   190
And forced ev'n me to see the damn'd at court.
Not Dante, dreaming all the infernal state,
Beheld such scenes of envy, sin, and hate.
Base fear becomes the guilty, not the free;
Suits tyrants, plunderers, but suits not me:
Shall I, the terror of this sinful town,
Care if a liveried lord or smile or frown?
Who cannot flatter, and detest who can,
Tremble before a noble serving-man?
O my fair mistress, Truth! shall I quit thee   200
For huffing, braggart, puff'd nobility?

Thou, who since yesterday hast roll'd o'er all
The busy, idle blockheads of the ball,
Hast thou, O Sun! beheld an emptier sort,
Than such as swell this bladder of a court?
Now pox on those who show a court in wax!
It ought to bring all courtiers on their backs:
Such painted puppets! such a varnish'd race
Of hollow gewgaws, only dress and face!
Such waxen noses, stately staring things—   210
No wonder some folks bow, and think them kings.

See! where the British youth, engaged no more
At Fig's,[174] at White's, with felons, or a whore,
Pay their last duty to the court, and come
All fresh and fragrant, to the drawing-room;
In hues as gay, and odours as divine,
As the fair fields they sold to look so fine.
'That's velvet for a king!' the flatterer swears;
'Tis true, for ten days hence 'twill be King Lear's.
Our court may justly to our stage give rules,   220
That helps it both to fools' coats and to fools.
And why not players strut in courtiers' clothes?
For these are actors too, as well as those:
Wants reach all states; they beg, but better dress'd,
And all is splendid poverty at best.

Painted for sight, and essenced for the smell,
Like frigates fraught with spice and cochineal,
Sail in the ladies: how each pirate eyes
So weak a vessel, and so rich a prize!
Top-gallant he, and she in all her trim,   230
He boarding her, she striking sail to him:
'Dear Countess! you have charms all hearts to hit!'
And, 'Sweet Sir Fopling! you have so much wit!'
Such wits and beauties are not praised for nought,
For both the beauty and the wit are bought.
'Twould burst ev'n Heraclitus with the spleen,
To see those antics, Fopling and Courtin:
The Presence seems, with things so richly odd,
The mosque of Mahound, or some queer pagod.
See them survey their limbs by Durer's rules,   240
Of all beau-kind the best proportion'd fools!
Adjust their clothes, and to confession draw

Those venial sins, an atom, or a straw;
But oh! what terrors must distract the soul
Convicted of that mortal crime, a hole;
Or should one pound of powder less bespread
Those monkey tails that wag behind their head.
Thus finish'd, and corrected to a hair,
They march, to prate their hour before the fair.
So first to preach a white-gloved chaplain goes,   250
With band of lily, and with cheek of rose,
Sweeter than Sharon, in immaculate trim,
Neatness itself impertinent in him,
Let but the ladies smile, and they are blest:
Prodigious! how the things protest, protest:
Peace, fools! or Gonson will for Papists seize you,
If once he catch you at your Jesu! Jesu!

Nature made every fop to plague his brother,
Just as one beauty mortifies another.
But here's the captain that will plague them both,   260
Whose air cries, Arm! whose very look's an oath:
The captain's honest, sirs, and that's enough,
Though his soul's bullet, and his body buff.
He spits fore-right; his haughty chest before,
Like battering rams, beats open every door:
And with a face as red, and as awry,
As Herod's hangdogs in old tapestry,
Scarecrow to boys, the breeding woman's curse,
Has yet a strange ambition to look worse;
Confounds the civil, keeps the rude in awe,
Jests like a licensed fool, commands like law.   270

Frighted, I quit the room, but leave it so
As men from jails to execution go;
For hung with deadly sins[175] I see the wall,
And lined with giants deadlier than 'em all:
Each man an Ascapart,[176] of strength to toss
For quoits, both Temple-bar and Charing-cross.
Scared at the grisly forms, I sweat, I fly,
And shake all o'er, like a discover'd spy.

Courts are too much for wits so weak as mine:
Charge them with Heaven's artillery, bold divine!   280
From such alone the great rebukes endure,

Whose satire's sacred, and whose rage secure:
'Tis mine to wash a few light stains, but theirs
To deluge sin, and drown a court in tears.
Howe'er, what's now Apocrypha, my wit,
In time to come, may pass for holy writ.

* * * * *

EPILOGUE[177] TO THE SATIRES.

IN TWO DIALOGUES.

(WRITTEN IN MDCCXXXVIII.)

DIALOGUE I.

Fr. Not twice a twelvemonth you appear in print,
And when it comes, the court see nothing in 't.
You grow correct, that once with rapture writ,
And are, besides, too moral for a wit.
Decay of parts, alas! we all must feel—
Why now, this moment, don't I see you steal?
'Tis all from Horace; Horace long before ye
Said, 'Tories call'd him Whig, and Whigs a Tory;'
And taught his Romans, in much better metre,
'To laugh at fools who put their trust in Peter.'   10

But, Horace, sir, was delicate, was nice;
Bubo[178] observes, he lash'd no sort of vice:
Horace would say, Sir Billy[179] served the crown,
Blunt could do business, Huggins[180] knew the town;
In Sappho touch the failings of the sex,
In reverend bishops note some small neglects,
And own, the Spaniard did a waggish thing,
Who cropp'd our ears,[181] and sent them to the king.
His sly, polite, insinuating style
Could please at court, and make Augustus smile: 20
An artful manager, that crept between
His friend and shame, and was a kind of screen.
But, faith, your very friends will soon be sore;
Patriots there are, who wish you'd jest no more—
And where's the glory? 'twill be only thought
The great man[182] never offer'd you a groat.
Go see Sir Robert—

P.   See Sir Robert!—hum—
And never laugh—for all my life to come?
Seen him I have,[183] but in his happier hour
Of social pleasure, ill-exchanged for power;   30

Seen him, uncumber'd with the venal tribe,
Smile without art, and win without a bribe.
Would he oblige me? let me only find,
He does not think me what he thinks mankind.
Come, come, at all I laugh he laughs, no doubt;
The only difference is, I dare laugh out.

F. Why, yes: with Scripture still you may be free;
A horse-laugh, if you please, at honesty;
A joke on Jekyl,[184] or some odd old Whig
Who never changed his principle, or wig: 40
A patriot is a fool in every age,
Whom all Lord Chamberlains allow the stage:
These nothing hurts; they keep their fashion still,
And wear their strange old virtue, as they will.

If any ask you, 'Who's the man, so near
His prince, that writes in verse, and has his ear?'
Why, answer, Lyttleton,[185] and I'll engage
The worthy youth shall ne'er be in a rage:
But were his verses vile, his whisper base,
You'd quickly find him in Lord Fanny's case.   50
Sejanus, Wolsey,[186] hurt not honest Fleury,[187]
But well may put some statesmen in a fury.

Laugh then at any, but at fools or foes;
These you but anger, and you mend not those.
Laugh at your friends, and, if your friends are sore,
So much the better, you may laugh the more.
To vice and folly to confine the jest,
Sets half the world, God knows, against the rest;
Did not the sneer of more impartial men
At sense and virtue, balance all again.   60
Judicious wits spread wide the ridicule,
And charitably comfort knave and fool.

P. Dear sir, forgive the prejudice of youth:
Adieu distinction, satire, warmth, and truth!
Come, harmless characters that no one hit;
Come, Henley's oratory, Osborn's[188] wit!
The honey dropping from Favonio's tongue,
The flowers of Bubo, and the flow of Yonge!
The gracious dew of pulpit eloquence,

And all the well-whipt cream of courtly sense,   70
That first was Hervy's, Fox's next, and then
The senate's, and then Hervy's once again.
Oh come, that easy, Ciceronian style,
So Latin, yet so English all the while,
As, though the pride of Middleton and Bland,
All boys may read, and girls may understand!
Then might I sing, without the least offence,
And all I sung should be the nation's sense;[189]
Or teach the melancholy Muse to mourn,
Hang the sad verse on Carolina's[190] urn,   80
And hail her passage to the realms of rest,
All parts perform'd, and all her children bless'd!
So—satire is no more—I feel it die—
No gazetteer[191] more innocent than I—
And let, a-God's-name! every fool and knave
Be graced through life, and flatter'd in his grave.

F. Why so? if satire knows its time and place,
You still may lash the greatest—in disgrace:
For merit will by turns forsake them all;
Would you know when exactly when they fall.   90
But let all satire in all changes spare
Immortal Selkirk,[192] and grave Delaware.[193]
Silent and soft, as saints remove to heaven,
All ties dissolved, and every sin forgiven,
These may some gentle ministerial wing
Receive, and place for ever near a king!
There, where no passion, pride, or shame transport,
Lull'd with the sweet nepenthe of a court;
There, where no father's, brother's, friend's disgrace
Once break their rest, or stir them from their place: 100
But past the sense of human miseries,
All tears are wiped for ever from all eyes;
No cheek is known to blush, no heart to throb,
Save when they lose a question, or a job.

P. Good Heaven forbid that I should blast their glory,
Who know how like Whig ministers to Tory,
And when three sovereigns died, could scarce be vex'd,
Considering what a gracious prince was next.
Have I, in silent wonder, seen such things
As pride in slaves, and avarice in kings;   110

And at a peer, or peeress, shall I fret,
Who starves a sister,[194] or forswears a debt?
Virtue, I grant you, is an empty boast;
But shall the dignity of vice be lost?
Ye gods! shall Cibber's son,[195] without rebuke,
Swear like a lord, or Rich[195] out-whore a duke?
A favourite's porter with his master vie,
Be bribed as often, and as often lie?
Shall Ward draw contracts with a statesman's skill?
Or Japhet pocket, like his Grace, a will?   120
Is it for Bond, or Peter, (paltry things)
To pay their debts, or keep their faith, like kings?
If Blount[196] dispatch'd himself, he play'd the man,
And so may'st thou, illustrious Passeran![197]
But shall a printer,[198] weary of his life,
Learn from their books to hang himself and wife?
This, this, my friend, I cannot, must not bear:
Vice thus abused, demands a nation's care:
This calls the Church to deprecate our sin,
And hurls the thunder of the laws on gin,[199]   130
Let modest Foster, if he will, excel
Ten metropolitans in preaching well;
A simple Quaker, or a Quaker's wife,[200]
Outdo Landaff[201] in doctrine,—yea, in life:
Let humble Allen,[202] with an awkward shame,
Do good by stealth, and blush to find it fame.
Virtue may choose the high or low degree,
'Tis just alike to virtue, and to me;
Dwell in a monk, or light upon a king,
She's still the same beloved, contented thing.   140
Vice is undone, if she forgets her birth,
And stoops from angels to the dregs of earth:
But 'tis the fall degrades her to a whore;
Let greatness own her, and she's mean no more:
Her birth, her beauty, crowds and courts confess,
Chaste matrons praise her, and grave bishops bless:
In golden chains the willing world she draws,
And hers the gospel is, and hers the laws,
Mounts the tribunal, lifts her scarlet head,
And sees pale virtue carted in her stead.   150
Lo! at the wheels of her triumphal car,
Old England's genius, rough with many a scar,
Dragg'd in the dust! his arms hang idly round,

His flag inverted trails along the ground!
Our youth, all liveried o'er with foreign gold,
Before her dance: behind her, crawl the old!
See thronging millions to the pagod run,
And offer country, parent, wife, or son!
Hear her black trumpet through the land proclaim,
That NOT TO BE CORRUPTED IS THE SHAME! 160
In soldier, churchman, patriot, man in power,
'Tis avarice all, ambition is no more!
See, all our nobles begging to be slaves!
See, all our fools aspiring to be knaves!
The wit of cheats, the courage of a whore,
Are what ten thousand envy and adore!
All, all look up with reverential awe,
At crimes that 'scape, or triumph o'er the law:
While truth, worth, wisdom, daily they decry—
'Nothing is sacred now but villany.' 170

Yet may this verse (if such a verse remain)
Show, there was one who held it in disdain.

* * * * *

VARIATIONS.

After VER. 2 in the MS.—

You don't, I hope, pretend to quit the trade,
Because you think your reputation made:
Like good Sir Paul, of whom so much was said,
That when his name was up, he lay a-bed.
Come, come, refresh us with a livelier song,
Or, like Sir Paul, you'll lie a-bed too long.

P. Sir, what I write, should be correctly writ.

F. Correct! 'tis what no genius can admit.
Besides, you grow too moral for a wit.

VER. 112 in some editions—'Who starves a mother.'

DIALOGUE II.

Fr. 'Tis all a libel—Paxton[203] (sir) will say.

P. Not yet, my friend! to-morrow, faith, it may;
And for that very cause I print to-day.
How should I fret to mangle every line,
In reverence to the sins of thirty-nine!
Vice with such giant strides comes on amain,
Invention strives to be before in vain;
Feign what I will, and paint it e'er so strong,
Some rising genius sins up to my song.

F. Yet none but you by name the guilty lash;   10
Ev'n Guthrie[204] saves half Newgate by a dash.
Spare then the person, and expose the vice.

P. How, sir! not damn the sharper, but the dice?
Come on then, Satire! general, unconfined,
Spread thy broad wing, and souse on all the kind.
Ye statesmen, priests, of one religion all!
Ye tradesmen, vile, in army, court, or hall!
Ye reverend atheists——

F.   Scandal! name them, who?

P. Why that's the thing you bid me not to do.
Who starved a sister, who forswore a debt,   20
I never named; the town's inquiring yet.
The poisoning dame——

F.   You mean——

P.   I don't.

F.   You do.

P. See, now I keep the secret, and not you!
The bribing statesman——

F.   Hold, too high you go.

P. The bribed elector— —

F.   There you stoop too low.

P. I fain would please you, if I knew with what;
Tell me, which knave is lawful game, which not?
Must great offenders, once escaped the crown,
Like royal harts, be never more run down?
Admit, your law to spare the knight requires,   30
As beasts of nature may we hunt the 'squires?
Suppose I censure—you know what I mean—
To save a bishop, may I name a dean?

F. A dean, sir? no: his fortune is not made,
You hurt a man that's rising in the trade.

P. If not the tradesman who set up to-day,
Much less the 'prentice who to-morrow may.
Down, down, proud Satire! though a realm be spoil'd,
Arraign no mightier thief than wretched Wild;[205]
Or, if a court or country's made a job,   40
Go drench a pickpocket, and join the mob.

But, sir, I beg you (for the love of vice!)
The matter's weighty, pray consider twice;
Have you less pity for the needy cheat,
The poor and friendless villain, than the great?
Alas! the small discredit of a bribe
Scarce hurts the lawyer, but undoes the scribe.
Then better, sure, it charity becomes
To tax directors, who (thank God) have plums;
Still better, ministers; or, if the thing   50
May pinch ev'n there—why lay it on a king.

F. Stop! stop!

P.   Must Satire; then, nor rise nor fall?
Speak out, and bid me blame no rogues at all.

F. Yes, strike that Wild, I'll justify the blow.

P. Strike! why the man was hanged ten years ago:
Who now that obsolete example fears?

Ev'n Peter trembles only for his ears.

F. What, always Peter! Peter thinks you mad,
You make men desperate if they once are bad:
Else might he take to virtue some years hence   60

P. As Selkirk, if he lives, will love the Prince.

F. Strange spleen to Selkirk!

P.   Do I wrong the man?
God knows, I praise a courtier where I can.
When I confess, there is who feels for fame,
And melts to goodness,[206] need I Scarb'rough[207] name?
Pleased, let me own, in Esher's peaceful grove[208]
(Where Kent and nature vie for Pelham's love)
The scene, the master, opening to my view,
I sit and dream I see my Craggs anew!
Ev'n in a bishop I can spy desert;   70
Secker is decent—Rundel has a heart—
Manners with candour are to Benson given—
To Berkeley, every virtue under heaven.

But does the court a worthy man remove?
That instant, I declare, he has my love:
I shun his zenith, court his mild decline;
Thus Somers once, and Halifax, were mine.
Oft, in the clear, still mirror of retreat,
I studied Shrewsbury, the wise and great:
Carleton's[209] calm sense, and Stanhope's noble flame,   80
Compared, and knew their generous end the same:
How pleasing Atterbury's softer hour!
How shined the soul, unconquer'd in the Tower!
How can I Pulteney, Chesterfield, forget,
While Roman spirit charms, and Attic wit:
Argyll,[210] the state's whole thunder born to wield,
And shake alike the senate and the field:
Or Wyndham,[211] just to freedom and the throne,
The master of our passions, and his own.
Names, which I long have loved, nor loved in vain,   90
Rank'd with their friends, not number'd with their train:
And if yet higher[212] the proud list should end,
Still let me say,—No follower, but a friend.[213]

Yet think not Friendship only prompts my lays;
I follow Virtue; where she shines, I praise:
Point she to priest or elder, Whig or Tory,
Or round a Quaker's beaver cast a glory.
I never (to my sorrow I declare)
Dined with the Man of Ross, or my Lord Mayor.[214]
Some, in their choice of friends, (nay, look not grave) 100
Have still a secret bias to a knave:
To find an honest man I beat about.
And love him, court him, praise him, in or out.

F. Then why so few commended?

P.   Not so fierce;
Find you the virtue, and I'll find the verse.
But random praise—the task can ne'er be done;
Each mother asks it for her booby son,
Each widow asks it for 'the best of men,'
For him she weeps, and him she weds again.
Praise cannot stoop, like satire, to the ground;   110
The number may be hang'd, but not be crown'd.
Enough for half the greatest of these days,
To 'scape my censure, not expect my praise.
Are they not rich? what more can they pretend?
Dare they to hope a poet for their friend?
What Richelieu wanted, Louis scarce could gain,
And what young Ammon wish'd, but wish'd in vain.
No power the Muse's friendship can command;
No power, when Virtue claims it, can withstand:
To Cato, Virgil paid one honest line;   120
Oh let my country's friends illumine mine!
—What are you thinking?

F.   Faith, the thought's no sin—
I think your friends are out, and would be in.

P. If merely to come in, sir, they go out,
The way they take is strangely round about.

F. They too may be corrupted, you'll allow?

P. I only call those knaves who are so now.
Is that too little? Come then, I'll comply—

Spirit of Arnall![215] aid me while I lie.
Cobham's a coward, Polwarth[216] is a slave,   130
And Lyttleton a dark, designing knave,
St John has ever been a wealthy fool—
But let me add, Sir Robert's mighty dull,
Has never made a friend in private life,
And was, besides, a tyrant to his wife.

But pray, when others praise him, do I blame?
Call Verres, Wolsey, any odious name?
Why rail they then, if but a wreath of mine,
O all-accomplish'd St John! deck thy shrine?

What! shall each spur-gall'd hackney of the day,   140
When Paxton gives him double pots and pay,
Or each new-pension'd sycophant, pretend
To break my windows if I treat a friend?
Then wisely plead, to me they meant no hurt,
But 'twas my guest at whom they threw the dirt?
Sure, if I spare the minister, no rules
Of honour bind me, not to maul his tools;
Sure, if they cannot cut, it may be said
His saws are toothless, and his hatchet's lead.

It anger'd Turenne, once upon a day,   150
To see a footman kick'd that took his pay:
But when he heard the affront the fellow gave,
Knew one a man of honour, one a knave,
The prudent general turn'd it to a jest,
And begg'd he'd take the pains to kick the rest:
Which not at present having time to do— —

F. Hold sir! for God's-sake where 'a the affront to you?
Against your worship when had Selkirk writ?
Or Page pour'd forth the torrent of his wit?
Or grant the bard[217] whose distich all commend   160
'In power a servant, out of power a friend,'
To Walpole guilty of some venial sin;
What's that to you who ne'er was out nor in?

The priest whose flattery bedropp'd the crown,
How hurt he you? he only stain'd the gown.
And how did, pray, the florid youth offend,

Whose speech you took, and gave it to a friend?

P. Faith, it imports not much from whom it came;
Whoever borrow'd, could not be to blame,
Since the whole house did afterwards the same. 170
Let courtly wits to wits afford supply,
As hog to hog in huts of Westphaly;
If one, through Nature's bounty, or his lord's,
Has what the frugal, dirty soil affords,
From him the next receives it, thick or thin,
As pure a mess almost as it came in;
The blessed benefit, not there confined,
Drops to the third, who nuzzles close behind;
From tail to mouth, they feed and they carouse:
The last full fairly gives it to the House. 180

F. This filthy simile, this beastly line
Quite turns my stomach— —

P.   So does flattery mine;
And all your courtly civet-cats can vent,
Perfume to you, to me is excrement.
But hear me further—Japhet,[218] 'tis agreed,
Writ not, and Chartres scarce could write or read,
In all the courts of Pindus guiltless quite;
But pens can forge, my friend, that cannot write;
And must no egg in Japhet's face be thrown,
Because the deed he forged was not my own? 190
Must never patriot then declaim at gin,
Unless, good man! he has been fairly in?
No zealous pastor blame a failing spouse,
Without a staring reason on his brows?
And each blasphemer quite escape the rod,
Because the insult's not on man, but God?

Ask you what provocation I have had?
The strong antipathy of good to bad.
When truth or virtue an affront endures,
The affront is mine, my friend, and should be yours. 200
Mine, as a foe profess'd to false pretence,
Who think a coxcomb's honour like his sense;
Mine, as a friend to every worthy mind;
And mine, as man, who feel for all mankind.

F. You're strangely proud.

P.   So proud, I am no slave:
So impudent, I own myself no knave:
So odd, my country's ruin makes me grave.
Yes, I am proud; I must be proud to see
Men not afraid of God, afraid of me:
Safe from the bar, the pulpit, and the throne,   210
Yet touch'd and shamed by ridicule alone.

O sacred weapon! left for truth's defence,
Sole dread of folly, vice, and insolence!
To all but heaven-directed hands denied,
The Muse may give thee, but the gods must guide:
Rev'rent I touch thee! but with honest zeal;
To rouse the watchmen of the public weal,
To virtue's work provoke the tardy Hall,
And goad the prelate slumbering in his stall.
Ye tinsel insects! whom a court maintains,   220
That counts your beauties only by your stains,
Spin all your cobwebs o'er the eye of day!
The Muse's wing shall brush you all away:
All his grace preaches, all his lordship sings,
All that makes saints of queens, and gods of kings,—
All, all but truth, drops dead-born from the press,
Like the last gazette, or the last address.

When black ambition[219] stains a public cause,
A monarch's sword when mad vain-glory draws,
Not Waller's wreath can hide the nation's scar,   230
Nor Boileau[220] turn the feather to a star.

Not so, when, diadem'd with rays divine,
Touch'd with the flame that breaks from Virtue's shrine,
Her priestess Muse forbids the good to die,
And opes the temple[221] of Eternity.
There, other trophies deck the truly brave,
Than such as Anstis[222] casts into the grave;
Far other stars than — — and — — wear,[223]
And may descend to Mordington from Stair:[224]
(Such as on Hough's unsullied mitre shine,   240
Or beam, good Digby,[225] from a heart like thine)
Let Envy howl, while Heaven's whole chorus sings,

And bark at honour not conferr'd by kings;
Let Flattery sickening see the incense rise,
Sweet to the world, and grateful to the skies:
Truth guards the poet, sanctifies the line,
And makes immortal verse as mean as mine.

Yes, the last pen for freedom let me draw,
When truth stands trembling on the edge of law;
Here, last of Britons! let your names be read;   250
Are none, none living? let me praise the dead,
And for that cause which made your fathers shine,
Fall by the votes of their degenerate line.

F. Alas! alas! pray end what you began,
And write next winter more 'Essays on Man.'

* * * * *

VARIATIONS.

VER. 185 in the MS.—

I grant it, sir; and further, 'tis agreed,
Japhet writ not, and Chartres scarce could read.

After VER. 227 in the MS.—

Where's now the star that lighted Charles to rise?
—With that which follow'd Julius to the skies
Angels that watch'd the Royal Oak so well,
How chanced ye nod, when luckless Sorel fell?
Hence, lying miracles! reduced so low
As to the regal-touch, and papal-toe;
Hence haughty Edgar's title to the main,
Britain's to France, and thine to India, Spain!

VER. 255 in the MS.—

Quit, quit these themes, and write 'Essays on Man.'

FOOTNOTES:

[1] We may mention that Roscoe and Dr Croly (in his admirable Life of Pope, prefixed to an excellent edition of his works) take a different view, and defend the poet.

[2] 'Preface: ' to the miscellaneous works of Pope, 1716.

[3] Written at sixteen years of age.

[4] 'Trumbull: ' see Life. He was born in Windsor Forest.

[5] 'Phosphor: ' the planet Venus.

[6] 'Wondrous tree: ' an allusion to the royal oak.

[7] 'Thistle: ' of Scotland.

[8] 'Lily: ' of France.

[9] 'Garth: ' Dr Samuel Garth, author of the 'Dispensary. '

[10] 'The woods, ' &c., from Spenser.

[11] 'Wycherley: ' the dramatist. See Life.

[12] This pastoral, Pope's own favourite, was produced on occasion of the death of a Mrs Tempest, a favourite of Mr Walsh, the poet's friend, who died on the night of the great storm in 1703, to which there are allusions. The scene lies in a grove—time, midnight.

[13] 'Stagyrite: Aristotle.

[14] 'La Mancha's knight: ' taken from the spurious second part of 'Don Quixote. '

[15] 'Unlucky as Fungoso: ' see Ben Johnson's 'Every Man in his Humour. '

[16] 'Timotheus: ' see 'Alexander's Feast. '

[17] 'Scotists and Thomists: ' two parties amongst the schoolmen, headed by Duns Scotus and Thomas Aquinas.

[18] 'Duck-lane: ' a place near Smithfield, where old books were sold.

[19] 'Milbourns: ' the Rev. Mr Luke Milbourn, an opponent of Dryden.

[20] Hall has imitated and excelled this passage. See his pamphlet, 'Christianity consistent with a Love of Freedom. '

[21] In this passage he alludes to Cromwell, Charles II., and the Revolution of 1688, and to their various effects on manners, opinions, &c.

[22] 'Appius: ' Dennis.

[23] 'Garth did not write: ' a common slander at that time in prejudice of that author.

[24] 'Maeonian star: ' Homer.

[25] 'Dionysius: ' of Halicarnassus.

[26] 'Mantua: ' Virgil's birth-place.

[27] 'Such was the Muse: ' Essay on poetry by the Duke of Buckingham.

[28] 'Caryll: ' Mr Caryll (a gentleman who was secretary to Queen Mary, wife of James II., whose fortunes he followed into France, author of the comedy of 'Sir Solomon Single, ' and of several translations in Dryden's Miscellanies) originally proposed the subject to Pope, with the view of putting an end, by this piece of ridicule, to a quarrel that had arisen between two noble families, those of Lord Petre and of Mrs Fermor, on the trifling occasion of his having cut off a lock of her hair. The author sent it to the lady, with whom he was acquainted; and she took it so well as to give about copies of it. That first sketch (we learn from one of his letters) was written in less than a fortnight, in 1711, in two cantos only, and it was so printed; first, in a miscellany of Ben. Lintot's, without the name of the author. But it was received so well that he enlarged it

the next year by the addition of the machinery of the Sylphs, and extended it to five cantos.

[29] 'Sylph: ' the Rosicrucian philosophy was a strange offshoot from Alchemy, and made up in equal proportions of Pagan Platonism, Christian Quietism, and Jewish Mysticism. See Bulwer's 'Zanoni. ' Pope has blended some of its elements with old legendary stories about guardian angels, fairies, &c.

[30] 'Baron: ' Lord Petre.

[31] Burns had this evidently in his eye when he wrote the lines 'Some hint the lover's harmless wile, ' &c., in his 'Vision. '

[32] 'Atalantis: ' a famous book written about that time by a woman: full of court and party-scandal, and in a loose effeminacy of style and sentiment which well suited the debauched taste of the better vulgar.

[33] 'Winds: ' see Odyssey.

[34] 'Thalestris: ' Mrs Morley.

[35] 'Sir Plume: ' Sir George Brown.

[36] 'Maeander: ' see Ovid.

[37] 'Partridge: ' see Pope's and Swift's Miscellanies.

[38] This poem was written at two different times: the first part of it, which relates to the country, in the year 1704, at the same time with the Pastorals; the latter part was not added till the year 1713, in which it was published.

[39] 'Stuart: ' Queen Anne.

[40] 'Savage laws: ' the forest-laws.

[41] 'The fields are ravish'd: ' alluding to the destruction made in the New Forest, and the tyrannies exercised there by William I.

[42] 'Himself denied a grave: ' the place of his interment at Caen in Normandy was claimed by a gentleman as his inheritance, the moment his servants were going to put him in his tomb: so that they

were obliged to compound with the owner before they could perform the king's obsequies.

[43] 'Second hope: ' Richard, second son of William the Conqueror.

[44] 'Queen: ' Anne.

[45] 'Still bears the name: ' the river Loddon.

[46] 'Trumbull: ' see Pastorals.

[47] 'Cooper's Hill: ' celebrated by Denham.

[48] 'Flowed from Cowley's tongue: ' Mr Cowley died at Chertsey, on the borders of the forest, and was from thence conveyed to Westminster.

[49] 'Noble Surrey: ' Henry Howard, Earl of Surrey, one of the first refiners of English poetry; who flourished in the time of Henry VIII.

[50] 'Edward's acts: ' Edward III., born here.

[51] 'Henry mourn: ' Henry VI.

[52] 'Once-fear'd Edward sleeps: ' Edward IV.

[53] 'Augusta: ' old name for London.

[54] 'And temples rise: ' the fifty new churches.

[55] The author of 'Successio, ' Elkanah Settle, appears to have been as much hated by Pope as he had been by Dryden. He figures prominently in 'The Dunciad. '

[56] This was written at twelve years old.

[57] This ode was written in imitation of the famous sonnet of Adrian to his departing soul. Flaxman also supplied hints for it. See 'The Adventurer. '

[58] See Memoir.

[59] 'But what with pleasure: ' this alludes to a famous passage of Seneca, which Mr Addison afterwards used as a motto to his play, when it was printed.

[60] Done by the author in his youth.

[61] Dr Johnson in the *Literary Review* highly commends this piece.

[62] This, it is said, was intended for Queen Caroline.

[63] 'Zamolxia: ' a disciple of Pythagoras.

[64] 'The youth: ' Alexander the Great: the tiara was the crown peculiar to the Asian princes: his desire to be thought the son of Jupiter Ammon, caused him to wear the horns of that god, and to represent the same upon his coins; which was continued by several of his successors.

[65] 'Timoleon: ' had saved the life of his brother Timophanes in the battle between the Argives and Corinthians; but afterwards killed him when he affected the tyranny.

[66] 'He whom ungrateful Athens: ' Aristides.

[67] 'May one kind grave: ' Abelard and Eloisa were interred in the same grave, or in monuments adjoining, in the monastery of the Paraclete: he died in the year 1142; she in 1163.

[68] 'Robert, Earl of Oxford: ' this epistle was sent to the Earl of Oxford with Dr Parnell's poems, published by our author, after the said earl's imprisonment in the Tower, and retreat into the country, in the year 1721.

[69] 'Secretary of State: ' in the year 1720.

[70] 'Work of years: ' Fresnoy employed above twenty years in finishing his poem.

[71] 'Worsley: ' Lady Frances, wife of Sir Robert Worsley.

[72] 'Voitnre: ' a French wit, born in Amiens 1598, died in 1648; a favourite of the Duke of Orleans, and member of the French Academy.

[73] 'Monthansier: ' Mademoiselle Paulet.

[74] 'Coronation: ' of King George the First, 1715.

[75] 'M. B.: ' Martha Blount.

[76] 'Southern: ' author of 'Oronooko, ' &c. He lived to the age of eighty-six.

[77] 'A table: ' he was invited to dine on his birthday with this nobleman, who had prepared for him the entertainment of which the bill of fare is here set down.

[78] 'Harp: ' the Irish harp was woven on table-cloths, &c.

[79] 'Prologues: ' Dryden used to sell his prologues at four guineas each, till, when Southern applied for one, he demanded six, saying, 'Young man, the players have got my goods too cheap. '

[80] 'Mr C. :' Mr Cleland, whose residence was in St James's Place, where he died in 1741. See preface to 'The Dunciad. '

[81] 'Trumbull: ' one of the principal Secretaries of State to King William III., who, having resigned his place, died in his retirement at Easthamstead, in Berkshire, 1746.

[82] 'Heaven's eternal year is thine: ' borrowed from Dryden's poem on Mrs Killigrew.

[83] 'Fenton: ' Pope's joint-translator of Homer's Odyssey. See Johnson's 'Lives of the Poets. '

[84] His only daughter expired in his arms, immediately after she arrived in France to see him.

[85] Lady Mary Montague wrote a rejoinder to this poem, in a caustic, sneering vein.

[86] 'Vindicate the ways, ' &c. : borrowed from Milton.

[87] 'Egypt's God: ' Apis.

[88] 'Thin partitions' from Dryden.

[89] 'Glory, jest, and riddle of the world: ' Pascal in his 'Pensees' has a thought almost identical with this.

[90] 'Good bishop: ' De Belsance, who distinguished himself by attention to the sick of the plague, in his diocese of Marseilles in 1720.

[91] 'Bethel: ' a benevolent gentleman in Yorkshire, a great friend of Pope's.

[92] 'Chartres: ' Colonel, infamous for every vice—a fraudulent gambler, &c. &c.

[93] 'Cromwell: ' it is not necessary now to answer this insult to the greatest of Britain's kings. It is a clever ape chattering at a dead lion.

[94] 'Good John: ' John Serle, his old and faithful servant.

[95] 'Mint: ' a place to which insolvent debtors retired, to enjoy an illegal protection, which they were there suffered to afford one another, from the persecution of their creditors. —P.

[96] 'Pitholeon: ' The name taken from a foolish poet of Rhodes, who pretended much to Greek. —P.

[97] 'Butchers, Henley: ' Orator Henley used to declaim to the butchers in Newport market.

[98] 'Freemasons, Moore: ' he was of this society, and frequently headed their processions.

[99] 'Bishop Boulter: ' friend of Ambrose Philips.

[100] 'Burnets, &c. :' authors of secret and scandalous history.

[101] 'Gildon: ' a forgotten critic and dramatist—a bitter libeller of Pope.

[102] 'A Persian tale: ' Ambrose Philips translated a book called the 'Persian Tales. '

[103] 'Bufo: ' most commentators refer this to Lord Halifax.

[104] 'Sir Will: ' Sir William Young.

[105] 'Bubo: ' Babb Dodington.

[106] 'Who to the dean, and silver bell: ' meaning the man who would have persuaded the Duke of Chandos that Mr P. meant him in those circumstances ridiculed in the 'Epistle on Taste. '—P.

[107] 'Sporus: ' Lord Hervey.

[108] 'The lie so oft o'erthrown: ' as, that he received subscriptions for Shakspeare; that he set his name to Mr Broome's verses, &c., which, though publicly disproved, were nevertheless shamelessly repeated. —P.

[109] 'The imputed trash: ' such as profane psalms, court-poems, and other scandalous things, printed in his name by Curll and others. —P.

[110] 'Abuse: ' namely, on the Duke of Buckingham, the Earl of Burlington, Lord Bathurst, Lord Bolingbroke, Bishop Atterbury, Dr Swift, Dr Arbuthnot, Mr Gay, his friends, his parents, and his very nurse, aspersed in printed papers, by James Moore, G. Ducket, L. Wolsted, Tho. Bentley, and other obscure persons. —P.

[111] 'Sappho: ' Lady M. W. Montague.

[112] 'Welsted: ' accused Pope of killing a lady by a satire.

[113] 'Budgell: ' Budgell, in a weekly pamphlet called *The Bee*, bestowed much abuse on him.

[114] 'Except his will: ' alluding to Tindal's will, by which, and other indirect practices, Budgell, to the exclusion of the next heir, a nephew, got to himself almost the whole fortune of a man entirely unrelated to him. —P.

[115] 'Curlls of town and court: ' Lord Hervey.

[116] 'Noble wife: ' alluding to the fate of Dryden and Addison.

[117] 'An oath: ' Pope's father was a nonjuror.

[118] Curll set up his head for a sign.

[119] His father was crooked.

[120] His mother was much afflicted with headaches.

[121] 'Fortescue: ' Baron of Exchequer, and afterwards Master of the Mint.

[122] 'Fanny: ' Hervey.

[123] 'Falling horse: ' the horse on which George II. charged at the battle of Oudenarde.

[124] 'Shippen: ' the only member of parliament Sir R. Walpole found incorruptible.

[125] 'Lee: ' Nathaniel, a wild, mad, but true poet of Dryden's day.

[126] 'Budgell: ' Addison's relation, who drowned himself in the Thames.

[127] 'And he whose lightning: ' Charles Mordaunt, Earl of Peterborough, a man distinguished by the rapidity of his military movements—a petty Napoleon.

[128] 'Oldfield: ' this eminent glutton ran through a fortune of fifteen hundred pounds a-year in the simple luxury of good eating. —P.

[129] 'Bedford-head: ' a famous eating-house.

[130] 'Proud Buckingham: ' Villiers, Duke of Buckingham.

[131] 'Aristippus: ' the licentious parasite of Dionysius.

[132] 'Sticks: ' Exchequer tallies—an old mode of reckoning.

[133] 'Barnard: ' Sir John Barnard, an eminent citizen of the day.

[134] 'Lady Mary: ' Montague, who was as great a sloven as a beauty.

[135] 'Murray: ' afterwards Lord Mansfield.

[136] 'Creech: ' the translator of Horace.

[137] 'Craggs: ' his father was originally a humble man.

[138] 'Cornbury: ' an excellent and high-minded nobleman, great-grandson of Lord Clarendon, the historian.

[139] 'Tindal: ' the infidel, author of 'Christianity as Old as the Creation. '

[140] 'Anstis: ' Garter King-at-Arms.

[141] 'Luckless play: ' Young's 'Buseris; ' the name of the spendthrift is not known.

[142] 'Augustus: ' referring ironically to George II., then excessively unpopular for refusing to enter into a war with Spain, which was supposed to have insulted our commerce.

[143] 'Skelton: ' poet laureate to Henry VIII.

[144] 'Christ's Kirk o' the Green: ' a ballad made by James I. of Scotland.

[145] 'The Devil: ' the Devil Tavern, where Ben Johnson held his poetical club.

[146] 'Horse-tail bare: ' referring to Sertorius, who told one of his soldiers to pluck off a horse's tail at one effort. He failed, of course. Sertorius then told another to pluck it away, hair by hair. He succeeded; and thus Sertorius taught the lesson of hard-working, patient perseverance.

[147] 'Gammer Gurton: ' one of the first printed plays in English, and therefore much valued by some antiquaries.

[148] 'All, by the king's example: ' a line from Lord Lansdown.

[149] 'Lely: ' Sir Peter, who painted Cromwell and all the celebrities of his day.

[150] 'Ripley: ' the government architect who built the Admiralty; no favourite except with his employers.

[151] 'Van: ' Vanbrugh.

[152] 'Astraea: ' Miss Bolin, author of obscene, but once popular novels.

[153] 'Old Edward's armour beams on Cibber's breast: ' the coronation of Henry VIII. and Queen Anne Boleyn, in which the play-houses vied with each other to represent all the pomp of a coronation. In this noble contention, the armour of one of the kings of England was borrowed from the Tower, to dress the champion. — P.

[154] 'Bernini: ' a great sculptor. He is said to have predicted Charles the First's melancholy fate from a sight of his bust.

[155] 'Colonel: ' Cotterel of Rousham, near Oxford.

[156] 'Blois: ' a town where French is spoken with great purity.

[157] 'Sir Godfrey: ' Sir Godfrey Kneller.

[158] 'Monroes: ' Dr Monroe, physician to Bedlam Hospital.

[159] 'Oldfield, Daitineuf: ' two celebrated gluttons mentioned formerly.

[160] 'Tooting, Earl's Court: ' two villages within a few miles of London.

[161] 'Composing songs: ' Burns imitates this in the 'Vision' —

'Stringin' blethers up in rhyme, For fules to sing. '

[162] 'Stephen: ' Mr Stephen Duck.

[163] 'Servile chaplains: ' Dr Kenett, who wrote a servile dedication to the Duke of Devonshire, to whom he was chaplain.

[164] 'Abbs Court: ' a farm over against Hampton Court.

[165] 'Townshend's turnips: ' Lord Townshend, Secretary of State to Georges the First and Second. When this great statesman retired from business, he amused himself in husbandry, and was particularly fond of the cultivation of turnips; it was the favourite subject of his conversation.

[166] 'Bu— —: ' Bubb Doddington.

[167] 'Oglethorpe: ' employed in settling the colony of Georgia. See Boswell's 'Johnson. '

[168] 'Belinda: ' in 'The Rape of the Lock. '

[169] 'Tips with silver: ' occurs also in the famous moonlight scene in the 'Iliad'—

'Tips with silver every mountain's head. '

[170] 'Adieu! ' how like Burns's lines, beginning—

" But when life's day draws near the gloaming, Farewell to vacant, careless roaming! " &c.

[171] 'Donne: ' Pope, it is said, imitated Donne's 'Satires' to show that celebrated men before him had been as severe as he. Donne was an extraordinary man—first a Roman Catholic, then a barrister, then a clergyman in the Church of England, and Dean of St Paul's, —a vigorous although rude satirist, a fine Latin versifier, the author of many powerful sermons, and of a strange book defending suicide; altogether a strong, eccentric, extravagant genius.

[172] 'Paul: ' supposed to be Paul Benfield, Esq., M.P., who was engaged in the jobbing transactions of that period; others fill up the blank in the original copy with Hall—as, for instance, Croly in his excellent edition.

[173] 'Hoadley: ' Bishop, whose sentences were wire-drawn.

[174] 'Figs: ' a prize-fighting academy; 'White's: ' a gaming-house, both much frequented by the young nobility.

[175] 'Deadly sins: ' the room hung with old tapestry, representing the seven deadly sins.

[176] 'Ascapart: ' a giant of romance.

[177] 'Epilogue: ' the first part of which was originally published as 'One thousand seven hundred and thirty-eight. ' It appeared the same day with Johnson's 'London. '

[178] 'Bubo: ' Bubb Duddington.

[179] 'Sir Billy: ' Tonge.

[180] 'Huggins: ' formerly jailor of the Fleet prison, enriched himself by many exactions, for which he was tried and expelled. —P.

[181] 'Cropp'd our ears: ' said to be executed by the captain of a Spanish ship on one Jenkins, the captain of an English one. He cut off his ears, and bid him carry them to the king his master. —P.

[182] 'The great man: ' the first minister.

[183] 'Seen him I have: ' alluding to Pope's service to Abbe Southcot, see 'Life. '

[184] 'Jekyl: ' Sir Joseph Jekyl, master of the rolls, a true Whig in his principles, and a man of the utmost probity. —P.

[185] 'Lyttleton: ' George Lyttleton, secretary to the Prince of Wales, distinguished both for his writings and speeches in the spirit of liberty. —P.

[186] 'Sejanus, Wolsey: ' the one the wicked minister of Tiberius; the other, of Henry VIII. The writers against the court usually bestowed these and other odious names on the minister, without distinction, and in the most injurious manner. —P.

[187] 'Fleury: ' Cardinal; and minister to Louis XV. It was a patriot-fashion, at that time, to cry up his wisdom and honesty. —P.

[188] 'Henley, Osborn: ' see them in their places in 'The Dunciad. '

[189] 'Nation's sense: ' the cant of politics at that time.

[190] 'Carolina: ' Queen-consort to King George II. She died in 1737. See, for her character, 'Heart of Midlothian. '

[191] 'Gazetteer: ' then Government newspaper.

[192] 'Immortal Selkirk: ' Charles, third son of Duke of Hamilton, created Earl of Selkirk in 1887.

[193] 'Grave Delaware: ' a title given that lord by King James II. He was of the bed-chamber to King William; he was so to King George I. ; he was so to King George II. This Lord was very skilful in all the forms of the House, in which he discharged himself with great gravity. — P.

[194] 'Sister: ' alluding to Lady M. W. Montague, who is said to have neglected her sister, the Countess of Mar, who died destitute in Paris.

[195] 'Cibber's son, Rich: ' two players; look for them in 'The Dunciad. ' —P.

[196] 'Blount: ' author of an impious and foolish book, called 'The Oracles of Reason, ' who, being in love with a near kinswoman of his, and rejected, gave himself a stab in the arm, as pretending to kill himself, of the consequence of which he really died. —P.

[197] 'Passerau: ' author of another book of the same stamp, called 'A Philosophical Discourse on Death, ' being a defence of suicide. He was a nobleman of Piedmont.

[198] 'A printer: ' a fact that happened in London a few years past. The unhappy man left behind him a paper justifying his action by the reasonings of some of these authors. —P.

[199] 'Gin: ' a spirituous liquor, the exhorbitant use of which had almost destroyed the lowest rank of the people, till it was restrained by an Act of Parliament in 1736. —P.

[200] 'Quaker's wife: ' Mrs Drummond, a preacher.

[201] 'Landaff: ' Harris by name, a worthy man, who had somehow offended the poet.

[202] 'Allen: ' of Bath, Warburton's father-in-law, the prototype of All-worthy in 'Tom Jones. '

[203] 'Paxton: ' late solicitor to the Treasury.

[204] 'Guthrie: ' the ordinary of Newgate, who publishes the memoirs of the malefactors, and is often prevailed upon to be so tender of their reputation, as to set down no more than the initials of their name. —P.

[205] 'Wild: ' Jonathan, a famous thief, and thief-impeacher, who was at last caught in his own train and hanged. —P. See Fielding, and 'Jack Shepherd. '

[206] 'Feels for fame, and melts to goodness: ' this is a fine compliment; the expression showing, that fame was but his second passion.

[207] 'Scarb'rough: ' Earl of, and Knight of the Garter, whose personal attachments to the king appeared from his steady adherence to the royal interest, after his resignation of his great employment of Master of the Horse; and whose known honour and virtue made him esteemed by all parties. —P.

[208] 'Esher's peaceful grove: ' the house and gardens of Esher, in Surrey, belonging to the Hon. Mr Pelham, brother of the Duke of Newcastle.

[209] 'Carleton: ' Lord, nephew of Robert Boyle.

[210] 'Argyll: ' see 'Heart of Midlothian. '

[211] 'Wyndham: ' Chancellor of Exchequer; for the rest, see history.

[212] 'Yet higher: ' he was at this time honoured with the esteem and favour of his Royal Highness the Prince.

[213] 'A friend: ' unrelated to their parties, and attached only to their persons.

[214] 'Lord Mayor: ' Sir John Barnard, Lord Mayor in the year of the poem, 1738.

[215] 'Spirit of Arnall: ' look for him in his place, Dunciad, b. ii., ver. 315.

[216] 'Polwarth: ' the Hon. Hugh Hume, son of Alexander Earl of Marchmont, grandson of Patrick Earl of Marchmont, and distinguished, like them, in the cause of liberty. —P.

[217] 'The bard: ' a verse taken out of a poem to Sir R. W.—P.

[218] 'Japhet, Chartres: ' see the epistle to Lord Bathurst.

[219] 'Black ambition: ' the case of Cromwell in the civil war of England; and of Louis XIV. in his conquest of the Low Countries. — P.

[220] 'Boileau: ' see his 'Ode on Namur. '

[221] 'Opes the temple: ' from Milton—'Opes the palace of Eternity. '

[222] 'Anstis: ' the chief herald-at-arms. It is the custom, at the funeral of great peers, to cast into the grave the broken staves and ensigns of honour. —P.

[223] 'Ver. 238: ' some fill up the blanks with George II., and Frederick, Prince of Wales—others, with Kent and Grafton.

[224] 'Stair: ' John Dalrymple, Earl of Stair, Knight of the Thistle. —P.

[225] 'Hough and Digby: ' Dr John Hough, Bishop of Worcester, and the Lord Digby.

END OF VOL. I.

www.ingramcontent.com/pod-product-compliance
Lightning Source LLC
LaVergne TN
LVHW041129050125
800559LV00034B/184